CRUISING THE MOVIES

SEMIOTEXT(E) ACTIVE AGENTS SERIES

Cruising the Movies © 2015 Felice Picano.
Originally published in 1985 by the Gay Presses of New York.

Published by Semiotext(e)
PO BOX 629, South Pasadena, CA 91031
www.semiotexte.com

Special thanks to Vince Aletti, Bill Arning, Mary Corliss, Bruce Eves, Stephen Greco, Billy Miller, Joseph Modica, Felice Picano, Tom Steele, and Jim Tamulis.

Boyd McDonald's essays in the section "Great Moments in Movies" originally appeared in *Christopher Street*, issues 74, 94, 96, 98, 99, 100, 101, 102, 103, 104, 106, and 107. All but issue 74 came out after the publication of the first edition of *Cruising the Movies*. "Art from the Post-Heterosexual Age" was pub-lished in *Art & Text* 20 (February-April, 1986).

Cover photograph by Georges Piette
Back Cover Photograph: Joseph Modica
Design: Hedi El Kholti

ISBN: 978-1-58435-171-9
Distributed by The MIT Press, Cambridge, Mass. and London, England
Printed in the United States of America

CRUISING THE MOVIES

A SEXUAL GUIDE TO OLDIES ON TV

Boyd McDonald

Introduction by William E. Jones

CONTENTS

Boyd McDonald at work in his room, 1980s.

INTRODUCTION
by William E. Jones

In *Cruising the Movies: A Sexual Guide to "Oldies" on TV* (1985), Boyd McDonald scrutinizes the anatomy of Ronald and Nancy Reagan with maniacal glee. The President is not only flabby and "sloppy assed," but also has tits and wears more makeup than Lucille Ball. In an essay on *John Loves Mary* (1949), Boyd writes mainly about Reagan's curiously feminine legs, and speculates that this display of flesh—he appears in the movie without pants not once but twice—is proof of the existence of heterosexuality in Hollywood. A homosexual would not have allowed such a casting error to occur. Reagan's lack of masculine attributes caused him to lash out at men whom he perceived (or, more likely, whom his speechwriters and handlers perceived) to be less than men, the homosexuals. The First Lady, a hard and remorseless political creature, exuded a skeletal and artificial femininity; she stayed thin by living on grapes and regularly flew a California manicurist to the White House to apply five coats of polish to her fingernails. In response to Kenneth Anger's claim that he had obtained a photograph of Mrs. Reagan's "twat" (taken back when she was Nancy Davis), Boyd asks to hear from any reader who has a picture of her "butt-hole."

These sorts of barbs, once common, are no longer much heard among cinema spectators, now that "oldies," which had formerly served as cheap programming for revival houses and independent television stations, have been elevated to serious archive screenings and expensive cable channels, where the odor of sanctity clings to them. Going to movies is not the collective ritual it once was, and internet blogs, written by lone spectators, are hardly an adequate replacement for spontaneous audience participation. Recent attempts to rehabilitate Reagan's image—"he wasn't as bad as the

Bushes," et cetera—cry out for renewed expressions of irreverence and further reminders that there was a time when, as Boyd told an interviewer, "It was shocking to have people like Nixon and Reagan in minor offices, let alone President."

At the end of *Cruising the Movies*, Boyd admits that the book "is not strictly about movies; it frequently uses them as an excuse for political, social, sexual, psychological, biographical, and autobiographical comments." Funnier than Robin Wood's *Hollywood from Vietnam to Reagan* (1986), more immediate in its style than Mark Feeny's *Nixon at the Movies* (2004), and haunting the scene as a kind of tactless plebeian predecessor of both books, *Cruising the Movies* was (and continues to be) a rare thing: a book of popular film criticism that is both unabashedly sexual and unapologetically political.

Boyd McDonald died on September 18, 1993. His obituary was a model of discretion: "Born July 11, 1925 in Lake Preston, South Dakota. He served in the US Army in World War II, attended and graduated Harvard University. Upon graduation he worked for *Time* magazine and IBM Corp. He pursued freelance writing up until the time of his death." After 20 years of what Boyd described as hack work, writing and editing copy for large corporations and nearly drinking himself to death, he dried out, went on welfare, and moved into a single room occupancy (SRO) hotel on New York's pre-gentrification Upper West Side. There he watched old movies at all hours of the day and night on a small black and white television set.

Like many of his fellow SRO residents, Boyd pursued something vaguely disreputable on the streets of New York, and from the late-1960s onward his "freelance writing" consisted chiefly of editing a series of chapbooks called *Straight to Hell*, compendia of "true homosexual experiences" collected from readers' contributions of their own personal stories. The direct yet suggestive title *Straight to Hell* was accompanied by various subtitles over the years: *Archives of the American Academy of Homosexual Research*, (in homage to Alfred Kinsey, whose work Boyd saw himself as continuing), *The Manhattan Review of Unnatural Acts* (an acknowledgment of *The New York*

ALLEN MacDONALD
26 Aspinwall Avenue
Brookline 46, Massachusetts
Brookline High School, Brook-
line, Mass.
Freshman Football

GORDON J. MacDONALD
Apatardo 66
San Luis Potosi
S. L. R., Mexico
San Marcos Academy, San Mar-
cos, Tex.
Freshman Crew

BOYD E. McDONALD
Lake Preston, South Dakota
Lake Preston High School, Lake
Preston, S. D.
The Crimson
U. S. Army

JAMES L. McDONALD
300 Forrer Street
Dayton 9, Ohio
Oakwood High School, Dayton,
O.

Boyd (lower left) in his Harvard Class of 1949 yearbook.

Review of Books, where Boyd placed an advertisement soliciting contributions to *STH*), *U.S. Chronicle of Crimes Against Nature*, and
many other parodic combinations of important-sounding words.
Straight to Hell offered its readers the truth about sex between men,
rigorously edited for style but never diluted or censored. In equal
measure masturbation fodder and fine literature, this modest publication run from a single room acquired a wide and appreciative
following, including Gore Vidal (who called it "one of the best
radical papers in the country," William S. Burroughs, Allen Ginsberg,
Christopher Isherwood, and Tennessee Williams.

The original *Straight to Hell* chapbooks were compiled in paper-
backs with admirably blunt titles: *Meat, Flesh, Sex, Cum, Smut,
Juice, Wads, Cream, Filth, Skin, Raunch, Lewd,* and *Scum.* Boyd's one
book that did not belong to this series, *Cruising the Movies*, collected
the columns he wrote for the gay literary magazine *Christopher Street*
between 1983 and 1985. While it did not appeal to readers'
prurient interests as directly as the *STH* anthologies—and conse-
quently sold a fraction of the copies they did—*Cruising the Movies*
gives a sense of more rarefied (and only a little less clandestine)
obsessions animating urban gay life, specifically the cinephilia in
which Boyd's generation indulged.

THE MAN~ HATTAN REVIEW OF UN~ NATURAL ACTS

$1

Photo: Ansonia Bookstore

No. 32

A cover and various pages from issues of *Straight to Hell*.
The last page is from issue 53 (1983) edited by Victor Weaver.

STH

(STRAIGHT TO HELL):
The Manhattan Review of Unnatural Acts.
Archives of the American Academy
of Homosexual Evidence.
Box 982, Radio City Station
New York City 10019.

COMBINED WITH
The American Jockey Shorts Journal
AND
The New York Review of Cocksucking.

*A magazine for the lower and upper classes:
always coarse, never common.*

The paper that made New York famous.

*In the long run, the only thing that has any
real class, or real dignity, or respectability
or responsibility, is the shameless truth.*

*Correspondents in principal pissoirs of
the world.*

*Homosexuality is not a handicap to overcome, but a
blessing to wallow in.*

"What a day is today! — that
is to say, what a day was
the day before yesterday."
—GERTRUDE STEIN

Photograph by AMG

Annual Report.

Your Company has doubled its paid circulation in recent months. I use all income to help STH grow, so that the magazine's revenues remain as gross as its editorial content. I do this not because I am selfless but because I want to do it. STH is what I want to spend money on. I don't want to acquire and display lovely things; STH is the loveliest thing my money can buy. Relations with your Company's printer remain distressingly satisfactory, offering no opportunity for paranoia, possibly because he has never bothered to examine the magazine, leaving it to a group of husky youths with swollen, dripping groins. Your Company still has no employees. I do not regard myself as an employee; to work on STH is to play. Work is what I do in offices by day. By night, at STH, I am even above the mere executive level. I do not execute policy, I make fucking policy, for Christ's sake.—THE EDITOR.

Professor Sees Ass-licking
As Over-emphasized in Issue 43.

--------UNIVERSITY.—I never go in for admiring assholes. But the one on P. 7, No. 43 was very tempting. Quite possibly, though, many readers will find objectionable the semi-scatological stuff that seems to excite some of your readers. When I get a chance, I will answer your questionnaire.

Thom Gunn, the Poet, Likes It.

FROM AN INTERVIEW IN *The Sentinel*, SAN FRANCISCO.]

THOM GUNN: Personally, I have been far more influenced by the wit and style of The Manhattan Review of Unnatural Acts *than I have been by the tiresome campiness of Ronald Firbank, who is usually taken as one of the chief exemplars of the aforementioned gay sensibility.''*

[EDITOR's NOTE: As I don't know from poetry, I enquired about Thom Gunn, an Englishman now living in San Francisco. A professor who is an STH subscriber assures me that Gunn is highly regarded.]

Photograph from *The Sentinel.*

Adultery in the Men's Room.

HAWAII.—I went down to a beach to watch the sun set, but was distracted by a tall, curly-headed young guy. He went into the restroom. I followed and sat in a stall with a glory hole, and soon he was stuffing his thick meat through. It was huge, cut and sweet-tasting. After I sucked on it for awhile he came around to the door and I let him in. He was even better looking up close. His cock was dripping and he pulled his jeans down so I could suck his heavy balls and smell the dampness between his legs. His cock was resting on my ear as I licked his balls. Then he pulled back and asked me to change positions. I stood up and he sat down and sucked my cock. He spread my butt and started to rub my asshole. He said, "It's dark now—let's go down to the beach." Before we left he stuck his tongue in my mouth and I was surprised, because he was married and most married men I know don't like to kiss the mouth (but kiss other things). We spread a blanket near the water and stripped and I started sucking that thick cock again. He put his legs up so I licked and sucked his balls. The smell from his asshole was shitty. I could tell he wanted to get fucked so I licked his hole till he begged me to stick my dick in. I spit on my dick and slowly put it in and bent way over to lick his dripping dick at the same time. He wiggled his asshole and I started fucking him hard. He said, "Fuck me harder. Make it last." I'd fuck his asshole until I was ready to explode, then I'd stop and tease him, lick his dick and pinch his nipples, until he'd say, "Fuck me, fuck me." Once my dick slipped out but I shoved it back in all at once. He started beating his meat. He said, "I'm glad you can fuck so long." We came together. One afternoon, I walked in to cruise a toilet in the Mall. I found both booths occupied and an enlisted man standing suspiciously in front of the toilet doors. I loitered by the sinks and sized him up. His sunglasses prevented me from looking him in the eye. I went outside to sit and watch the comings and goings. Soon I was back on the inside, ass on the toilet next to the enlisted man. Through a hole I could see his pants were pulled up to his thighs and his shirt covered his crotch, so I couldn't see anything but his hand between his legs, and he wasn't just scratching. I sat back and played with myself; I wanted him to know I was interested. He was slow. Several times we were interrupted by legitimate customers (though I don't know what could be more legitimate than sex). After awhile, he gradually exposed his cock. I was awed at the size and thickness of it. It was cut and reddish. The biggest cock I've seen in years. He beat off slowly, but he still didn't expose his cock hair or balls. My balls ached to dump their heavy load, but more than that I wanted to taste his fat cock. Suddenly he lowered his pants and pulled back his shirt. I was dizzy with excitement at the sight of the soldier's heavy cock poking out of a self-cut hole in the red women's bikini underpants. The top and sides were edged with lace. As he leaned back to stick his rod in the air, I caught a glimpse of a black garter belt attached to dark

6

READERS: Please do not ask when STH is due. I publish as often as I can. You pay for 12 numbers, not 12 months.

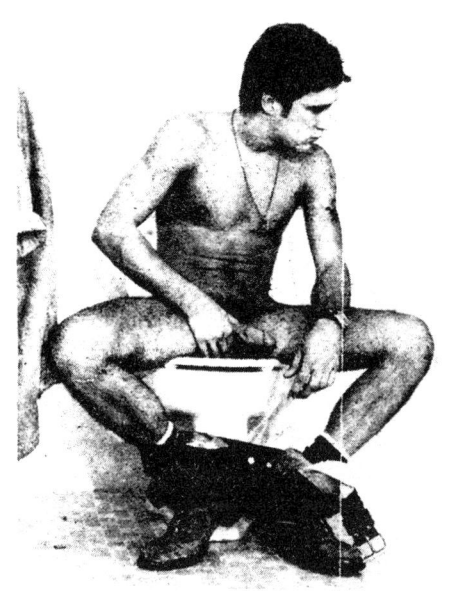

STRAIGHT TO HELL
THE MANHATTAN
REVIEW OF
UNNATURAL ACTS

Pro homosexual.
Pro women.
Pro children.
Anti "straight" male.

Libertarian and Libertine.

Love and hate for the American straight.

Always coarse, never common.

America's best-loved journal of cocksucking.

The paper that made New York famous.

Open All Nite.
6 Booths 6;
No Waiting.

PÈRE ANNOYED, Founder.
Cash Casino, Comptroller.
Loretta Jung, Psychiatric Advisor.

SUBSCRIPTION: 12 issues, $9.
Foreign, $10.

BACK ISSUES:
$1 the copy

Please make checks payable to cash and mail to:
Box 982
Radio City Station
New York, New York 10019

Published by
HI KLASS PRESS.

Fine products for the American home since 1973.

"In journalism, the only things that have any real class are white space and the truth."

–PÈRE ANNOYED
(1925-   )

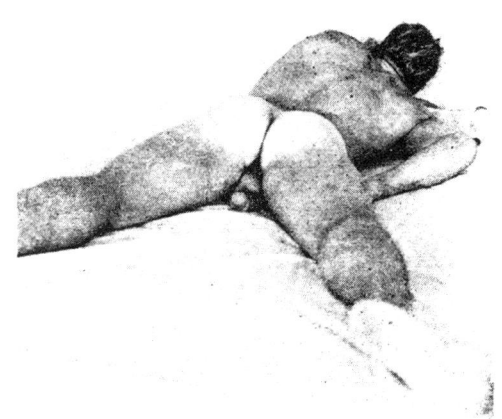

Photos: Ansonia Bookstore

COOKIE MUELLER

TAYLOR MEAD

FRAN LEBOWITZ

JOHN WATERS (right, with your favorite editor.)

JACKIE CURTIS

In case some of you in the know think I'm trying to take all the credit for these Sunday parties, the real shaker won't let me mention his name due to the highly sensitive nature of his day job. But believe me, if I thought I could get away with taking all the credit, I would. Lots of you ask about Boyd Mc-Donald. In addition to *Meat, Flesh,* and *Sex, Cum* has just been published, and he has two more books on the way. He's also a regular columnist for the magazine "Christopher Street." Me, I'm dying to get all this off to the printer so I can have a break. Till next time.

Straight to Hell's insistent focus on "true homosexual experiences" recalls the passage in Juan Goytisolo's autobiography *Forbidden Territory* (1985) describing the first time he met Jean Genet:

> Suddenly he turns to me and asks point-blank:
> "What about you? Are you a queer?"
> In my confusion, I reply that I have had homosexual experiences—something that until then I had never revealed in public… I suppose I blushed when I answered—makes no impression on him at all.
> "Experiences! Everybody has had experiences! You talk like an Anglo-Saxon pederast! I meant dreams, desires, fantasies."

For almost anyone born and raised in the 20th Century, the phrase "dreams, desires, fantasies" conjures an association with the movies, and that locus of fantasy *par excellence*, the movie star.

The phenomenon of the star arose spontaneously "from below" among popular audiences during the second decade of the 20th Century. Up until that time, producers, unaware of the commercial potential of actors as personalities and afraid that they would demand too much money, had used performers without credit. As Kenneth Anger describes it in *Hollywood Babylon* (1965),

> when crowds all over the country seemed to be flocking to see favorite performers known only as "Little Mary," "The Biograph Boy," or "The Vitagraph Girl," the disdained actors, until then thought of as little more than hired help, suddenly acquired ticket-selling importance. The already-famous faces took on names and rapidly-rising salaries: the Star System—a decidedly mixed blessing—was born.

There was more to the star than economics; there was a religious aspect to the phenomenon as well. Anger calls the early movie palaces "Wonder Sanctuaries where millions worshipped," and the development of movie cults, aided by the studios' publicity departments, as "this novel and pagan religion." The choice of the word "pagan" is not an idle one. The movie gods (always plural) appealed to their devotees in ways that harkened back to the Greek gods, who were worshiped in ecstatic rituals, who possessed human passions like anger, lust, and jealousy, and who acted on these passions capriciously.

In his French translation (more of an adaptation) of the Reverend George W. Cox's *Manual of Mythology* (1868), Stéphane Mallarmé made a significant change. He writes, "Si les dieux ne font rien d'inconvenant, c'est alors qu'ils ne sont plus dieux du tout"— in English, "If the gods do nothing unseemly, then they are no longer gods at all." The original text reads, "If the gods do aught unseemly, then they are not gods at all." (This sentence is itself a translation from Euripides.) It is possible that Mallarmé misunderstood the English word "aught" to mean "nothing" rather than its dictionary meaning of "anything." It is also possible that the typesetter changed the text. Or perhaps Mallarmé, obsessive that he was, made a subversive revision on purpose. If so,

> Twenty-five centuries of morality—pagan, Christian, and secular—seem to fall away before these words. Can it be, then, that in order to be a god one *must* be involved in unseemly behavior? Can it be that that vast repertoire of unnamable acts as come across in the ancient fables is itself the code through which the gods make themselves manifest? Such a theological vision would demand long and considered reflection.

Roberto Calasso raises these questions in his book *Literature and the Gods* (2001). Mallarmé died in 1898; he did not live to see the development of movie star cults and the gilded excesses of the silent era. Yet this idea, that gods are worshiped not because they are perfect but because they embody human failings on a superhuman scale, would have a great future in the minds of the credulous in the predominantly monotheistic, Judeo-Christian culture of the United States. With the success of the movies, a bunch of former proletarians who had skill in pantomime, pretty faces, and impressive physical endowments were elevated to god-like status, and suddenly deemed capable, just by setting a bad example, of toppling centuries of morality.

During the early 1920s, scandals involving actors cracking up and misbehaving caused periodic public relations crises for movie studios with investments of millions of dollars to lose. Kenneth Anger colorfully describes the reaction to revelations about the unseemly personal lives of stars: "Professional do-gooders would brand Hollywood a New Babylon whose evil influence rivaled the legendary depravity of old." The film industry's response was to form the Motion Picture Producers and Distributors of America, and to appoint someone to oversee Hollywood's public morality. The producers chose Will Hays, who was the Postmaster General of President Warren G. Harding's famously corrupt administration, and who, like most of the Harding cabinet, had been implicated in the Teapot Dome scandal. Hays was paid $100,000 a year, and earned his salary by placating concerned citizens while the producers did more or less whatever they pleased for the rest of the decade.

In 1930, the Motion Picture Producers and Distributors of America adopted the Motion Picture Production Code, which was enforced from 1934 until 1968, when it was abandoned in favor of the MPAA ratings system currently in use. These rules were the guidelines by which the film industry policed itself, and thereby circumvented formal US government censorship.

The premise that if corrupt people make movies, then these movies will corrupt their audiences, with an underlying insistence on a Christian notion of evil, finds florid expression in the prose of a Jesuit priest named Daniel Aloysius Lord (1888–1955).

Art can be morally evil in its effects. This is the case clearly enough with unclean art, indecent books, suggestive drama. The effect on the lives of men and women are [sic] obvious.

Note: It has often been argued that art itself is unmoral, neither good nor bad. This is true of the THING which is music, painting, poetry, etc. But the THING is the PRODUCT of some person's mind, and the intention of that mind was either good or bad morally when it produced the thing. Besides, the thing has its EFFECT upon those who come into contact with it. In both these ways, that is, as a product of a mind and as the cause of definite effects, it has a deep moral significance and unmistakable moral quality.

This passage comes from Lord's major work, the original version of the Production Code dating from 1930. Lord wrote it with help from Martin Quigley, publisher of the *Motion Picture Herald*, and Cardinal Mundelein of Chicago. Producers accepted the text of the Code almost unedited. (For instance, they retained the repeated use of all capital letters, which in this case suggests condescension to the reader.) Lord was a well known Catholic writer who also edited a publication called *The Queen's Work*. His collaborator and superior in the church led a rather lurid personal life, as a submission "from a priest" published in Boyd McDonald's *Meat* (1981) attests:

> At the death of George Mundelein, Cardinal Archbishop of Chicago from 1915 to 1939, four cops were needed to eject the harem of bumboys which His Eminence had lodging right there in his palace with him.

There is no further description of the bumboys. The rest of the text concerns the loss of jewelry, such as a heavy gold and amethyst ring stolen from the Bishop of Worcester, Massachusetts, and pawned by a young Marine; another episcopal ring was flushed down the toilet.

The Production Code declared vast areas of human experience, including bumboys and toilets, off limits to American movies. The proscriptions most pertinent to Boyd's later work included the following:

> —The sanctity of the institution of marriage and the home shall be upheld. —Pictures shall not infer that low forms of sex relationship are the accepted or common thing....
> —Sex perversion or any inference to it is forbidden....
> —Miscegenation (sex relationships between the white and black races) is forbidden....
> —Certain places are so closely and thoroughly associated with sexual life or with sexual sin that their use must be carefully limited.

Regarding the penultimate item on the list, Boyd reminds us in *Scum* (1993) that "black and white men were sexually integrated long before this nation integrated them in schools and jobs." The phrase "certain places" in the last item was generally understood to mean brothels and the offices of abortion doctors. Lord may have had other locales in mind as well, places mentioned in the pages of *Straight to Hell*, e. g., public toilets, parks, locker rooms, and even the palaces of the Catholic Church's hierarchy. All were possible venues for the queen's work.

The Production Code was decisive in shaping the consciousness of millions of movie fans, and Boyd McDonald was no exception. These "Don'ts and Be Carefuls" were promulgated in an attempt to control public discourse from the year Boyd entered elementary school (1930) until the year he left the workplace (1968). Later, the Production Code and the assumptions behind it defined the targets of Boyd's satirical writing, whether the subject was a film or not. Especially important to him were two related effects of the restrictions on popular cinema: first, the homosexual was obliged to construct a life for himself without the aid of self-affirming images; and second, the benighted majority was lulled into a complacency untroubled by any thoughts about the homosexual. Men had sex with each other constantly without anyone but the interested parties—including "dirt" (as vice cops were called) and the occasional "do-gooder"—paying attention. When homosexuals went to the movies, they had little expectation of seeing anyone resembling themselves, so in the absence of actors going after cock, their fantasies revolved around actresses who could go after men (if not their cocks) as enthusiastically as the Production Code would allow them.

In the context of a review of Pauline Kael's *5001 Nights at the Movies* (1982) called "A Hearty Heterosexual Looks at the Picture Biz" in the *STH* volume *Cum* (1983), Boyd explicitly presents his point of view as a writer about film. He also expresses his preference for actresses and reveals something about his viewing habits.

> In fact Kael is the only real man, in the classical sense, among the huge mob of picture reviewers (or as they prefer, film

critics) in New York. She is typically heterosexual in her frequent, and suspect, use of the adjective "bitchy" to depict women, and shows no awareness that it is boys and men who are the real bitches in our culture; the entire cast of *The Women*, who after all restrict their fighting to people they know, do not add up to anything as "bitchy" as a single sexually-distressed boy or man who calls a perfect stranger "fag."

Motion pictures are for people who like to watch women; the men in pictures, as Bette Davis and Kael herself have said, are not *men*. There's better stuff on the streets, any street; the streets are my cinema, the male whores my Brandos of the boulevard, the only time I see on the streets men like those who appear in pictures—Warren Beatty, Ronnie Reagan, Robert Taylor, Ryan O'Neal, Robert Redford and so on—is when by coincidence I pass, just as it is letting out, a dancing school. I haven't gone to the movies since 1969 (*The Damned*); that picture, according to Kael, has "gorgeous naked boys in black lace panties," an observation that, if it had appeared in any other magazine, could be reprinted... as its "Neatest Trick of the Week." But I watch oldies on TV.

Thus Boyd McDonald encapsulates the inspiration for his own book, *Cruising the Movies*.

The people appearing in films interested Boyd more than the people working behind the camera. He belonged to an old-fashioned generation of film fans who populated the audiences of revival houses and special screenings around New York. In a *Village Voice* article from 1975, Mark Jacobson describes what he calls a "film freak":

Tad is a Bette Davis fan. He got his hair rinsed blonde and sometimes he uses a curling iron on it. He walks with his hand in his back pocket. He says "what a dump" a lot. He also spends at least 15 hours a week watching movies.... Tad usually can be seen at any Bette movie at the Theatre 80 St. Marks, or MoMA, or in front of his "erratic little TV."

This form of idolatry—still with us among those who remember Bette Davis and other stars—has been supplanted in respectable circles by a more intellectual form of idolatry that takes its distance from the effusive rhetoric of fan magazines.

The "auteur theory" is an American variation on (or bastardization of) the *politique des auteurs*, the policy of French film critics, first at *Cahiers du Cinéma* in the mid-1950s, then in other cultural journals, to elevate the director from someone who simply kept the actors from running into the furniture to the main creative artist shaping a motion picture, especially one that has a distinct visual style. (An *auteur* can also be a producer or screenwriter, but usually one with directing responsibilities, credited or not.) The original French version was a program of advocacy, a partisan form of connoisseurship, and the critics who adopted it held that if popular films could be great art, then they must have artists behind them. The *politique des auteurs* diminished the contributions of the many other creative workers involved in making movies, and it has been widely criticized, yet has nonetheless proven durable, because it is useful in film criticism. It reached a wide audience in the US when "Notes on the Auteur Theory" by Andrew Sarris appeared in the *Village Voice* in 1962, and what had been a *politique* congealed into a *théorie*. By the time Boyd stopped going to movie theaters in 1969, the movie star fans—in the eyes of outsiders, not especially classy or educated, and very queeny—were in retreat, as the auteurists took over the scene. The auteurists sought publication in journals, programming opportunities, positions in academia, and ultimately, legitimacy for film studies. While Boyd probably would not have had sex with a bleached blonde Bette Davis fan, he did tend to align himself politically with a more colorful element among film fans.

Cruising the Movies conducts a subtle polemic against the *politique des auteurs*. The book includes essays about films directed by some of the auteurists' biggest heroes: Fritz Lang, Nicholas Ray (with *Macao* being the work of Ray and Joseph von Sternberg), and Frank Capra (who has less snob appeal); but Boyd does not once use their names.

He acknowledges only a few directors, and all of them in passing. The Richard Widmark quotes appearing in Boyd's essay "Kiss of Death" mention two directors: "Henry Hathaway didn't want me"; and "Otto [Preminger] just didn't know what he was doing." To Boyd Vincente Minnelli was "one of the swishiest men in Hollywood history." In another essay, "Star of Stars," he calls Bob Mizer of Athletic Model Guild "the DeMille of posing strap pictures." Boyd also exposes the *New York Times* obituary of Henry Hathaway as plagiarized from Ephraim Katz's *The Film Encyclopedia* (1982).

During his years as a film critic, Boyd never wrote about Louise Brooks, possibly because Kenneth Tynan had already published a famous essay on her in *The New Yorker* (a magazine Boyd read regularly) in 1979, and because it was almost impossible for someone who didn't go to theaters to see silent movies in the 1980s. Perhaps Brooks was too highbrow—or worse, middle-brow striving for high—to interest Boyd. She had, after all, made her greatest films, *Pandora's Box* and *Diary of a Lost Girl* (both 1929), in Europe. Nonetheless, Louise and Boyd had a few things in common; for one, he would have agreed with her in denouncing the tendency to value directors over stars, a subject which she, having once been a movie star, approached from an informed point of view. John Kobal included an interview with Louise Brooks in his book *People Will Talk* (1986), which Boyd reviewed for *Christopher Street*. In one of her lengthy and some-times caustic responses to Kobal's questions, Brooks defends Mae Murray, the star of *The Merry Widow* (1925) directed by Erich von Stroheim, against her detractors.

> It's so unfair the way they treat people. Now, for instance, von Stroheim has become an idol, you see, and so Mae Murray just stinks all around, all over. Now, she was the most ridiculous woman, and the most ridiculous actress, and let us say insane. In a way. On the other hand, she was a great success, and anyone who made a success in the business has something, believe me. It is the roughest, toughest, most humiliating and degrading job in the world. So they will not allow her to be even fairly good,

let's say in *The Merry Widow*. It was the best performance she ever gave, and it is cruel, when she was an old woman, not to give her credit for what she had: a lovely body, a certain kind of grace, a kind of silly personality. The fact is, her pictures kept old man [Louis B.] Mayer going at Metro for a long time, so she must have had something, for in the end it is the public that matters with films…. It isn't like great literature which very few people can understand and those few people have to pass it down from century to century. Anyone who goes to a movie can understand it; whether it catches them emotionally or not isn't the answer. All you have to have is an eye and an ear, to have lived, spoken, felt, eaten, drunk, and so forth.

Mae Murray experienced a brief, heady vogue, outlived her fame by almost 40 years, and died indigent. The same thing nearly happened to Louise Brooks, but for the support of a few wealthy admirers and an encounter with the film fans living across the hall from her New York apartment. These young men threw a party and used an image from a Louise Brooks film on the invitation, which she noticed, and was very angry until they convinced her that she was not the butt of a joke. One of her neighbors knew the director of the film archive at George Eastman House, James Card, who said some months later, "I would give anything to talk to Louise Brooks." Soon after-wards, Brooks's resurrection began. Like Boyd, she stopped drinking after decades of alcoholism and reinvented herself as a writer of unflinching honesty and precise style. Before she wrote her autobiography, *Lulu in Hollywood* (1982), she was merely a has-been. For many years, the former colleagues she saw in public would look through her as though she wasn't even there; only a few homosexuals cared.

From the mid-1960s to the late 1980s, Richard Lamparski made it his mission to track down as many "has-beens" as he could find and interview them for his radio show. He wrote books based upon these interviews, a series of 11 volumes with the title *Whatever Became Of…?* Lamparski was an important reference for Boyd, and as he asserts in *Meat*, "so crucial to American culture that one no longer uses his first name, Richard." Lamparski is rarely discussed today, because his type of celebrity journalism has become commonplace, and because almost all the people he interviewed are now long dead, replaced in the public's affection by many subsequent generations of celebrities.

When Lamparski began this work, his idea was so new that few believed it had any merit, even though he had no lack of material; there were many actors who had not appeared in movies for years, and had no way of reaching the audiences that once flocked to their movies. As Lamparski explains in a 2012 interview,

> I had a close friend [who] was very encouraging to me, but he really wasn't very interested in what I was doing, he was only interested in movies, not movie stars…. He said to me once, "I hope you're not gonna spend a couple of years of your life trying to get this thing underway and not succeed…. How are you gonna find, I don't know, Gale Sondergaard?" I said, "Well, we know she's alive—that's a clue. And number two, I'll look her up in the phone book under her husband's name." We knew him because he'd been sent to prison as part of "the Unfriendly 10" [leftist writers and directors who were convicted of contempt of Congress for refusing to answer questions about their political affiliations before the House Un-American Activities Committee in 1947]. I picked up the New York phone book and I see her—Mrs. Herbert Biberman. And he looked at me and said, "You can do it."… And now to get the permission. I called while he was there, called cold, and told Biberman who I was. He said, "Well, she's having a bath just now, but I'll tell her. We both listen to WBAI…. Give me your telephone number and Gale will call you in the next day or so."
>
> Years later, she told me that she was in the tub… and he came and stood in the doorway and… said, "You can go on the air, no commercials, and tell about what happened to you…. So either you'll do it or you won't." She said, "I was never really sure if I had a chance to speak I would….

He forced me into it, and I realized it was the right thing to do." So I changed her life in a way and I proved I could do it.

On Lamparski's radio program, Gale Sondergaard told the story of her husband's and her own blacklisting, as well as the harassed production and distribution of the independent film directed by Biberman, *Salt of the Earth* (1954), about a New Mexico zinc miners' strike. The interview was broadcast in May 1966, and it came at the beginning of a career revival for Sondergaard. While she was blacklisted, she had done some theater acting (mainly summer stock and off-Broadway one-woman shows), but in the late 1960s, she returned to movies, made appearances on television shows, and continued to speak publicly about the Hollywood Blacklist.

Originally trained in the theater and reluctant to act in movies, Gale Sondergaard scored a triumph in *Anthony Adverse* (1936), winning the first Academy Award for Best Supporting Actress for her first screen role. She was the choice of Mervyn Leroy, *The Wizard of Oz*'s original director, to play the Wicked Witch of the West. She made two screen tests: one as a slinky villainess (her preference), and the other as an ugly hag (the studio's). Wary of the effect hideous prosthetic makeup would have on her image as a glamour girl, she turned down the part in favor of a role in *The Life of Emile Zola* (1937), a prestige picture and Academy Award winner that hardly anyone remembers anymore. She followed this role with many others, mainly exotic types. She played a Eurasian widow exacting revenge upon the "other woman" (Bette Davis) who shot her husband in *The Letter* (1940), and in *Anna and the King of Siam* (1946), she played a Thai courtier, a role for which she received an Oscar nomination.

Not limiting herself to prestige pictures, Sondergaard did some of her most memorable work in horror and suspense movies while under contract at Universal Studios. As the title character in *The Spider Woman* (1944), she enlivened an average Sherlock Holmes movie, and unbeknownst to her, inspired a little boy who would become an important Latin American writer, Manuel Puig. Years before he began his novel *Kiss of the Spider Woman* (1976), Puig

Rondo Hatton and Gale Sondergaard in *The Spider Woman Strikes Back* (1946).

wrote to his friend and fellow author, Guillermo Cabrera Infante, about his first experience of success, "I feel like Gale Sondergaard in *Return of the Spider Woman.*" (This may have been a mistake introduced by a translation of a translation; the title of the film is actually *The Spider Woman Strikes Back*.) *The Spider Woman Strikes Back* (1946) features the same lead actress and was produced by the same studio, but otherwise bears no relation to *The Spider Woman*. The plot concerns a woman (played by Sondergaard) wreaking vengeance on the town her family once owned. She poses as a kindly blind woman while surreptitiously draining the blood of her paid companion (Brenda Joyce) to feed a rare poisonous plant in her basement. Attended by her grotesque assistant (Rondo Hatton), she performs these tasks in a sequined gown. As she pours blood into a blossom, a tendril of the plant grabs her arm, and she exclaims, "You beautiful creature!" It is a sublime scene in the midst of a numbingly pedestrian movie.

Because she was blacklisted, Gale Sondergaard disappeared from the screen, and her fans were deprived of the opportunity to observe her fade away gradually. Manuel Puig must have been disappointed, because one of his greatest obsessions was locating the exact moment when an actress was at her absolute peak of beauty and allure. Puig did not take a cruel pleasure in describing an actress's decline, because he identified completely with women in movies. He felt deep down that he was a woman, and in speaking with intimates except his mother, he referred to people exclusively using the feminine gender, which has an even stranger effect in Spanish than in English. He also noted in excruciating detail the decline of his own middle-aged body (male pattern baldness, a stooped posture) and its result: diminishing attention received from men in public. Above all, Puig wanted a husband; he never found one.

By contrast, in *Cruising the Movies*, Boyd McDonald turns his obsessive gaze on actors, or as he calls them, "eating stuff." He holds that talent is not only irrelevant, but a distraction from the main point of movies, the exhibition of beautiful and exceptional people simply being rather than acting. A star is above all a person millions of spectators want to rim, suck, and fuck. Boyd cites the example of Guy Madison. He was discovered by Henry Willson, a closeted homosexual legendary for his eye for male beauty and despicable politics. A native of Pumpkin Corner, California, Madison made his first appearance on screen in the patriotic snoozer, *Since You Went Away* (1944), while on leave from the Navy. Wearing his own uniform, with a cascade blond curls spilling over his forehead, and speaking in a languorous, untrained voice, he seems to have been imported from another, more lascivious movie. Madison in his screen debut sounds a bit like Jack Smith, though he does not ask embarrassing questions about men getting indelible lipstick on their cocks, as Smith asked Frances Francine on the soundtrack of *Flaming Creatures* (1963) two decades later. Madison's character has a sexless three-way, going on a date with a girl and her boyfriend (Robert Walker, in an Army uniform). Before the sort of action described in *Straight to Hell* can transpire, the sailor catches his bus and exits the scene. Madison creates an indelible impression during a few minutes in the middle of a three-hour movie. The popular reaction, in the form of thousands of fan letters, was immediate. Studio executives signed up Madison once he was discharged, but

Guy Madison in a mid-1940s publicity still.

they insisted he take acting lessons, voice lessons, and dancing lessons to become a "real" actor. He never learned much; he merely got older and tired.

Boyd's taste in actresses displayed a range of interests: he appreciated women of impressive physical bearing (Jane Russell, Hope Emerson), glamorous antagonists (Gail Patrick, Lynn Bari), and tough leading ladies (Barbara Stanwyck, Gloria Grahame). The only thing he could not abide was a display of mere talent. (Katherine Hepburn was a favorite object of scorn.) He had special affection for any actress who maintained a sense of humor about the absurd situations in which she found herself. All of the women Boyd admired were adept at delivering a wisecrack, and this ability, learned from countless hours of movie viewing, found its way into his writing and conversation. He did not want to be Barbara Stanwyck, but he aspired to the contemptuous way she treated men, who were, after all, only sex objects.

Boyd's sensibility became fixed during his youth in the 1930s and '40s. The models of behavior he observed at that time haunted him (and society as a whole) for decades, if only as standards against which to react. Manuel Puig called these models "the subdued woman and the dashing male." The actresses of the era had to strike a balance between frank sexual interest, which was unacceptable, and complete passivity, which did not hold the attention of spectators. Wisecracks and double entendres enabled women on screen to be less subdued, and they offered a way of rebelling against convention for the homosexual, whose desires could not be openly expressed except in private. The dialogue of classic Hollywood movies became a *lingua franca* for gay men to use in recognizing each other, venting their frustrations, and talking about the "eating stuff" all around them. Among many (though by no means all) homosexual men in the twentieth century, identification with film actresses—their transports of emotion, how they moved and spoke, what they wore—was so profound and complex that few who experienced it were able to analyze or explain the phenomenon to outsiders. Those who could do so (like Puig) risked being dismissed as silly queens. It was not just a question of strategy or subversion, and the term "camp" does not quite encompass it, either. What was seen and heard at the movies altered the very texture of daily life, simultaneously imprisoning several generations' imaginations and giving voice to their innermost desires.

When the movie studios began licensing their giant libraries of films for broadcast in the US, the airwaves were flooded with artifacts from the 1930s and 40s. To people watching (and re-watching) these films in the 1960s, 70s, and early 80s, it was as though the glory days of Hollywood had never entirely gone away. They are vanishing now. A publicity machine postponed oblivion for decades, but the future has finally arrived; to most contemporary spectators, the aesthetic of these films seems utterly remote. A way of life influenced, even engendered, by movie-going is on its way to extinction, like Latin, transformed beyond recognition into vulgar new languages and kept alive in its classical form by a priestly and scholarly caste which must struggle to remain relevant, or else resign itself to insignificance. The old gods have been cast down, and their graven images no longer hold the masses in awe. The artifacts of the original cults—posters, autographs, bits of production ephemera—are lately being treated with something less than respect. Former treasures end up in landfills, on the sidewalk in front of dead collectors' houses, or at best, in cold storage.

Boyd McDonald found most of the images used in *Cruising the Movies* at the Museum of Modern Art Film Stills Archive, a collection of four million photographs, one of the largest archives of its kind. Production stills for studio films, taken on dressed and lit sets with performers in full make up and costume, do not correspond exactly to any of the shots in a film. Although they are staged, they do not represent dramatic action in motion, and in their frozen glamour, they can reveal what a spectator watching a film might miss. Boyd was always on the lookout for telling erotic details: Gloria Grahame's and Gary Cooper's lips (both wearing lipstick), the bulges in David Nelson's and Michael Callan's skin-tight costumes, and other objects of fascination. A number of his essays were inspired more by stills than by the films from which they came.

Very few of these stills, integral as they are to *Cruising the Movies*, are presently available for reasons that deserve comment. In an article from 2012, Richard Corliss, *Time* magazine's film critic, writes about what happened to the archive directed by his wife Mary:

> On the morning of January 11, 2002, Mary Lea Bandy, chief curator of the MoMA Department of Film and Video, told the two Stills Archive staff members that at the end of the business day two things would happen: the facility would be shuttered and the staffers would be laid off—until, and unless, the Museum found space for the Stills Archive when MoMA returned from its temporary home in Queens to an enlarged Manhattan premises in 2005. The collection was mothballed in the Film Department's vault in Hamlin, Pennsylvania, where it remains today, inaccessible to scholars and journalists, and to the head of the Archive, Mary Corliss.

A *Village Voice* report by Anthony Kaufman from ten years earlier provides further information:

> Corliss had always planned for the archive to stay open to the public during the museum's reconstruction. Together with architects from Cooper, Robertson & Partners, she helped supervise the final plans for a mezzanine-level space in MoMA Queens to house the stills.
>
> But then on April 28, 2000, Corliss, along with 250 MoMA staffers, went on strike. And when she returned in the fall after a bitter 134-day walkout, plans for a Film Stills Archive in Queens no longer seemed to exist. According to Corliss, repeated attempts over the following months to find out about the status of the Stills Archive space in Queens were rebuffed.
>
> "I think it's retribution," says Terry Geesken, who worked alongside Corliss for more than 18 years.... Geesken and Corliss were both active participants in the strike by United Auto Workers union Local 2110... and they suggest the layoffs are related. The coincidence is not lost on many film scholars.

"Mary was a vocal supporter of the strike," says film historian Eric Myers, "and this is one way they have of getting rid of her."

At MoMA, no one is suggesting a link between the strike and the layoffs; [Glenn] Lowry told the *New York Times* that there was no connection. MoMA director Lowry has received much attention for his vocal (and theatrical) opposition to the strike…. An ambitious fundraiser and marketer, Lowry is also known for his willingness to slash staff. During his tenure at the Art Gallery of Ontario, he cut half of the museum's 400 employees during a fiscal crunch and later fired four curators….

With the highest salary of any US museum director, Glenn Lowry makes a lot of money; that much is clear. Exactly how much he makes, in what form it comes to him, and its sources—these are complex questions. When the New York state attorney general's office made inquiries in 2007, the *New York Times* discovered the facts relating to Lowry's actual income. In its effort to recruit Lowry for the job, MoMA created the New York Fine Arts Support Trust, which supplemented his official salary and later rewarded him when the strike was broken. Between 1995 and 2003, Lowry earned $5.35 million in addition to his salary, bonus, and benefits, which totaled $1.28 million for those years. When the Museum Tower was completed, he moved into one of its apartments valued at $6 million and lived there rent-free. According to a *World Socialist Web Site* report in 2000, "At the time of the strike, the median wage for MoMA employees [was] $28,000 a year, and the starting salary for 40 of the workers [was] $17,000 a year." At the time of this writing, the Museum of Modern Art Film Stills Archive remains inaccessible to the public.

In an essay she wrote for Roger Ebert's book, *The Great Movies* (2002), Mary Corliss reflects on the experience of working with film stills:

When I rummage through bulging "personality files" of movie star stills, I can see a compressed life story: the freshness and gawky promise of a young actor; the radiant maturity as the star's appeal is complemented by the filmmakers' artistry;

then, as age writes its cruel lines on a face, the poignant battle against decay, waged with heavy makeup and lighting that is ever more carefully soft-focus. Any of these personality files is a flip-book that grants me a God's-eye view into both the intoxicating nature of human beauty and the inevitability of mortality. In a film still, though, an actor can remain forever at the apogee of his appeal.

When asked about Boyd McDonald, Mary Corliss responded with the following message:

> I fondly remember Mr. McDonald as a frequent visitor to the Film Stills Archive who was keenly intent on finding the perfect images to illustrate his literary projects. Although he was always professional and extremely knowledgeable about film history, our discussions, albeit friendly and professional, never extended to any subjects other than cinema, film stills, and MoMA's exhibitions.

Film fans generally develop a solitary devotion, for while a group of people comes together at an appointed time to see a screening, the experience of watching a movie in the darkness of a theater isolates them. Each spectator—understood in this case to be a male homosexual, like John Kobal, Richard Lamparski, Boyd McDonald, et al—sees his own movie, has his own list (perhaps not even acknowledged to himself) of fetishes for which he looks. He lies in wait until he is ravished by the sight of *that* actor, *that* gesture, *that* bit of exposed flesh or suggestive fold of cloth. Many of the objects of fascination are really mistakes which a costumer or set dresser, editor or censor forgot to correct, but which become unintended gifts to the fetishist. In discussions after a movie is over, the fetishist argues for what he loves above all with his fellow film fans, but only a sympathetic few will ever understand.

After his withdrawal from public movie-going in 1969, Boyd cultivated a circle of friends with whom he could enjoy movies without leaving home. He writes about the experience in *Cruising the Movies*'s essay on *Stallion Road* (1947). The film features a shot of a double rear view: the screen is filled by Ronald Reagan's "sloppy ass" on top of a horse's ass. Boyd, without a VCR to record and review this moment, can hardly believe what he sees.

"My God Almighty!" I cried over the 'phone to a friend when I saw Reagan stick his big butt in the camera, and my friend, watching the picture on his own receiver 60 blocks to the south of me, released a simultaneous cry of astonishment. *Stallion Road*, like most pictures, is not complete in itself and requires audience participation—additional dialogue supplied by the viewers. This is best done at home; it would annoy patrons in the theater. *Stallion Road* is so bleak that my friend and I, connected by telephone as we watched it, supplied not only additional dialogue (all of it unprintable) but also imaginary conversations among the cast and crew between camera set-ups....

It seemed probable to us that Zachary Scott would discuss with Alexis [Smith] their co-star: "That's some butt Ronnie's got on him, isn't it? I've seen better on a fucking elephant. Shit, he's not a piece of meat, he's only Spam."

Boyd's main companion in this activity was his editor, Tom Steele, who describes their camaraderie:

Back in the 1980s and '90s, I had to work in my office until the wee hours of each morning in order to prepare our publications, *New York Native* and *Christopher Street*. (I was the only editor at the time.) Practically the only person I knew who was still wide awake was Boyd, and many nights I would go to his single-room-furnished to visit. Boyd was a recovered alcoholic, but he kept a bottle of vodka on hand for me to unwind with.... Even if I didn't go to Boyd's apartment, I would usually call him at two in the morning or so, and we would chat for an hour or more. Often, we watched the same late-night movie on our TVs while talking on the phone, and he usually wrote about those movies for *Christopher Street*. *Cruising the Movies* was the eventual result.

At times the book reads like the transcript of an evening with a circle of gay men sitting around watching movies and providing their own acerbic commentary. Boyd McDonald's *Cruising the Movies* serves as a tribute to this most ephemeral cultural activity.

According to journalist and activist Arthur Bell, publicity stills of Tom Cruise compelled Boyd to break his moratorium on going to movie theaters. Boyd emerged from his single room to see *All the Right Moves* (1983), which he called a "heterosexual training film," a remark no writer reviewing films for a general audience could make. Most critics were so "plot crazed," as Boyd put it, that they could not acknowledge the obvious, even when it was highlighted by telling details. For example, the teen sex scenes, strenuous calisthenics, and locker room dramas of *All the Right Moves* play out in a fictional town with the evocatively phallic name of Ampipe.

After taking a break from contemporary movies for a whole decade in the 1970s, Boyd must have been disoriented by an American popular cinema that had become ever more infantile and jingoistic since Ronald Reagan was elected president. In *All the Right Moves*, Boyd saw a representation of the white working people who got piped, and who would be conned a year later into reelecting Ronnie the loveable shyster, formerly an omnipresent corporate spokesman, who was nothing if not their class enemy. Boyd did not often write about the movies of the Reagan '80s; no doubt they were too transparently cynical and manipulative to interest him very much. He preferred the highly coded and chaste films of his youth.

Watching "oldies" on television in the middle of the night, Boyd McDonald, declassed Ivy Leaguer and film fan, would write about the details that not only caught his attention but moved him to howl and applaud. He exposed the subtexts that made Hollywood films immensely popular yet could not be named. *Cruising the Movies* is his account of the return of the repressed. The book encourages us to enjoy the products of mass culture against the grain, which is to say politically, in ways that are at once anarchic, knowing, and intensely pleasurable.

CRUISING THE MOVIES

A SEXUAL GUIDE TO OLDIES ON TV

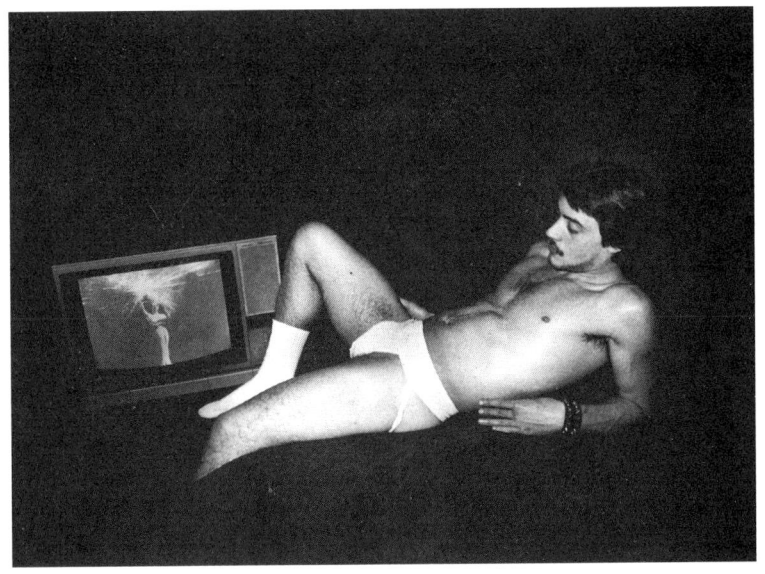

Boyd McDonald

Gay Presses of New York

PREFACE

Most of these articles ran in *Christopher Street*. A few ran in *New York Native*, *Connection*, and *Philadelphia Gay News*.

I asked Tom Steele, editor of *Christopher Street*, not to take cream in his coffee, as I take mine black and don't like people who aren't like me. He refused to give up cream but he has met Anne Baxter, and on the strength of that I have continued to work with him, as with the other editors.

I am indebted to Gregory McVay, who devoted his life to drinking and watching movies, for some insights that would not without him have occurred to me. Not only did he have a friend who interviewed Ginger Rogers, but Gregory himself knew Tallulah Bankhead.

Many of my readers, it turns out, have met many movie stars. Some movie stars in retirement seem to have nothing better to do than to call their fans, sometimes while plastered. It is distressing that the magnificent Mary Astor is living in a "home" for retired players when there are millions of men who would care for her in a home of her own and watch, with her, old Mary Astor movies.

Most homosexuals are authorities on movies and my comments in this book, however much they may seem like hasty judgments, are the result of prolonged discussions with other authorities. One of my editors and I, for example, spent the better part of 1984 speculating about David Nelson's butt, and our discussions are continuing in 1985.

I have confined my studies to pictures which are available on commercial TV. I watched them on a GE b/w receiver. It cost $80 and has brought me an estimated $80 million worth of ecstasy.

I have, finally, no wife to thank for typing my manuscript. Unlike "straight" writers, if I had a wife I'd want her to do something that's more fun than typing my manuscript.

—Boyd McDonald, *New York City, March, 1985*

A still of such extreme beauty as this could only come from one studio: AMG (Athletic Model Guild). One of the butt-holes shown—I don't believe I have to say which one—is arguably the finest ever photographed.

AMG is the smallest and finest studio in the film capital. The only other studio which was anywhere near as interesting was Monogram, and even Monogram was far behind. Ever since the 1950s, decades before photographs of bareassed men became a staple product on newsstands, Bob Mizer, founder of AMG, has been supplying movies and still photographs of the finest male flesh obtainable. He has had trouble with cops and other sexually deranged people and has survived as a hero of modern homosexuality. By now he has accumulated what is doubtless the world's greatest treasure of photographs of naked men and of men in posing straps and jock straps, including some of the finest pieces of ass in the military (or AWOL from the military). Virtually any AMG butt selected at random is superior in quality to those of Cary Grant, Gary Cooper, Clark Gable, in fact to almost any star at the bigger studios with the exception of David Nelson and Bobby Jordan. The AMG collection is overwhelming; there is nothing I can say about it. But nothing has to be said; the AMG photographs speak the international language of lust.

Unlike the other movies mentioned in this book, Mizer's are not shown on TV. I recommend sending him $6.00 for a couple of issues of *Physique Pictorial*, his photo magazine, which shows some of the AMG meat available. The address is: Bob Mizer, AMG, 1834 West 11th Street, Los Angeles, California 90006.

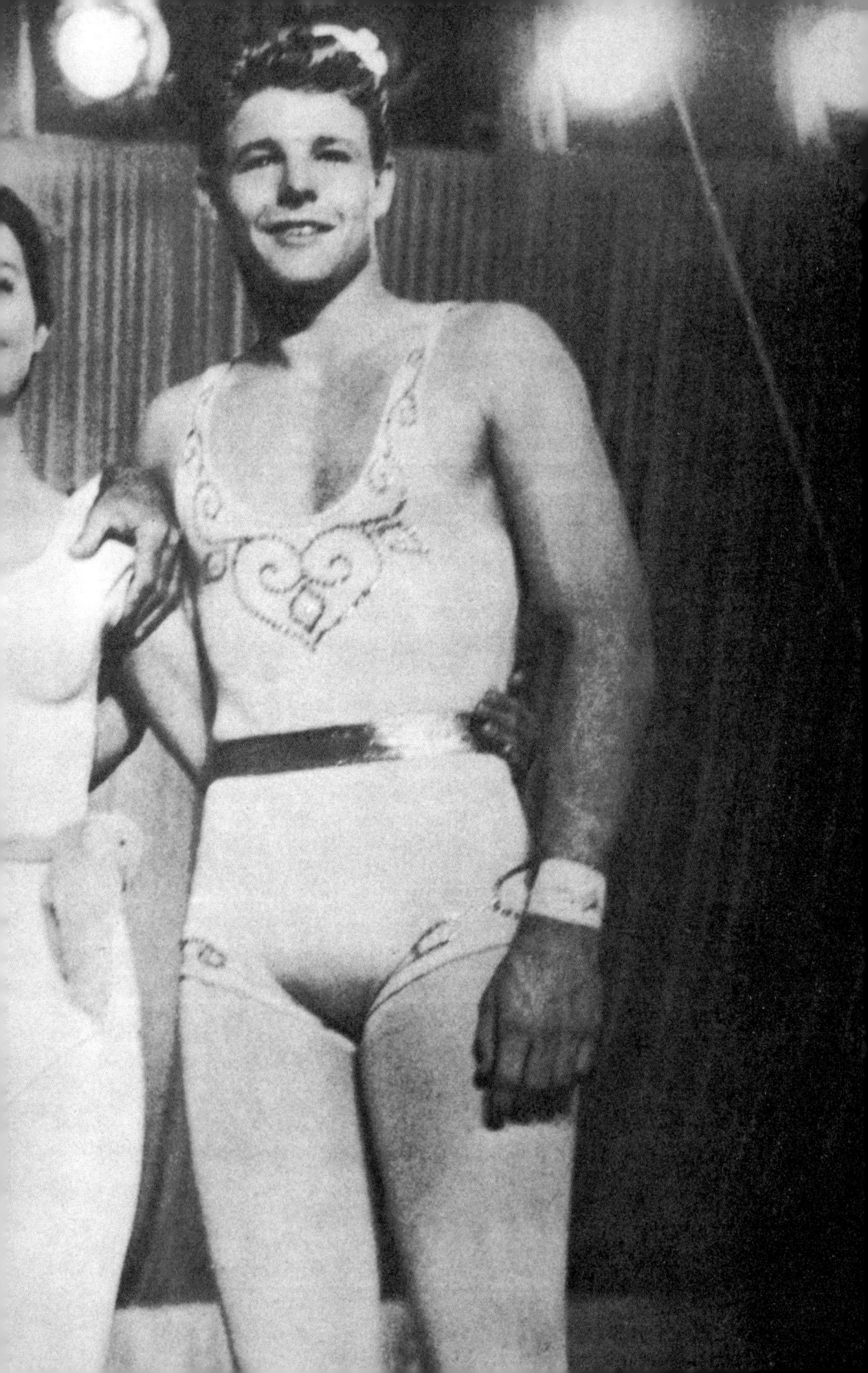

THE BIG CIRCUS

The David Nelson story is largely unprintable, not because of anything David has done but because of what men would like to do with him. Fortunately, there is no need to tell the story in words; it is pretty much contained in stills and glossies of David. Stills from *The Big Circus* (1959), in which he wore white trapeze tights, are especially articulate; I don't think I have to list the various parts of that body that men would like to "eat," as I believe they call it.

I always depend upon the art director and editor to run photographs that supply graphic evidence for my sermonettes; I especially need them now to tell my story in a glossy, for the exact details of the lust David inspires are best left in the bedroom (or if you prefer, as I do, in the bushes, alleys, offices, cars, trucks, theater balconies, and public terlets). I am not privy to advance knowledge of what glossies run with my articles and I was shocked—but pleasantly—to see in my study of Richard Widmark that the art director and editor had actually added a vital new concept by running a still of Widmark with his thighs spread and his left hand resting on his succulent groin. The photograph revealed an inspiring quality in Widmark's nature that I had not even dared, in my text, to suggest (or in my mind, to hope). A man's hand resting on his bulge is eloquent body language which says that he enjoys his meat and lets others enjoy it too; with that slight but overpoweringly obscene gesture, a man suddenly gives the shocking signal that his meat, up to then merely an impossible dream, is in reality available. (I mean of course men generally, not Widmark specifically.)

Even if he had made no other pictures than *The Big Circus*, David Nelson would still rank as one of Hollywood's premier suck objects. On or off the trapeze, his body composes a variety of images for which the word "historic" would not be an exaggeration, and when, on rare occasions, he turns his butt to the camera, the white fabric clinging ecstatically to his crack can only draw gasps from men who have an aesthetic sense (for it is the kind of butt they like to wallow in like pigs, the dirty things). At gatherings of serious cineastes, speculation sooner or later turns to David Nelson's asshole—his "vital center," in Arthur Schlesinger's phrase. (Schlesinger did do some picture reviews, but he used the phrase to describe centrist political goals rather than David's asshole.) In the absence of any published data—David married twice, but if either of his wives had any special interest in or knowledge of his asshole, she has not written of it—the only thing film scholars can do is extrapolate from information visible on his face, mainly his eyebrow hairs and pink lips. Most would conclude, I think, that his hole, and the hairs which formed its ornamental frame, were among the finest in the film capital. By contrast, the heavy black brows of Brooke Shields and Matt Dillon threaten the possibility that these two newer players are, literally, bushy-tailed.

Simply by giving men the right kind of look with his jewel-like eyes—eyes of the sort the lyricist probably had in mind when he wrote:

> Jeepers, creepers,
> Where'd you get those peepers?
> Jeepers, creepers,
> Where'd you get those eyes?

—David could, had he wanted, have spent his life being licked. But such a routine would soon lead to skin irritations on various parts of his body, and instead of thus satisfying mere thousands of men utterly, he chose to satisfy millions of them partially by appearing for over a decade on TV with his parents, Ozzie 'n' Harriet, and his brother Eric (commonly known as Ricky), and by making at least five pictures, including *Day of the Outlaw*, which sounds especially worthwhile; *The Remarkable Mr. Pennypacker*, whose star, Clifton Webb, possibly gave his evaluation of David's thighs in correspondence with Noel Coward or someone similar; *30*; and *Peyton Place*, in which, David said in a 1957 interview at Fox while clad in blue jeans, loafers and an "untucked" shirt, he is "red-blooded and all-American" and "the only normal character in the picture."

He "wondered if girls went out with him only because he was famous." He would have no such worry had he "gone out" with boys, who not only would not want publicity but would actually have wanted to keep it secret since, in all likelihood, their sole interest in "going" with him would be to play with his peter, nuts, and, in some cases, his asshole. I don't have to tell you how nasty boys are. David played football at USC, sired two sons, who are in all probability embarrassingly handsome, and indulged in one of the two main California vulgarities, driving a Porsche, but not, so far as is known, in the other one, cocaine. In 1974 Lamparski's *Whatever Became Of...?* quoted David as saying that "life really began" for him and his wife "when we accepted Jesus Christ as our Savior"; the following year he accepted a new wife, according to a cutting from *Variety* in his file at the Lincoln Center Library.

In white tights in *The Big Circus*, seen at 3 p.m., April 14, 1984, on Channel 5, David's body is more starkly erotic than one that is "stark naked." The dazzling white of his costume erases all human imperfections and distractions, such as body hairs, blemishes, scars, pores, and so on, and purifies and idealizes his body while still displaying its exact form. A noticeable percentage of the male population, perhaps around 35 percent, would probably like to examine David's body under any circumstances, including nudity. But even the middle class can regard David's groin and butt, when wrapped tightly in pure white, as being in good taste, and he was, moreover, an authentic athlete, having trained and performed with a couple of trapeze artists who had the fascinating names of Del and Babs. So that he was eligible for the admirations of men who normally cannot permit themselves to worship the male body except under the guise of sports lovers, a phrase which is breathtakingly apt. *In toto*, adding up David's honest sexual fans, the middle class (who dare admire him in white tights), and the sports lovers (who can pretend, perhaps even believe, that it is his athletic skill they like), perhaps as much as 80 percent of the male population would be interested in *The Big Circus*. His body thus was potentially one of the most valuable properties in Hollywood, yet it was scarcely used cinematically or, for all I know, sexually. If there were ever an actor ideally suited for such poses as sitting back in his jock strap with one leg over the arm of a chair, it is David Nelson. This is the sort of image men like to crawl and grovel for. But *The Big Circus*, made when he was about 23 years old, is the only picture which displayed his body and even in this picture his body is seen only fleetingly until the climax. Then it is seen in all its glory in a chase sequence as David climbs up the trapeze rigging and walks the tightrope; even his shadow moving against the circus tent is awesome.

Characteristically, the *Times* schedule ignored David's tempting body and did not even include his name in its listing; hundreds of thousands of New Yorkers who have no other source of information than the *Times* were thus unaware of the opportunity to see perhaps the greatest exhibition of a perfect male body in action ever recorded on film. The plot-crazy *Times* TV schedule writer complained that *The Big Circus* has "every big-top cliché invented." Any hack writer can construct a plot, but, to paraphrase the renowned hack poet, Joyce Kilmer, only God can make a butt. A reviewer who is blind to such beauty and complains of "clichés" would ask for franks 'n' beans in a Chinese restaurant.

Comprehensive though the images of David's white-clad body may be, they only arouse questions—questions which someone on the crew of *The Big Circus* could answer, and I hope will answer in a Letter to the Editor. Did David have his own private dressing room for this picture? When he changed into his circus tights, where did he leave his street clothes? Did he wear Jockey shorts? Where did he toss his shorts when he pulled them off? Were they ever stolen from his dressing room? Did he bring his own trapeze costumes from his act with the adorable Del and Babs, or did the studio supply them? Did the wardrobe department do fittings and alterations on his tights? Did he wear anything under his tights to, as it were, "catch the drip?" Did he wear anything to hold back his dick and nuts, which did not form a satisfying bulge in his costume, or was he simply, like so many men, not well hung? Where did he toss his tights after a day's shooting? Were they picked up by the studio laundry? Did collectors ever steal, or try to buy, his used tights? If David owned them himself and took them home with him, did he launder them himself? Did he examine them before laundering them? If so, in what sense? Where did he buy them? Where did he try them on? What did he think of his appearance in the mirror? Did he get a hard-on while dressing or undressing? Did his dick leak or drip when he thought of romance? Did anyone in the crew whistle when he walked onto the set in his tights? How, in such a complex costume, did he go about taking a leak, or taking a shit, during the day's shooting? Did anyone from the Fox wardrobe department ever sell his used tights? Laundered or unlaundered? I assume the wardrobe people were hip enough to know that the tights would be worth a goodly sum unlaundered.

BOMBA AND THE HIDDEN CITY

Starting in 1939 at the age of eight, Johnny Sheffield made at least eight Tarzan pictures as "Boy." In his late teens and early twenties, he made at least five and perhaps as many as 11 Bomba the Jungle Boy pictures, starting in 1949. His flesh, especially in the Tarzan pictures, can efficiently be summarized as perfect; inevitably, by the end of the Bomba period some slight decomposition had begun to set in. Still his body always looked better than any other available on the screen, then or even now.

His *oeuvre* comprises the principal filmed record of the growth during a decade of a boy's flesh, from beginning to end silken, hairless, perfectly rounded. He is seen, almost naked, while standing, lying down, sitting with one or both knees up, squatting, running, jumping, swimming, wrestling, swinging on vines, climbing trees and hills. More people have seen more of his flesh than that of any other player. Before puberty his body was a child molester's dream; in his post-paederast period, as he grew to 190 pounds, he arrested the attention of men who like a husky youth.

Throughout his career, as both "Boy" and Bomba, he wore only a loin cloth which was revealing even by today's standards and especially *avant-garde* for the 1940s and 1950s: a narrow flap in front and a wider one in back. Since the nakedness of his hips between the two flaps was marred only by a string around his waist, he could not have been wearing briefs underneath. I assume he wore a pouch holding his nuts; I know he wore a piece of black cloth covering most, but by no means all, of his butt. In *Bomba and the Hidden City* (1950), seen on Channel 9 on September 10 at 5:30 a.m. (yes, a.m.), I saw for the first time the scanty black cloth under his back flap. Photographed from below and behind as he scampered up an artificial hill on the studio back lot, the flap, which normally guards his butt carefully, fell aside. The undercloth covered the top two-thirds of his butt, but the lower third—smooth and creamy—was bare.

I have never seen the corresponding pouch in front. I don't believe, in all his exertions, the front flap has ever fallen aside to reveal the pouch underneath. If it had, someone would have written me. Since his pictures, the Bombas even more than the Tarzans, were low budget pictures, it seems unlikely that there were a lot of re-takes; and I assume the front flap was sewn to the pouch beneath. At all times, his round thighs are generously and comprehensively displayed; in profile, he shows a couple of inches—but they are the two most crucial inches—of his bare butt where it begins its curve out from his thighs. When he squats, an opportunity for the audience to see the obscene little strip connecting the front pouch with the seat is sabotaged by the fact that Sheffield—suspicious for one so young, and rightly so in light of the millions of eyes waiting for a glimpse of his secrets—holds his perfect knees together.

Of course it is the chance for such a glimpse, rather than anything in the scripts, which are noticeably less aesthetic than Sheffield's body, that constitutes the real suspense in his pictures and holds the viewers' concentration more than do ordinary pictures. Television is therefore the ideal medium for them; were it not for the commercials, viewers would have no chance to take coffee or other refreshments, and uninterrupted concentration on an entire Sheffield picture in a theater would tire the brain, to say nothing of the balls.

The literature classifies Sheffield as popular among audiences of children, and it is certainly true that young boys like to see and play with each others' peters. But it is not until they are older that they normally begin to crave more intimate examinations of each others' bodies; it is a craving that grows more maddening—but in a pleasant, even ecstatic way—as the years and decades go by, and I believe it is millions of dirty old men in their 20s and on up, as much of the audience of children, who support the Sheffield pictures. It is these men for whom Sheffield is a really huge star. Many of his pictures are available on TV, so that his chaste but occasionally fickle loin clothes provide not just a great moment in movies, strictly speaking, but many great hours.

Sheffield's face was too friendly and contented to qualify as a red hot Class 1 sex object (he was, after all, born and raised in Pasadena); Ivan Lendl, the churlish Czech, is so fantastically unfriendly, so sullen, grouchy, mean, touchy, impatient, arrogant, contemptuous, rude, selfish, and inconsiderate that I couldn't help but become deeply interested in him (but not deeply enough to show up at Bloomingdale's when he made a PA there late in August to promote some tasteless Adidas athletic drag). Moreover, Lendl wears it on the right, and this type comes closer to the ideal of the male slut than do conventional men who let it hang on the left; the male slut differs from his female counterpart in that while she is blatantly willing to please, he, like Lendl, seems more interested in humiliating.

In our sex-shy culture, Sheffield is not even listed in most of the movie literature. The *Times* did not even list *Bomba and the Hidden City* in its daily TV schedule, even though it was the principal TV attraction of September 10 (and they call that "the paper of record"). A clue to what the *Times* would think of Bomba, if it thought of him, can be seen in Janet Maslin's condemnation in that paper of a film showing naked Swedish schoolboys as "prurient;" decoded, this means merely that Maslin is not interested in naked boys. She is an attractive young woman and I wish her luck in acquiring whatever partner she does desire, if any; but her mind is not her best feature. Steven H. Scheuer's *Movies on TV* lists such unnecessary players as Maureen O'Sullivan and Charles Bickford in the cast of *Tarzan's New York Adventure* (1942), but not Sheffield; this is a picture I'm eager to "catch," for it acts out what must be everyone's dream (Boy gets kidnapped). Though not even listed in Scheuer, Sheffield would be anatomically at least the star of the picture, and a professor in London spoke for millions when he wrote me upon seeing Tarzan on TV during Christmas holidays in northern Scotland, "After watching Johnny Weissmuller's tits grow rounder and fuller with each Tarzan movie, as alas his belly followed suit, I found that, divine as his mammoth butt promised to be, I turned my attention increasingly to Boy, Johnny Sheffield."

The professional reviewers, without exception, lack the professor's taste and intelligence. Those who do mention Sheffield at all are patronizing. They judge pictures by their budgets rather than by

their aesthetic value. Leslie Halliwell, whose *Film Guide* reveals him to be considerably more regal than his sovereign, Elizabeth R., calls the Bomba pictures "cut-rate hokum," and Leonard Maltin's *TV Movies* reports that Bomba's producer, Walter Mirisch, "has gone on to far greater things" when what he means is "far more expensive things." Ryan O'Neal, for example, is far more expensive than Johnny Sheffield but scarcely "greater;" O'Neal's embarrassingly thin ankles, so thin as to raise the question of whether he has some Negro blood, detract from any favorable impression made by his bare ass, which anyway, forgetting his trivial ankles, comes within ounces of the heavyweight class (a claim that could hardly be made for his acting talent). The prognosis is that eventually he may suffer from the "ice cream cone legs" which afflicted Judy Garland toward the end. Nancy Reagan suffers from the opposite malady: her ankles are the biggest in show biz, almost as big as her calves.

The failure of the movie writers to mention Sheffield and the snotty remarks they made about the cost of his films render their work useless for reference; I sought help from a librarian at the show biz branch of the public library in Lincoln Center. I knew I was in the hands of a confident intellectual as soon as I mentioned the name Sheffield; he said at once, "Bomba the Jungle Boy." He helped me find what material the library has on Bomba. For the benefit of those who did not read an Associated Press interview in the Baltimore *Sun* in 1939, I'll report that Sheffield wore for the interview "nothing but a leather breech-cloth, tan make-up and blue bedroom slippers"; the blue bedroom slippers are an especially obscene touch for the precocious little tease. After he stopped making the Bomba pictures, his life took a tragic turn; according to Lamparski, he married and became a father.

But he bequeathed a priceless and unique filmed legacy and it warrants a well-illustrated book, a book that would give the details of how he got the job, what the audition consisted of, why the other applicants were rejected, plus the details of his costume design and fittings and the atmosphere in his dressing room and the make-up room, with reminiscences from assorted technicians about his appearance and behavior both on and off camera as the years went by.

CLASH BY NIGHT

Unlike so many movie stars, Robert Ryan was able to portray a real heterosexual. But Barbara Stanwyck in *Clash by Night* (1952), seen on Channel 11 at 2 a.m. March 30, 1983, is not impressed. It is very, very, very hard to impress Barbara Stanwyck. She is authentically blue collar in this picture, utterly credible when she says she used to sell sheet music in a dime store, and able to make us forget that she is a glamorous millionaire movie star. She drinks what she calls a "slug" of whiskey out of a shot glass with no chaser and holds a cigarette in her teeth when she lights it. The picture would not be the same without cigarettes; the climax for me occurred not when the director intended it but earlier in the picture when Ryan, fairly tough himself but of course no match for Stanwyck, lit two cigarettes and handed one to her. She accepted it but looked at it with an easy, graceful scorn for just a fraction of a second and tossed it over her shoulder. I was so shocked I didn't notice what Ryan did. I believe he did nothing; what could he do?

CRY OF THE CITY

In *Cry of the City* (1948) and, according to her file at Lincoln Center, in life, Hope Emerson liked to cook and eat. She had a body to show for it, an overwhelming body, 230 pounds and 6'2". In a brief but memorable breakfast in the picture, even though both her cheeks are bulging with wheatcakes, she sticks still another morsel in her mouth; an embarrassingly tall stack of cakes awaits her on a plate. She was a real sport; only Anne Revere in *Scudda Hoo! Scudda Hay!* (also 1948) eats with comparable gusto. By contrast, Nancy Reagan, according to Susan Brownmiller, lives on grapes and Jackie Kennedy Onassis will have just salad for lunch—salad, mind you, without dressing. Presumably they want to keep the boyish figures which are so alluring to men. I prefer people who can get away with eating, drinking, smoking, and so on; who live, not just prolong life. Less hairdressing and more salad dressing would humanize people like Jackie. Hope Emerson said she never dieted. She was exempt by nature from the beauty rat race, seemed perfectly content to be, and was better off than women who depend on men; at Fox, which made *Cry of the City*, Carole Landis was called the "studio hooker," had to provide sex for Darryl Zanuck, and killed herself at age 29 after breaking up with a married actor (Rex Harrison). Emerson, instead of resenting the fact that she was "different," cashed in on it. She became a cult goddess, one of the very finest Hollywood toughs, a great American goon, up in a class with the pockmarked and profoundly grim Marc Lawrence. Emerson couldn't possibly have known how adorable she was.

She was not frightened or troubled, in *Cry of the City* or in life. Why worry. She said she never had stage fright and didn't mind cracks about her size, and she seemed to find it charming when she sat down in a play once and the chair broke.

Her breakfast companion in the picture, Richard Conte, does not eat; he's in trouble. Apart from the fear that Emerson will steal the scene and the fact that only last night she started to strangle him, the two are about to go to an 18th Street subway station to get some stolen jewels from a locker—and they are double-crossing each other. Though not specifically identified as such in the script, they are clearly Reagan Republicans—people who don't give a shit for anything except money. But Emerson and Conte are not offensive like Reaganites; they are charmingly honest about their greed and do not conceal it under piety and patriotism. Conte, the Italian George Raft, did appear in other pictures as a war hero; hoods and soldiers were his specialties. In thus demonstrating how similar these two occupations are, Hollywood unwittingly told us something. Had Conte portrayed athletes also, his career would have encompassed the three principal non-sexual ways in which American men try to be, or seem, or feel heterosexual; to experience and display heterosexuality. Conte was an absolutely reliable player; I'd watch a picture for him alone. But he never made it to the top; he didn't have the asshole of a star. That is, he was not perceived as having the asshole of a star. There was nothing about his face, body, or manner that made large numbers of men wonder about his asshole as they probably wondered, for example, about those of Jackie Searle, Tito Guizar, Bruce Cabot, and so on. I know no more about Conte's or any other Hollywood asshole than do the readers—and I undoubtedly know less than some readers (I don't have to tell you how promiscuous the stars are.)

Simple greatness is harder to recognize than mere talent. The great, in writing and in acting, do not display technique or education, as do the talented. The *New York Times* and Leonard Maltin's *TV Movies* fully appreciate talent at, for example, the tap dancing level, but neither the *Times* nor Maltin even lists Emerson in their little notices on *Cry of the City*, seen on channel 9 at 8:30 p.m. July 25, 1984. To see her is not to see an actor acting but a person being, manipulating the audience by her mere existence rather than by technical effort. Perhaps, as happens so often in the picture business, only members of a sexual elite—that is, outlaws—can instinctively appreciate the grandeur of an Emerson. Maltin is far too common and ordinary to be gay, but I sometimes wonder about the *Times*. Its use

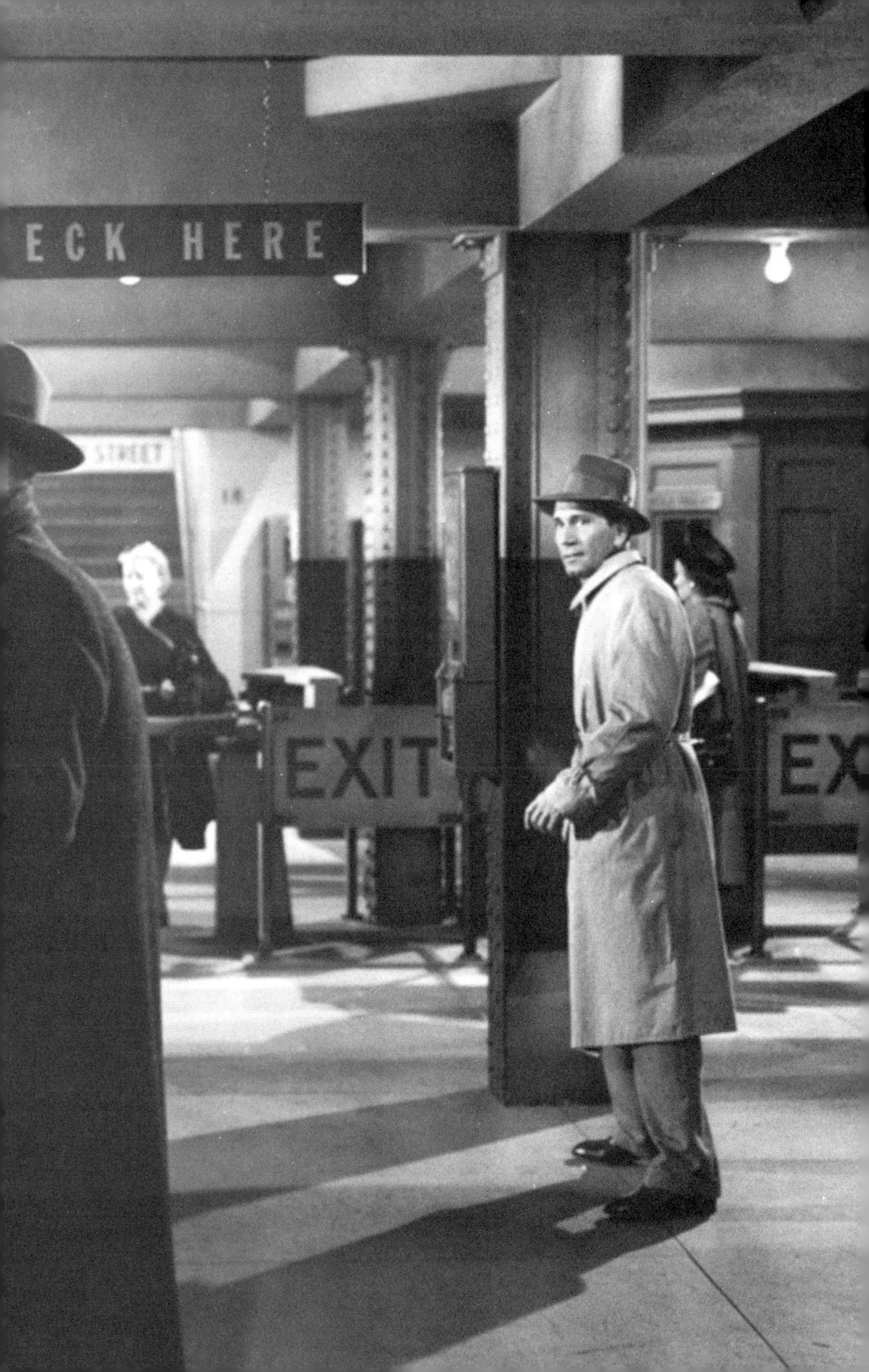
ECK HERE
STREET
EXIT
EX

of "divinely subdued" for *The Gay Divorcee* (1934) is hardly the work of a man trying to seem "straight" but its listing for *Charro!* (1969), the Elvis Presley masterwork, not only omits the exclamation point, which is the sort of thing a complacent heterosexual would do, but describes the picture as having "plenty color" [sic], a sufficiently barbaric remark to have been written by a hockey fan from Long Island. Maltin does not include Emerson in the cast of *Adam's Rib* (1949), either; viewers who do not care to watch the conventional scenery-chewing of the star he does list (Katherine Hepburn) might thus unknowingly miss Emerson's representation—which must be one of her finest—of a circus strong woman. She also played a lady wrestler on Broadway and a prison matron in *Caged* (1950), getting for this an Academy Award nomination (the winner was Josephine Hull).

The stills shown here are from the Museum of Modern Art. I believe the Museum has literally a million stills and it is they, rather than the Picassos and so on, which comprise the Museum's real treasure (paintings are sloppy). The stills here display Emerson's main physical asset, apart from her large size: her depressed, "down" face with its fantastically cold eyes. She makes no attempt in *Cry of the City* to act interesting or attractive, or even to act at all. She doesn't smile;

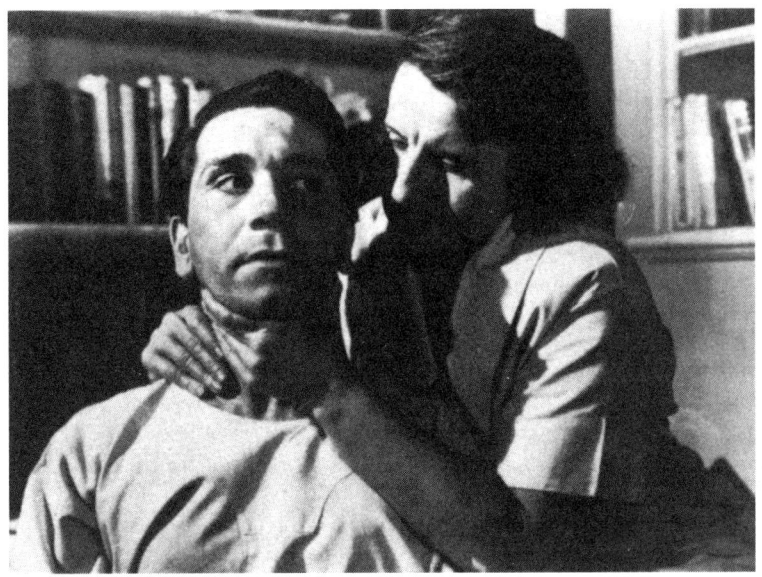

she doesn't display actor's diction but talks in a flat whine; she doesn't walk theatrically but schleps, in a tired way, in a wrinkled dress. Her first entrance is a prolonged star entrance unequalled by any I've seen since Mae West's dazzling entrance in *Catherine Was Great* on Broadway. Conte knocks on the door of Emerson's massage parlor; through the frosted glass we see a weary hulk walk slowly along a long hallway to the door. Conte needs money and has to get out of town.

EMERSON: Will South America be all right?

He tells her that her massage feels good. "I have the touch," she says. "It's only given to a few." Abruptly, and with extraordinary charm, she gets a stranglehold on his neck and says quietly, "Give me the key, Martin." It is absurd (but wonderfully so) because a woman in Emerson's position naturally has a gat. In fact she pulls it on Conte in a taxi en route to the subway. What a thrill, to be riding in a cab and have Emerson pull her heater on you. She has her way with the audience as easily as she does with Conte. The thing to do with her is give her her way, give her anything she wants, and you'll have a chance for survival. Had I been a Lesbian, I assume only she could gratify my

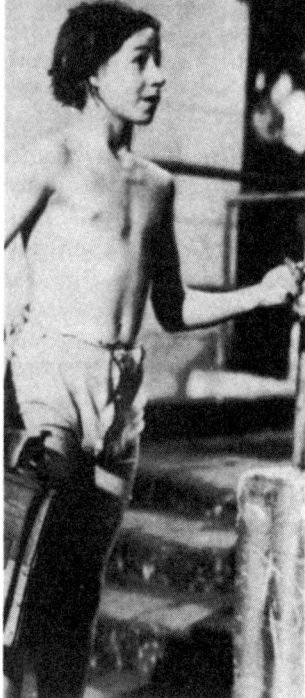

supposed lusts; what a thrill to have Emerson throw you around. But I'm crazy for her even though I'm not a Lesbian. (My remark does not mean that Emerson was Lesbian, any more than my fondness for Bobby Jordan, the Dead End Kid, means that *he* was a Lesbian. I "fell," as it were, for Bobby when I saw him in an especially obscene bathing suit and was able to sustain my love for him in another picture even though he remained fully clothed in a soldier's costume.)

It took three cops to subdue Emerson at the subway lockers (for Conte had ratted on her, the dirty double crosser). I hated to see it but knew, because of the Hays Office, the Catholic Legion of Decency, "Crime Does Not Pay," and so on, that I'd have to. I wanted Emerson to get away with the jewels. I'm normally on the side of movie hoods; I suppose most sensitive people are. Emerson's death in 1960 at age 63 was tragic not because age 63 is exactly premature but because she got such a late start in pictures; she didn't make *Cry of the City,* her first important picture, until she was about 51, and she was busy in pictures really only during the last decade of her life. But she did make about 20 pictures in that time. Because of the shocking negligence of such standard TV guides as the *Times* and Maltin, I'll list here some Emerson pictures to watch for: *That Wonderful Urge, House of Strangers, Thieves' Highway, Roseanna McCoy, Dancing in the Dark, Copper Canyon, Double Crossbones, Belle le Grand, Westward the Women, The Lady Wants Mink, Casanova's Big Night, Untamed, Guns of Fort Petticoat, All Mine to Give, Rock-a-Bye Baby.* (I've only seen *Cry of the City*.)

Her work before she went into pictures is lost to posterity. On Broadway, she won the accolade "vastly entertaining" for *Street Scene* in 1947 from Brooks Atkinson, and a review in her file from the *New York World Telegram* under date of June 8, 1946 evaluates her act at No. 1 Fifth Avenue, the night spot, as "rowdy, rough, and revealing." The *Peter Gunn* TV series, in which, according to an NBC press release dated September 18, 1958, Emerson plays a night club owner, warrants reviving on a local re-run station for that reason alone, apart from any charm Peter Gunn may have had.

Were she alive today, she would provide a valuable antidote to the poisonous treatment of women on film; in recent years, "straight" men have increasingly made it official that they hate women, and by now even such nasty little creatures as Prince (Nelson) are abusing women on screen (his *Purple Rain*, to judge from reviews, is a real slapathon). Nobody would slap Hope Emerson around.

When a player is that overwhelming, so overwhelming as to put many cineastes into deep and apparently irreversible trauma, the most trivial details of her life are as valuable as the relics of a saint. It thus struck me as important that Emerson's favorite food, as listed on a press agent's questionnaire in her file, was "fried chicken and corn on the cob" (as befits a native of Hawarden, Iowa). I reported this to my editor at once. He hadn't known, and was glad to learn it. Two weekends later, he told three men on Fire Island, and they too were interested in the information. In a gesture almost sickening in its sentimentality, like the sacrament of communion in church, I have been eating fried chicken and corn on the cob since my discovery that Emerson did.

After "greatest extravagance" on the questionnaire she wrote "perfume." I bet she smelled good.

A DATE WITH THE FALCON

I got up at 5:30 a.m. on April 21, 1984 to see *A Date with the Falcon* (1941) on channel 9, and was in ecstasy throughout. It is only one of the picture's comprehensive collection of charms that it probably contains more slaps per reel than any picture outside the Abbott-Costello *oeuvre*. But the bullying, psychopathic quality of Bud Abbott's constant slaps of Lou Costello is defused in this Falcon picture by the fact that it is the adorable Wendy Barrie, about 29 when she made the film, who does all the slapping. Her slap object, George Sanders, about 35 in this picture, is the only actor—indeed, the only man—I can think of who is fully 100 percent cool, and can easily take Wendy's slaps without the slightest physical or

psychological discomfort. The slaps, even though they are occasioned by such flimsy excuses as Sanders being late for a date, are the least of the dangers he faces in the picture; but he faces all danger not merely without fear but even without condescending to recognize the existence of danger. When two of Mona Maris's goons force Sanders into her limo he merely says, when he is pushed against her in the back seat, "Hello again." That's *cool*.

Mona, a creature of incomparable glamour and menace, was fantastically South American. When a South American woman plays *femme fatale*, she can be more femme and more fatale than her California counterparts. Whenever Mona walks into a frame, she exudes an almost nauseating danger without losing any of her hypnotic beauty. She was never a well-known player and by now has become as obscure as she was glamorous. I had thought, in my arrogance, that I was the only person apart from her husband who knew of her, so that there was a faint amount of disappointment mixed in with my main feeling of delight that the Museum of Modern Art Film Stills Archive was able to unearth from its digs the still shown here. For her exquisitely frightening part in this *Falcon* picture, Mona, a native of Buenos Aires, conceivably drew upon her education in a French convent, than which there is nothing more horrifying.

Mona married a Dutch millionaire and retired to Lima, Peru, where I hope she is living in the same luxury she displays in this still, and where I hope her utter glamour is better appreciated than it was in Hollywood.

Sanders, whose manner was as ornate and stately as the chair he is sitting on in the still shown here, always turned in a perfect performance, but he is guilty, in the still, of one gross error (perhaps the only one in his long career in pictures). I refer, of course, to the fact that he fails to show an inch or so of shirt cuff at the end of his coat sleeve. To readers who are impatient with me for waiting this long to mention this barbarism, I apologize for being a tease.

Sanders carried hauteur, cynicism, and elegance as far as they could be carried in heterosexuality, up to within an inch of the point where he would be liable to be called a piss-elegant queen. But he was apparently quite heterosexual. He married, among others, two

of the Gabor sisters, and the following dialogue, condensed from *Legend* by Fred Lawrence Guiles, demonstrates how Sanders operated offscreen, in this case when he tried to pick up Marilyn Monroe in the days before she became well-known:

> **Sanders:** My dear young lady, do come and sit by my side … I presume you also have a name.
> **Monroe:** I'm Marilyn Monroe.
> **Sanders:** You will forgive me for not having heard it before. May I have the honor of asking you to marry me? You are naturally a little reluctant to marry one who is not only a stranger, but an actor. I can understand your hesitancy— particularly on the second ground … Blonde, pneumatic, and full of peasant health—just the type meant for me … Please think it over, Miss Monroe. I can promise you only one thing if you marry me. You'll become one of the most glamourous stars in Hollywood. I'll help you. Word of honor.

The episode demonstrates how, in the heterosexual trade, men may offer material rewards rather than, as in homosexuality, sexual gratification.

It is startling to read that anyone as fascinating as George Sanders gave, in a note found in his hotel room in Barcelona, boredom as the reason for his suicide.

FIREBALL 500

No star in Hollywood history has been endowed with such an endearing lack of talent as Annette Funicello (b. 1942). The literature is in unanimous agreement (a rare occurrence in a discipline where one man's piece of meat is another's poison) that she is not especially beautiful nor can she sing, dance, or act much better than many of the millions who worship at her casually-shod feet. But this only makes her triumph all the sweeter. Any asshole with talent can succeed in show biz; Funicello made it on the strength of overwhelming niceness alone. In a medium where almost everyone has a talent for something (if only for such a simple thing as sucking cock), her refreshing lack of talent provides a welcome relief; it is especially calming to watch a Funicello picture after being overexposed to such excessively gifted players as Liza Minnelli, who relentlessly ram their talent up the viewer's ass.

Funicello never tries to compensate for her lack of talent by striving to please and she is a bigger star even than Bette Davis in this one sense: that while Davis takes parts of a quality a kindergarten tot might well reject on the ground that they are bad for her image, she always works very hard; Funicello seldom bothers. Nice girls don't have to put out—in cars or on camera. It is one thing for a creature like Davis, whose mere walk was worth millions on the Warner assets ledger, to complain about the shoddy quality of her scripts; it shows a fascinating ingratitude for Funicello to resent, as she appears to in precious moments, the fact that she has for some reason to be what everyone in America is dying to be (a movie star).

Lesser stars like Tommy Tune, a "tops in taps" type, may pride themselves on their ability to keep in step; what the culture needs is men and women like Funicello who clearly don't give a shit—who

are leaders of men, not followers of them. Funicello's complacency, bordering on audacity and backed up by box office numbers, is nothing less than magnificent. Minnelli and Eddie Murphy, the black comedian, are as rich and famous as can be, yet they still are so insecure they do 100% fake gestures like bend over in pained laughter at lines that can be no more amusing to them than they are to the audience. Funicello is above all that sort of thing; she is above nearly everything.

But she is, like Barbara Stanwyck, prompt, prepared, and professional. But here again it is one thing for Stanwyck, who after all can turn on a menacing personality at the sound of "Roll 'em," to be anxious to get a printable take and get on to the next one in a businesslike fashion; it is considerably more valiant for Funicello, who has nothing really to turn on, poor darling, to act with her eyes on the sound stage clock and her ears cocked for the 5 o'clock whistle.

She is a principal beneficiary of a perversion inherent in the picture business, to wit, that bad pictures are better than good pictures. Alerted by the *Times* TV schedule, which evaluates her *Fireball 500* (1966) as a "turkey," and by Leonard Maltin's judgment in *TV Movies* that the picture is a "bomb," I determined to catch its scheduled showing at 12:30 a.m. September 21, 1983 on channel 7. My conviction that if these dreadful people thought the picture bad it must be good was only strengthened by Ephraim Katz's failure to even list Funicello in *The Film Encyclopedia*, a failure which calls into question not merely his judgment but his very sanity, especially in light of the regard he gives to such cinematic deadbeats as Charlton Heston, who manages, with his cold announcer's school competence, to botch even parts that were drawn from a promising original property (the Bible).

Fireball turned out to be one of the worst—that is to say, best— pictures ever canned. Its central stroke of genius was the selection by its writer-director—who, to the surprise of no one familiar with Funicello's *oeuvre*, was William Asher—of stock car racing as the picture's *mise en scène*. For most people sports car racing, such as that indulged in by Paul Newman, is sufficiently regressive to satisfy their most infantile cravings for competitive aggression on the track; but for the advanced *aficionado* of motorized machismo only stock cars—

ordinary Fords and Chevys and so on that are "souped up"—will do. The only tackier scene in the track genre is of course the "demolition derby," where cars are purposely, rather than accidentally (as in the stock and sports car races and on the highways), totalled.

In *Fireball* Funicello and her co-star, Frankie Avalon, look a little weather-beaten, perhaps from their series of beach pictures; *Beach Blanket Bingo* the year before had been especially sandy. The two stars by now were aged 24 and 27, respectively. As a young girl Funicello, like all Americans I suppose, had hung her future co-star's glossy in her bedroom along with likenesses of Ricky Nelson, Paul Anka, and Dick Clark. For her wedding in 1965 to an agent 12 years her senior Avalon had given her eight sterling goblets and a check in the amount of $100.00, the barbarism of giving money at all being topped by the mutually debasing sum. By now—by *Fireball*—they knew they'd gone as far as they could go. Hard work would not win a promotion, nor could they be fired for not working hard; they were too adorable. At this stage in their careers instead of being fired they'd have had to be impeached, like a president. But neither of them committed even petty crimes, let alone the high crimes which have characterized our recent presidents. They were in the same fix as Robert Benchley, who claimed he realized late in his literary career that he had no talent but couldn't stop writing because by then he was too successful.

The Funicello of *Fireball* is at the height of her powers, in utter mastery of her situation. In her one musical number she shows, understandably, no interest in the material and, like opera singers in rehearsal, makes no attempt to be heard. In fairness it should be pointed out that she apparently was given no electronic help what-soever and that in all probability she is no worse as a singer than the next generation of pop singers, the English and American male heterosexual cocksuckers whose trivial voices were magnified by millions of dollars worth of equipment.

Funicello's bullet-proof hair by now is also at its height. Like so many truly great stars—Queen Elizabeth, Mae West, and so on—Funicello is rather short (5'2") and she elevated her hair to give the illusion of height. But there was no need to do so; shortness doesn't photograph. No one would know, for example, from seeing them

on TV, that Dick Cavett and Norman Mailer are virtual dwarfs. But in seeking to look taller Funicello displayed the same innocence and lack of show biz savvy that had made her such a charming—and vulnerable—juvenile; Walt Disney, that miserly predator, paid her a mere $200 a week for a time and when she reached her majority and collected her earnings as a Disney child star they came to little more than 40 grand. Characteristically Funicello used the money to take her parents to Hawaii and had some money left over.

Fireball is apparently a "come as you are" picture; costumes seemingly were not issued to the cast and Funicello appeared throughout in the same casual clothes, usually slacks, which she might wear for a drive to Encino to have her oil checked at her father's gas station; that admirable man, unlike movie fathers who live off their daughter's pay, continued to operate his gas station even after Annette achieved full stardom. Her sole concession to the cameras seems to have been the removal of hair curlers, but even this is more than can be said for the thrillingly careless extras in the Elvis Presley beach picture, *Girl Happy* (1965), who did not bother to remove theirs. (That picture is memorable also for the unwitting wisdom of a Presley tune which warns that "you'll land in jail in Fort Lauderdale" if you don't get a girl; an acquaintance of mine was arrested and jailed in that city for accepting a cop's sexual proposition in a men's room.)

For *Fireball*, Asher went to the trouble (although he wouldn't have had to, really) of concocting the second most complex plot (after *The Big Sleep*, 1946) of any important picture. It is impossible to guess before the final pairing off whether Avalon or the second male lead, Fabian, will "get" Funicello. At the climax it is not Funicello but the second female lead, Julie Parrish (whose North Carolina mansion is seemingly copied from the *belle époque* of motel design), who is given a line which for half a century has made possible many a successful entrance in to many a gay bar: "I want a man." Her challenge, even though it is almost insultingly indiscriminate, is accepted by one of the two male leads—which one, will not be revealed here on the slight chance that there is still someone even at this late date who has not seen the picture and will want to catch it next time it is shown. The only clue I'll give is that

Fabian's dick—which, according to Martin Greif's *Gay Engagement Calendar*, is unusually long—was not a deciding factor. No information on Avalon's is available; he has small hands, but eight children.

Funicello and her husband separated in 1982. Since it was not a divorce, her evaluation of him as a husband is not a matter of public record. But there is some reason to believe that she should have dropped him as her agent as well as her husband; the last work he got her, according to her file at the show-biz branch of the public library in Lincoln Center, was a peanut butter commercial in 1977. Even though it was a leading brand (Skippy), it was hardly enough to satisfy the millions of Americans still irreversibly traumatized by Funicello. She and Avalon appeared with Asher on *Entertainment Tonight* on November 11, 1983. They want to make a comeback. One ideal picture would be a demolition derby picture; though they still look infuriatingly good they probably don't want, at ages 41 and 44, to go back to the bathing suit genre.

THE FLYING FONTAINES

Michael Callan's unnerving groin in this still from *The Flying Fontaines* (1959) is an especially welcome contribution from the Museum of Modern Art Film Stills Archive; groin shots give balance to a book which, like this one, emphasizes keisters, and the film critic, whatever his or her own perversions, must strive to do justice to both dicks and butt holes. (The writer has never pretended to comprehend the allure of twat and leaves that subject to heterosexual reviewers, if any.)

Sometimes my requests for stills are so concupiscent that the Museum cannot honor them; other times, as in the still shown here, the Museum puts out more than I dared hope. The Museum does put out when it can and I value that quality in a museum as I do in a man.

I have reason to believe that Michael has a size L or even XL "fuck prong," if I may use the expression of a classics professor in London who advises me by mail. (English academicians apparently are more vigorous than their cautious counterparts in America; A.L. Rowse casually characterizes one figure in English history as "a stinking shit.") That Michael may be what I believe is called "hung like a mule" is suggested by the fact that even though his tool is held back by at least two layers of tight trapeze drag, it still gives an insistent thrust. Freed of the bandage-like restraints of his costume and left to flop about naturally, it might well turn out to be his best feature.

In fairness, it should be pointed out that the shadow cast on Michael's meat by the left arm of one of his fellow aerialists may render it more alluring than it really is. (I've asked the art director to crop out the other players in the still, lest they draw attention away from Michael's bulge. In so doing, I copied Mae West, who

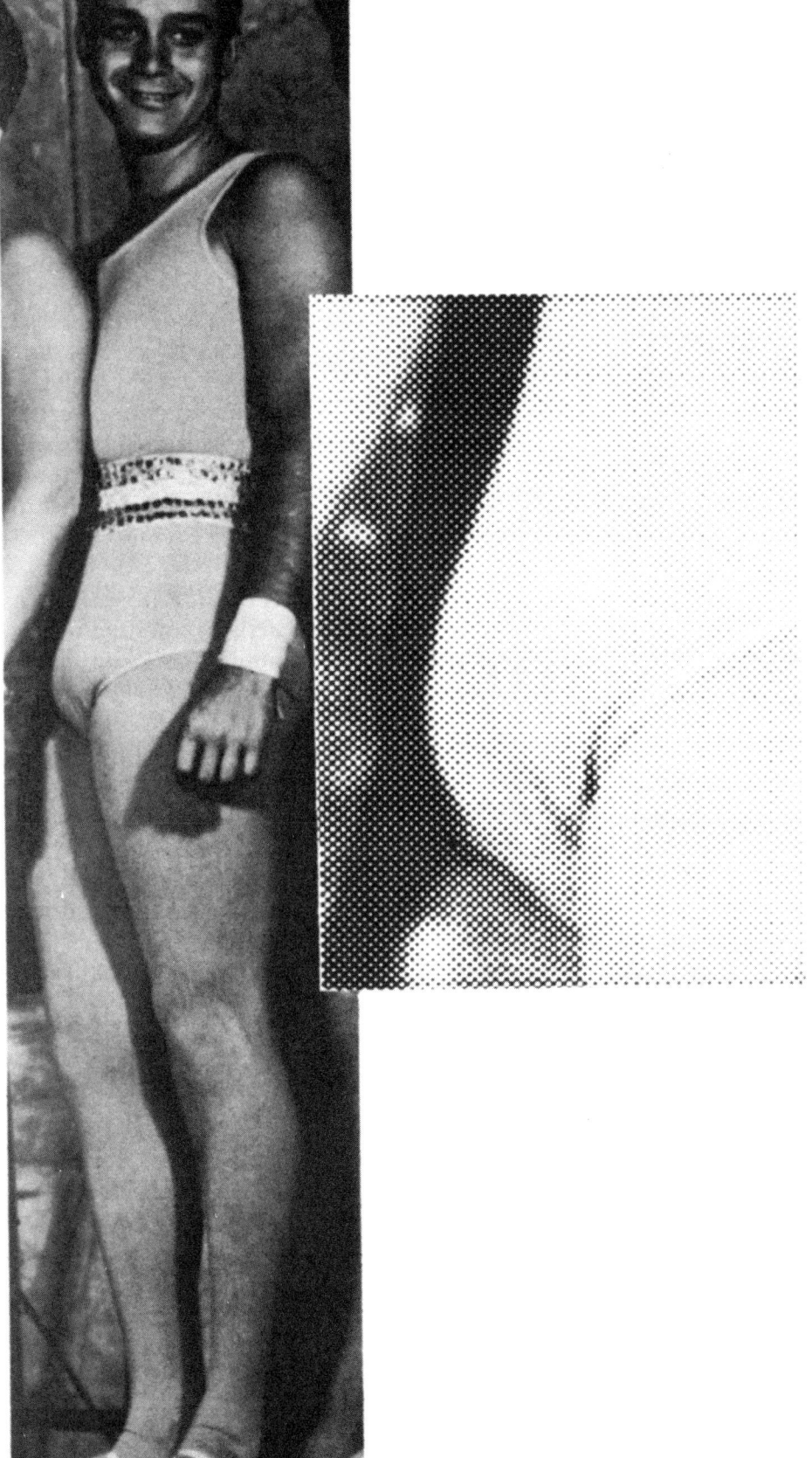

insisted that other players remain paralyzed while she was talking or moving so that all eyes would remain on her.)

The question of how Michael is hung could probably be settled by a cast or crew member of the Broadway musical *West Side Story*, in which Michael appeared before he went into pictures. The only comment Michael has given on his appearance, according to his file at the Lincoln Center Library, is one he gave to a *New York Post* writer in 1964 when he said that in his first audition for *West Side Story* he was told that he was "too handsome for the role." Michael added, "I don't think I'm too good looking, do you?" The *Post* writer did not reply, not in his published article anyway, and failed also, after mentioning that at the Savoy Plaza interview Michael "lounged in tight blue pants [and] matching short sleeve shirt with … the top buttons open and chest bared," to mention whether his chest was hairless and whether his butt in 1964 retained its beauty as displayed in *The Flying Fontaines* five years earlier.

Michael auditioned several more times for *West Side Story*. Finally, three experienced appraisers of male flesh—Stephen Sondheim (lyricist), Arthur Laurents (writer), and Jerome Robbins (choreographer) who had apparently wanted a hood for the part, gave it to Michael anyway. At one performance, a Hollywood talent scout "discovered" him. He made at least 16 pictures, at least two of them with titles that suggest a prominent display of his groin and butt. One is *Gidget Goes Hawaiian* (1961); the word "Hawaiian" suggests bathing suits, but perhaps I have an oversimplified notion of life in those islands, as I do of life on Manhattan Island. The other is *13 West Street* (1962); if this be the homosexual West Street, the one on the Manhattan waterfront, the picture warrants watching, but it may be worthwhile anyway as what Leonard Matlin in *TV Movies* calls "a taut actioner." I enjoy actioners, especially taut ones.

I suspect, however, that the reason Michael failed to become a star is that producers and directors failed to recognize what a valuable property he was as a piece of meat. By 1981, to judge from an appraisal on file at the library, it was too late. David Galligan wrote in an article published under date of November 26 of that year that "a few lines crease around the eyes and the bottom two buttons of his shirt strain tightly." If by this Galligan means that Michael had let his stomach "go," I assume he no longer had hopes of playing sexual parts. Unaccountably, for one who examined Michael so carefully, Galligan failed to mention whether he had gotten fat assed.

Michael has had at least one wife and at least two children (daughters), but as a dancer he must inevitably have some knowledge of homosexuality as well. I do not wish to suggest that he has carnal knowledge of homosexuality but anyone who, like Michael, began dancing lessons at 13, worked as a production line dancer and singer in night clubs in his native Philly, and did a dance act at the Copacabana in Manhattan before he landed in *West Side Story* would have worked with more homosexuals than heterosexuals,

I am glad to have Michael in my book as a piece of Jew butt to mix in a virtual melting pot of butt of all nations, without regard to race, creed, color or taste. Michael, like many Jews (and an even larger number of gentiles), does not look like a Jew; the only thing he looks like is a male Suzanne Pleshette. I deduce his Jewish extraction from a remark he made to an interviewer, "that his father is the only Jew he knows who runs two Italian restaurants." As a youth, Michael, then yclept Martin Harris Calineff, "helped out" in his father's "luncheonette" (one of my favorite words).

I scarcely noticed his groin in *The Flying Fontaines* (seen at 1 a.m. on February 15, 1984, on channel 7), so entranced was I by his butt in general and its crack in particular as revealed by his trapeze tights and photographed, for example, from below when he climbed a rope ladder to a trapeze. Too few photographers are aware that one of the very best ways to capture on film the qualities of a man's butt is to photograph him climbing a ladder. Michael's ass was about 23 years old when he made this picture and its full glory is displayed generously throughout the film.

I had never heard of Michael when I saw *The Flying Fontaines*; I watched the picture as a matter of policy (I watch all trapeze pictures and also go to the circus at the Garden). It is the only Michael Callan picture I've seen. It is one that the aforementioned professor regrets not having seen: "May I say how shocked, nay hurt, I am that you should imagine I have no memory of or interest in Michael Callan's rear? I remember him well from certain movies of the early Sixties in which his beauty of thigh and butt (never, alas, bared) approached that of the Divine Ricky [Nelson]. That I have missed seeing him in a trapeze outfit comes as a cruel blow so late in my filmgoing career when the chance of catching him so attired is well nigh zero. I remember him doing a reasonably inept dance in a Columbia movie called *Pepe*. It was still a high point of the film in that he was called upon to rotate his pelvis and splay his thighs, which he did splendidly. I don't know why they wanted to go on to more ambitious moves which taxed his abilities, since most of the audience could have watched more of the same for the rest of the dance number (or movie, in the case of more obsessive Callan-admirers). I am unusually keen to be among the first to see your movie star book. Anybody who immortalizes the underappreciated but coterie-revered Callan… must be fulfilling a kind of destiny."

The author of the *Times*'s listing for *The Flying Fontaines*, unable to appreciate the beauty of Michael's butt, sought gratification in the picture's plot but failed, finding it "the old story." Homosexuals get more out of watching a movie (or walking down a street); hence the title of my book, *Cruising the Movies*.

FRATERNITY ROW

Lured by the painting used in its ads, I went to a theater in 1977 to see *Fraternity Row*. I was sucked into the theater but not sucked off inside the theater; nor were any of the other men. I prefer theaters in which men strip completely bareass in the balcony and slouch down in their chairs with one foot on the chair (or shoulder) in front of them, whilst other men crawl up the balcony steps on all fours, meaningfully.

Students from UCLA, which I believe stands for the University of California in Los Angeles, were used in the film. The school is not noted for intellectual ambience, but there is nothing wrong, in *Fraternity Row* at least, with the butts of its student body nor with the underpants in which they are wrapped.

I don't know who modeled for the painting, details of which are reproduced here, but the figures, their butts, and their underpants are without flaw and without peer in art. In an El Greco or Delacroix grouping, perhaps only one or at most two men may look to be worth sucking off; in the *Fraternity Row* painting every single one does. By excruciating use of shadow on the underpants, the artist managed to limn vividly the butt cheek and crack values inside the pants; the sensitive art lover can almost taste and smell them. The dazzling white of the underpants imparts an enticing, and probably misleading, quality of purity to the sexual parts, both front and rear, of the youths wearing them.

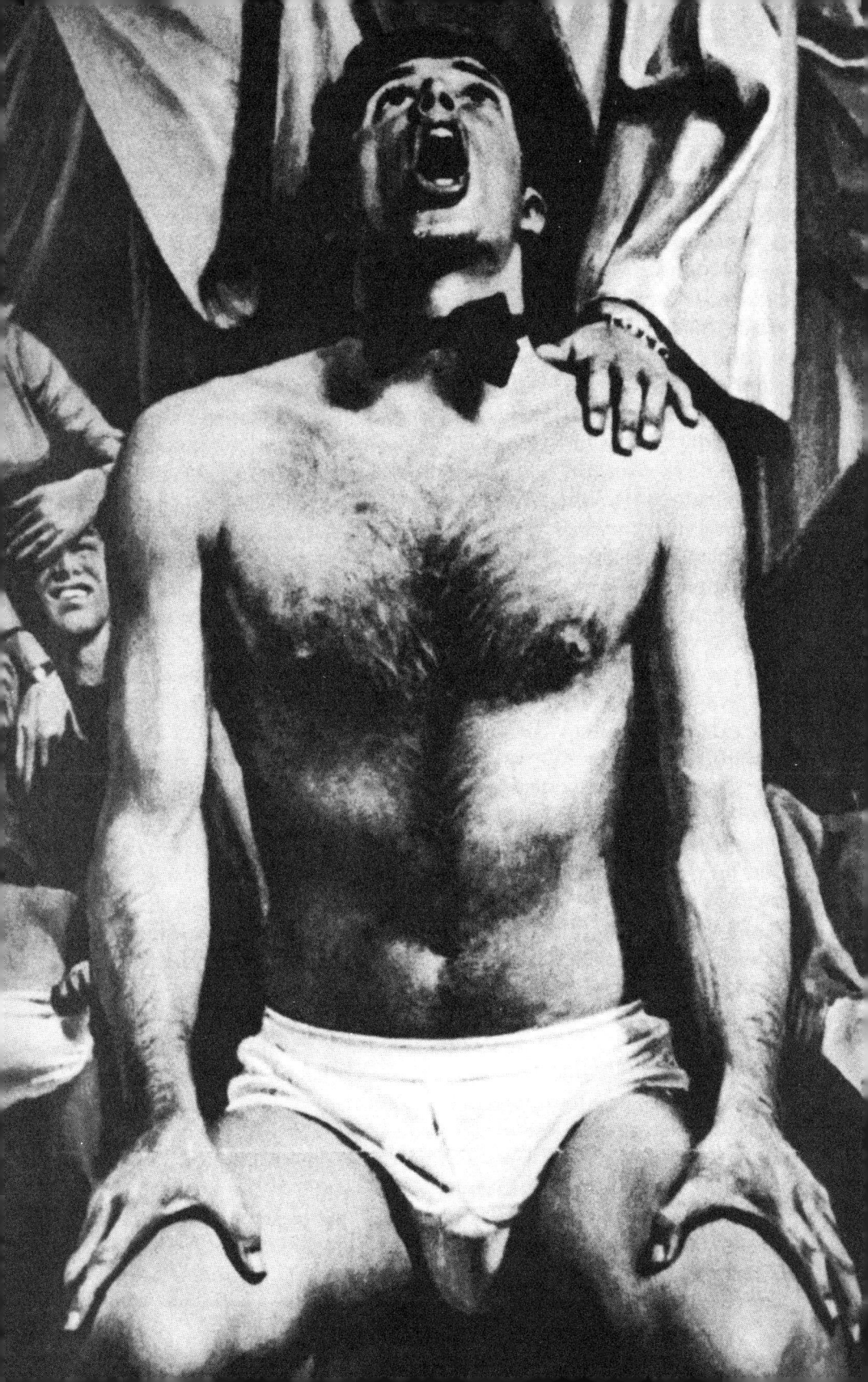

The painting is a fantastic tease, showing students about to pull down their briefs and surrender their bare butts in an initiation rite. Most men have seen in showers, locker rooms, and so on, as many dicks as they care to (the trick of course is to see the dick of someone fully clothed who arouses curiosity), but the butt hole, hidden and forbidden, is a considerably more intimate and personal sight than the dick. A man's butt hole can be seen only when, like the students in the painting, he voluntarily or involuntarily surrenders it abjectly.

The *Fraternity Row* painting is a masterwork of representational art, one which deserves the highest accolade that can be given to a painting, *viz.*, that it is almost as good as a photograph. I very frankly prefer it to a Chagall, for example. Chagalls of course have a higher dollar value than the *Fraternity Row* painting, but paintings of alluring men in their underpants could be said to be even more valuable than a Chagall in the sense that, for men who like this sort of thing, they are priceless. This is a point for men to remember the next time they are haggling with a male whore who is precisely what they want.

It occurred to me that the *Fraternity Row* ad art I'd seen seven years ago would provide an aesthetic experience for the reader also. I called Jim Tamulis, perhaps the nation's (and thus the world's) leading authority on Jockey shorts, in hopes that he would have seen the ads too and would have some idea how I might obtain a copy at this late date. I was astonished (but oughtn't to've been, in light of his comprehensive collection of classic portrayals of men's briefs) to hear that he owned a one-sheet (poster) of the painting. He brought it to lunch at the Cafe Loup, where the sauce on my roast pork was as sweet as the baked sugar-cured California hams limned in the painting. In fact the painting turned out to be even better than I'd remembered; the artist was conscientious enough to show, above at least one youth's elastic waistband, the beginning of the crack of his ass.

Coming home from lunch with Jim, I saw a youth in full athletic drag near the West Side "Y," where businessmen go to see and be seen in their jockstraps. On the seat of his sweat pants were the Greek letters of some fraternity. My knowledge of these decadent organizations is so slight that I don't know whether the youth's fraternity owns, at least temporarily, rights to his rear end. I have reason to suspect, extrapolating from his visible signs, that his ass was a nasty, hairy one. Coming home from another meeting with Jim (this one to return the poster I'd borrowed at the previous one), I saw from my cab window an Italianate youth in jeans standing at the entrance to an office building and bidding goodbye to two young "buddies," as they are called, by using the method of bending his knees, sticking his groin out, grabbing it tightly in one hand, and shaking the whole bulge, dick and nuts, up and down vigorously. He was laughing of course, but I viewed it as seriously sexual. He gave me a chance to see again what I had seen many times before, how non-college youths engage in homosexual horseplay in the same way fraternity brats do (by making fun of it).

Fraternity Row portrays some of this heterosexual homosexuality so rampant in college fraternities, which attract straight queers. In fraternities, as in prisons, Navy ports, and so on, men make homosexual activity socially acceptable by making it customary, like war; making it butch, brutal, and abusive—forced, rather than voluntary; and by masking homosexual pleasure under punishment and profit, (prostitution). Fraternity brothers, prisoners, sailors, and so on take advantage of these opportunities for homosexual action in organizations where it is the custom and they do not have to take personal responsibility for it.

HARPER

Paul Newman appears in boxer shorts in *Harper* (1966), seen at 4:30 p.m., September 25, 1983 on channel 1; men were not wearing Jockey shorts on camera in those days. But even in 1966 Newman was able to enjoy the thrill of one contemporary media custom. Frank Sinatra, one of America's best-guarded bigots, had pioneered years before by introducing the word "queen" on network TV (the Carson show), and in *Harper* Newman gave an early movie rendition of the word "faggot"—he called a man who was beating him up "you fish-eyed faggot." In light of Newman's off-screen life, it was an inappropriate word for him to use; but perhaps for that very reason it was all the more fun.

The picture also boasts a powerful performance by the distinguished American baritone, Lauren Bacall, who later, according to a columnist, as part of her agreement to appear on Broadway in *Woman of the Year*, stipulated that two (2) rolls of toilet tissue be delivered to her dressing room daily. I don't think stars should leave anything as important as toilet tissue in the care of others, but should always carry their own supply, either in purses or pockets.

HONEYMOON

It was Sidney Skolsky's genius, or perhaps just his honesty, to sense that the public's real interest is in what, if anything, the stars wear to bed.

An actor with just a routinely dirty mind might say, as Guy Madison did in Skolsky's column of October 26, 1946, that he sleeps in the nude. Skolsky repeated this news in another column about Madison on August 22, 1948, this time developing the concept a little further, adding that Madison feels more comfortable naked than clothed and that he likes to sleep in a large bed so that he can roll around. Give the public what—don't you see?—it wants.

But is that, is nudity, what the public wants? Not necessarily. I contend that a man who wears anything at all in bed is more advanced erotically than one who sleeps bareass, more challenging, because he offers the opportunity for sexual advances and resistance, for seduction and conquest. It is impossible to conquer a man who's naked: he's already conquered. Few men are more boring than those whose private parts are excessively accessible; as Shakespeare put it in a more romantic setting in *Troilus and Cressida*,

> Things won are done;
> Joy's soul lies in the doing.

By August 2, 1953, Madison had progressed to the point where he reported in Skolsky's column that he sleeps in "white broadcloth shorts." These are of course less interesting than white Jockey shorts but still, at least to start with, more interesting than utter nudity.

Guy Madison's underpants are not something I care to go into, but I daresay many other men would. He arrested the attention of,

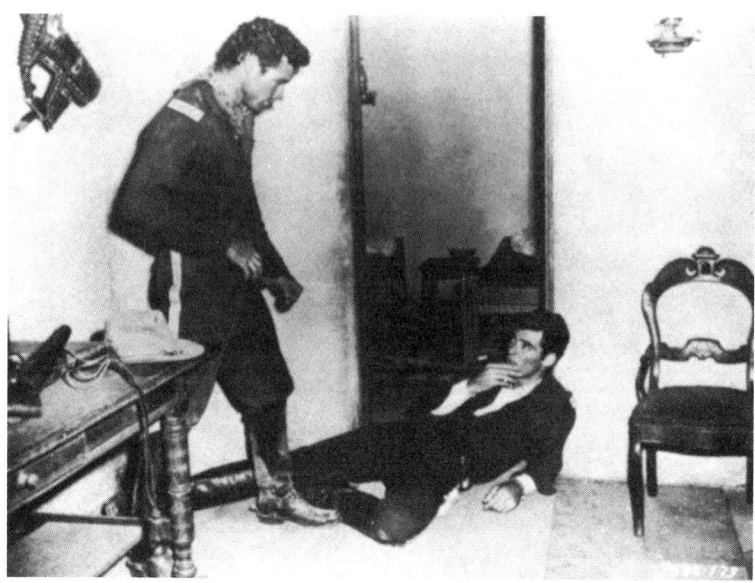

among others, Gore Vidal, who has written positively of him (albeit briefly and non-committally, in a way not unlike the way he wrote of Maria Montez). People Vidal enjoys (e.g., Logan Pearsall Smith) are likely to be generally enjoyable, just as anyone he dislikes (e.g., William F. Buckley, Jr.) is almost certain to be of the wrong set. For this reason only, I watched Madison in *Honeymoon* (1947) at 1 p.m., March 14, 1984 on channel 9.

For once, Vidal may have made an error in taste and thus have expressed an incorrect opinion. Madison's face, in *Honeymoon*, is fancy; he walks funny; his hind end is pear shaped, and it's placed 2" to 3" lower on his body than is the Caucasian custom. Though he was only about 25 when he made this picture, he already seemed tired.

Henry Willson, an agent who handled Rock Hudson and Tab Hunter, had picked Madison up—or to use the preferred Hollywood term, discovered him—three years earlier when Madison was Robert Ozell Moseley and in the Navy. Willson took his prize to Fatso Selznick, Jennifer Jones's husband, who, though not particularly homosexual, knew a piece of saleable meat when he saw one. Fatso put Madison at once into *Since You Went Away* (1944).

Madison made the picture while he was still in the Navy and still in his sailor suit, which was more obscene than anything the studio designers could have dreamed up, and he created a sensation. Practically all men, with the possible exception of Frank Sinatra, who once shrunk to 100 pounds and who at all times has been blatantly exempt from military service, look better in a sailor costume than out of it.

But once the studio took Madison's uniform off and sent him to acting, voice, and dancing classes, he apparently became denatured, almost de-balled. "Don't act, just *be*" is what the directors should have told Madison. By *Honeymoon*, a decay in his allure had become noticeable; he went on a long skid and wound up in Italian westerns. Italy is intellectually no more remote from the pioneer days of the American west than is Hollywood, yet somehow the Italian westerns normally managed to achieve only a chickenshit quality, not the real bullshit which characterizes the westerns conceptualized in Bev Hills, Bel Air, and Westwood.

The main problem was probably that Italian westerns were made by cast-offs of all nations and dialogue was dubbed after filming, seemingly by any old cab driver or telephone operator who happened to be passing by the dubbing studio when a little speech was needed. This was a mistake. The spoken word is at least 10% of the charm of "talkies" (the other 90% of course is the groins and butts of the actors).

One of the most recent cuttings in Madison's file in Lincoln Center's "library of the stars" quotes him as saying he can no longer even get in to see people who are hiring for pictures. Hired originally for his beauty, he was treated as actresses are treated when their beauty is gone.

Whilst rifling through his file, I saw out of the corner of my left eye a youth making his his way across the vast room with unusually long strides. Walking from his asshole down, as everyone should, he was more a star than Madison. I turned in my chair and shamelessly watched his progress. He had a big smile and a medium-sized butt, whose perfect half circle (rare in a world of elliptical nates) was displayed to advantage with each of his long strides. He reported to a small, bearded scholar who abandoned his research at once and the two of them left—for what purpose, it is too painful to imagine; the dirty things.

I returned to Madison's file. That Skolsky, who died recently, did not die of overwork is suggested by a comparison of the endings of his three columns on Madison. 1946: "He will tell you that he would like to be sophisticated." 1948: "He will admit that he would like to be sophisticated." 1953: "He admits he'd like to be sophisticated."

Louella O. Parsons didn't exactly bust her balls either, but all that matters really is who in Hollywood is getting what parts, sexual and cinematic, and Lolly supplied daily data on these subjects for the Hearst papers. Her semi-literate columns, rich in exclamation points, had a standard sign off:

That's all for now. See you tomorrow!

It was a style as comfortable as an old shoe, and as shoddy; still she made such other movie writers as James Agee less interesting, if more respectable. Lolly complimented Madison for his "patience" with his first wife, Gail Russell, a gifted drunk; Lolly was herself a pissy-assed old drunk and thus able to write of the Madison-Russell marriage with a special comprehension. I do not wish to seem disapproving of Parsons's boozing; it enhanced her ferocious charm and that of any gathering she staggered into, as did Betty Ford's White House tippling, which showed more sensitivity than anything her husband, the president, did. At her peak, according to one White House aide, Mrs. Ford was so stewed she couldn't get her shoes on, which is adorable. Lolly checked out in 1972 and Betty Ford has gone off the sauce, becoming just an ordinary president's wife like the rest (but not as ordinary as Nancy Reagan). I don't suppose I have to add that Betty Ford, Lolly Parsons, and women in general are less destructive drunk than most men are sober. I have often wished my mother could have been a lush, but she only took a little wine.

Madison is from Bakersfield, California, a city which, with its large reserves of rednecks, tends to produce more erotic men than L.A. He once worked as a telephone linesman in Bakersfield, but by *Honeymoon*, after the studio's ill-advised attempts to make him artistic, cultured, and refined, he no longer seemed capable of doing anything more with a telephone than dialing Shirley Temple, his co-star.

Temple, aged 19 when she made *Honeymoon*, was suffering under a handicap similar to Madison's: she was not using her basic strengths on camera. Had the studios known then, as her career after pictures was to prove, that she has what it takes to run for Congress on the Republican ticket and win a political appointment from Richard Nixon, they could have groomed her to be the new Mayo Methot. For any woman who can, as Temple did, operate in the savagely greedy and corrupt world of California Republican politics is a tough cookie indeed (as Nancy Reagan also demonstrates), and well equipped to replace the sorely-missed Methot in gun moll and prison riot pictures. (I would not, however, wish Temple to duplicate with her husband, Charles Black, an executive, Methot's drunken marital brawls with Humphrey Bogart—not, at least, in public, like Methot and Bogart.)

Instead, Temple made a long struggle to adapt to adulthood the adorable Wee Willie Winkie persona of her childhood stardom. It didn't work, and she finally debarked from the Good Ship Lollipop and boarded the lethal submarine that is the Republican Party.

IN A LONELY PLACE

Gloria Grahame is a high school boy's dream of cool, of real, effortless masculinity as opposed to the effort to act masculine made by her co-star in *In a Lonely Place* (1950), a poseur named "Humphrey Bogart." She had the sullen, bored walk and talk of someone who can't be shocked, isn't afraid and just doesn't give a shit. But she was perfectly feminine; the badge of her femininity was the fantastically sharp outline of her lips, or, more precisely, her lipstick. Of public figures, only Margaret Whiting, the pop singer, has a pair of lips so sharply painted. Grahame's male co-stars, no matter how they posed and swaggered, had no weapon to compete with her lipstick; without the slightest effort, simply by standing there with those lips, she stole scenes from everyone else on the screen. I never take my eyes off her lips, but just sit waiting for her to open them and say something. When she does she says it well, in a cool, understated way. A detective in *In a Lonely Place*, seen on channel 9 at 1 p.m. March 29, 1983, makes the mistake of asking her if she and Bogart are going to get married. The detective is a total stranger, his question is not germane to the murder he is investigating and Grahame is the first person to realize that it is just none of his fucking business. So she answers, "We'll send you an invitation if we do." It's a good line in itself and the effortless contempt of Grahame's reading makes it a great one.

JOHN LOVES MARY

Ronnie Reagan's bizarre legs are sufficient reason to watch *John Loves Mary* (1949), a picture so *ordinaire* it needs this bizarre touch. When the faces in this historic still from the Museum of Modem Art are cropped, Reagan could pass for a butch lez from the Women's Army Corps who is about to put the old make on a fluff (Patricia Neal).

Ronnie was about 38 when he made the picture; his body "went" early. "Mommy," as he called Nancy Reagan, didn't have him until three years later (they married in 1952, attended by a married couple, Mr. and Mrs. William Holden, who were not speaking to each other). The big fat tits Ronnie developed later supplied an

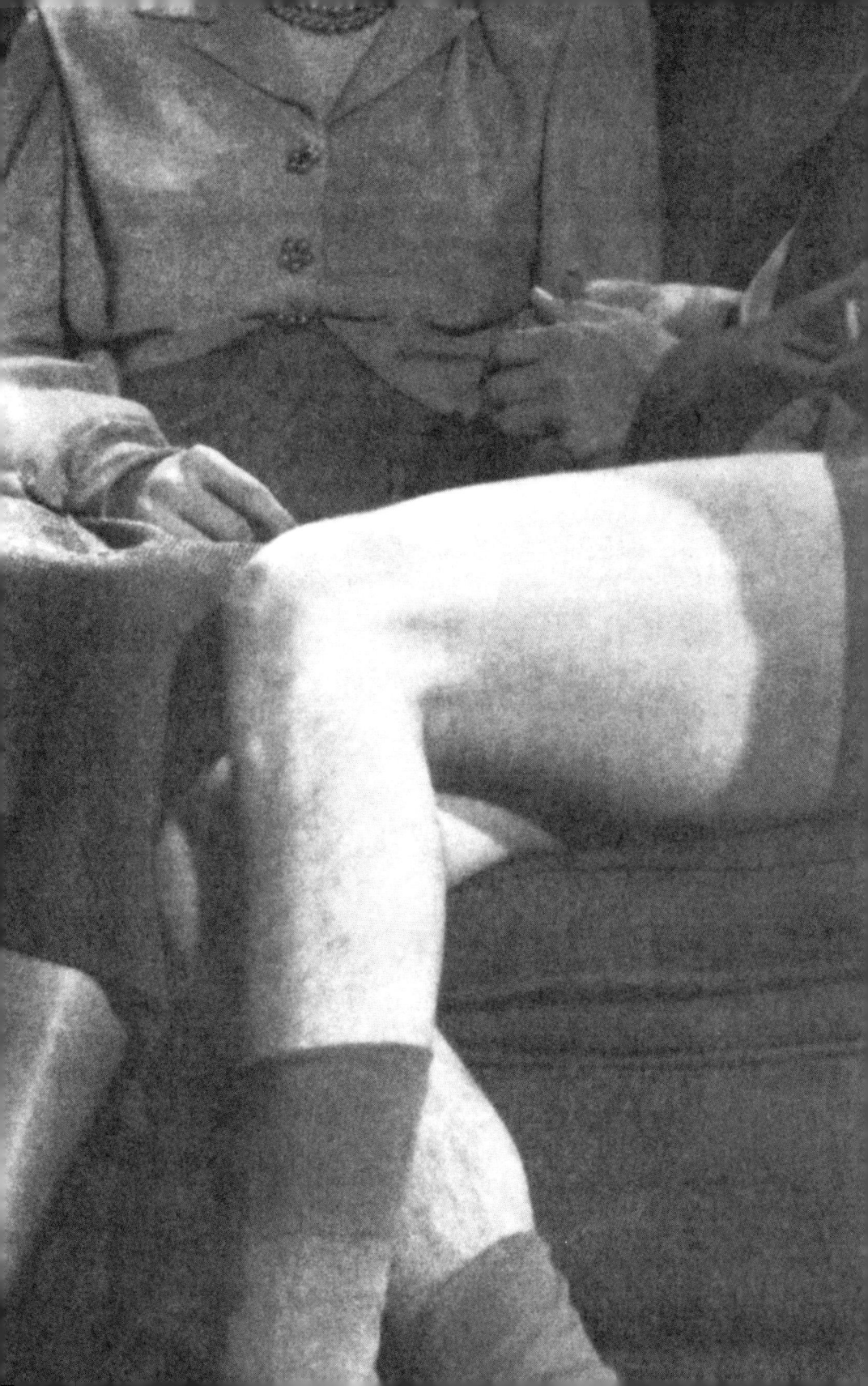

additional incentive to make himself feel manly by issuing, as President of the United States, an anti-homosexual statement. What a hero.

John Loves Mary, seen at 2 a.m. November 14, 1984 on channel 5, requires him to remove his pants twice. However ladylike his gams (they bear an embarrassing resemblance to Mae West's), what they really reaffirm is the existence of heterosexuality. Only heterosexuals could have cast this picture; homosexuals are more demanding and would have to see an actor's legs before "inking" him for a picture that displays them twice. A polite homosexual, upon seeing Ronnie's legs in audition, would say, "I'm sorry"; a rude one would use the emphatic homosexual word for no, "*Please*."

His co-star, as was the custom, was about 15 years his junior. It was Pat Neal's first picture; very soon, she went on to better things—better pictures, better men. She had an affair, for instance, with Gary Cooper, her co-star in *The Fountainhead*, which was released the same year as *John Loves Mary*. "Coop," to be sure, was 25 years her senior and had a skinny, hairy body; but his face was arguably the most beautiful of any actor's, ever, and he had a big dick which was fairly easy to see thanks to his habit of hanging out bareass in his dressing room or trailer. I saw him strolling out of the Pierre a year or two before his death. His face was still embarrassingly beautiful, and he looked embarrassed by it. His skin had the "treated" high executive look of the presidents in those days of CBS, IBM, GM, and GE. But he did look his age and he was by then I think a man only a woman would go to bed with (according to the literature, he'd had, as do most men who are not physically or spiritually deformed, some homosexual experience when he was younger). He looked self-conscious and wary of strangers after 40 years of being stared at, but he didn't look as though he'd be mean to any stranger who approached him, merely bored.

Although she is a native of Packard, Kentucky, Pat developed over the years the Locust Valley Lockjaw, or Ivy League, accent. Years after her Hollywood heyday, she made a TV commercial for Maxim's coffee which has become a cult classic among lovers of this ferociously snotty speech. Her commercial in fact is as memorable as any of her 30 pictures. A requirement of the accent (along with an "o" before "i" and an "a" before "o," so that "Christ, no!" becomes "Chroist nao!") is a lisped "s," and the very first sentence of Pat's commercial for Maxim (Macshim in her accent) gave her four opportunities for this. She took macshimum advantage of the opportunities:

My hushband ish a writer, and like mosht writersh ...

It's not easy for an actress to find work after age 25 (by contrast, actors play romantic leads when they're so old they practically have to be wheeled onto the set). Nonetheless I was saddened to learn in 1985 that Pat, at about 59, had accepted a gig at the second Presidential inauguration of her co-star in *John Loves Mary* and *The Hasty Heart* (also 1949), who was 74 by then. In Reagan's first term as President, John Updike, the novelist, was among those who attended one of the regular group dinners at the White House. People who accepted these invitations only encouraged the Reagans in their worst vices and gave them the delusion that they are acceptable. They are acceptable only to the 60% of the populace that is cold.

KISS OF DEATH

Richard Widmark wasted his youthful beauty in radio and on Broadway; he did not get into pictures until he was 33. For some reason he wanted badly the part of Tommy Udo, the goon in *Kiss of Death* (1947), seen at 8 p.m. January 28, 1984 on channel 5, and tried for it twice. It was an odd ambition for a man who was known as nice, quiet, friendly, polite, and intelligent, who likes to read and listen to music, who was to live all his life with just one wife (their child married the baseball star, Sandy Koufax).

"Henry Hathaway didn't want me," Widmark told an interviewer; "he said I was too clean cut." Widmark tried again with wax in his upper gums, which apparently helped him talk tougher, and this time he got the job. He is so savage in the part that when he asks his doxie, "Do you want something?" it is clear that by "something" he means a beating; and his co-star, Victor Mature, thought him a creep for real and gossiped about him on the set, wondering if he was married.

This of course is the picture with that historic scene in which Widmark shoves Mildred Dunnock down a flight of stairs in her wheelchair. But from a certain point of view there is an even more sensational scene, the one in which Widmark slowly emerges from the shadows of a restaurant back room to confront Victor Mature in the dining room. Widmark pauses, and poses, when the light reveals his face. It is a fantastic face, expertly lit; anyone who sees it must decide whether the image is more terrifying than beautiful. I suppose most people keep their decision secret. In life fear normally wins out but since this is, in Hitchcock's phrase, "only a movie," I can say Widmark looks good. Hathaway did well to change his mind; it is especially menacing when a man that beautiful can act that tough.

A pity he's not a film critic; he has a strong style. Of *St. Joan* (1957), he said, "The picture was awful. I was also awful. Otto [Preminger] just didn't know what he was doing. Jean Seberg was ridiculous."

Beats John Simon.

LITTLE GIANT

It is easier to understand why "straights" normally tell lies about homosexuality (especially their own) than it is to understand why, on rare occasions and for no apparent reason, they briefly flirt with the truth.

Thus in *Little Giant* (1933), seen on channel 5 at 2:30 a.m. November 26, 1983, it is understandable when Edward G. Robinson makes a scornful remark about "fags with handkerchiefs up their sleeves," but there can be no understanding of the scene in which, while visiting a mansion, Robinson puts his fat hand on the bare black butt of a statue and holds it there while he comments on the good build of the nude statue. His remark is made in a safely heterosexual context—the immortal Mary Astor is with him. But she does not appear to understand his unaccustomed honesty any more than I do. It is totally gratuitous and I could not have been more astonished had Tyrone Power, in romantic dialogue with Loretta Young, abruptly scratched his asshole (which, to judge from Hector Arce's biography, was an exceptionally hairy one).

However impure their motives, such valiant pioneers as Frank Sinatra, Paul Newman, Edward G. Robinson, *inter alia* helped build a tradition which today makes it easy for network TV shows such as *Bay City Blues* (channel 4) to bring the word "faggot" right into the lovely homes of our lovely families and make the word a part of our lovely traditional family values.

LOVE ME TENDER

If it be my duty to mention that *Love Me Tender* (1956) is a grammatically incorrect title, I must say also that there is nothing wrong with the body language of its star. Elvis Presley (1935–1977) was the first pop star to invite attention to his prick and subdued versions of the messages he projected with his crotch in concert are apparent in the pictures he's made. Yes, the word "pop" is redundant in that stars in others fields—Luciano Pavarotti, Jerry Falwell, Ronnie Reagan, or whoever—have never flapped their thighs or caressed their crotches, at least not on camera.

Love Me Tender, seen at 8 p.m., December 1, 1984, on channel 5, is the first of Elvis's 33 pictures and as thrilling as the rest. It is set in 1865. The Civil War has just ended, as has Elvis's virginity; He was about 20 when he made the picture and married in it to Debra Paget.

Not that it matters, but I was favorably impressed by her. I'd never seen her and was prepared (from certain unflattering references in the literature and from having seen the cheap blondes in the later Presley pictures) for a real tramp. But she turned out to be cool.

Elvis's older brother, Richard Egan, shows, in his one bare-chested scene, the bizarre effects of regular attendance at gymnasia (even though it was not the custom in Civil War days for men to "work out"), but there is no gym routine that can account for his sensual, sharply-outlined lips. He wants to use them on his kid brother's wife, but he's a gentleman and he solves the problem by leaving the family farm.

In thus portraying Egan as wanting only Debra, the picture panders shamelessly to the heterosexual market. It would have been more credible, at least to homosexual viewers, had Egan's conflict

MEN'S WARDROBE
PIC. A.780 DATE 8/28/56
TITLE - RENO BROS.
DIR. - R. WEBB
ACTOR - ELVIS PRESLEY
PART OF "CLINT"
CHANGE #1
WORN
Sc. 46 THRU 60
EXT.
RENO FARMHOUSE

been compounded by an irresistable urge to lick his kid brother's dick, balls, and butt hole. To begin with, Egan reportedly was "grossed out" by the fact that Colonel Parker, Elvis's manager, went about the set in his undershirt; a man so hypersensitive could not have remained insensitive to the beauty of Elvis's nose, the finest in show biz; of his full lips, of his mascara (which the cast and crew made fun of), and of his substantial and authoritative rear end. The chances are that, if Elvis and Egan were like so many other brothers, especially those who live on isolated farms, they played with each other's peters when they were boys, before *Love Me Tender* begins. Elvis had grown up during Egan's four-year absence in the war and it seems likely that the older man would be eager to check out, upon his return to the farm, the progress Elvis had made in growing a man-sized dick and pubic hairs. Egan might even have wanted to examine what the youth had in the way of butt hairs. These things happen all the time among brothers and among friends who are anxious to compare each other's sex parts and ornamental hairs. The mere fact that no mention of it is made in *Love Me Tender* is hardly sufficient reason to assume that Elvis and Egan were exempt from this natural curiosity. Moreover, we can already see in this first Presley picture signs of the flirty Presley of six years later in *Follow That Dream* (1962); when a social worker in that picture asks him if anyone had ever told him he's handsome, he replies, in all seriousness: "Only girls."

Debra in fact tells Egan that Elvis loves him as much as he loves her, a fact which I already suspected when I watched the brothers' ecstatic embrace upon Egan's return from the war; Elvis similarly (according to *Elvis* by Albert Goldman) "took Ricky [Nelson] in his arms and lifted him" when they first met at a party in the Beverly Wilshire, which I believe is a hotel in California. Ricky was 15½ at the time, but already 5'10". Then "Elvis took Ricky by the shoulder," according to another witness, "and led him into another room and shut the door." Both were in full bloom as juicy pieces of eating stuff. In fact Ricky still is, as is his brother David; now middle-aged, they are two of the oldest pieces of eating stuff in America (but this does not mean that they are available for eating). Ricky was "thrilled," the book says, by Elvis, and Elvis by Ricky, whom he'd seen on the *Ozzie 'n' Harriet* TV show. It would be pleasant to be able to report that, behind the closed door at the Beverly Wilshire, the two succulent youths continued the embrace they had begun out in the party room and advanced to the point where they unzipped each other's pants, pulled each other's Jockey shorts down, and at least felt of, or even tasted, each other's dick and nuts. I cannot believe they didn't think of it: "All that night," according to Elvis, "the two of them never took their eyes off each other." What can this mean, other than that each wondered how the other was hung? With my mind thus set, I like to died when I began the next sentence in *Elvis*: "When [Marcia] Borie talked to Ricky later, he said that Elvis had filled him up..." But the rest of the sentence was a total turn-off: "... with do's and don'ts." (Ricky had sought Elvis's counsel on staging his own act.) There is thus no ground for suspecting that Elvis and Ricky had an experience that was actually sexual, rather than merely homo.

Elvis was in danger of coming closer, perhaps even of coming, with what Goldman calls "the only man whom he would ever befriend in the movie colony," the blond, blue-collar Nick Adams, a minor actor with major allure. Adams, Goldman says, had already

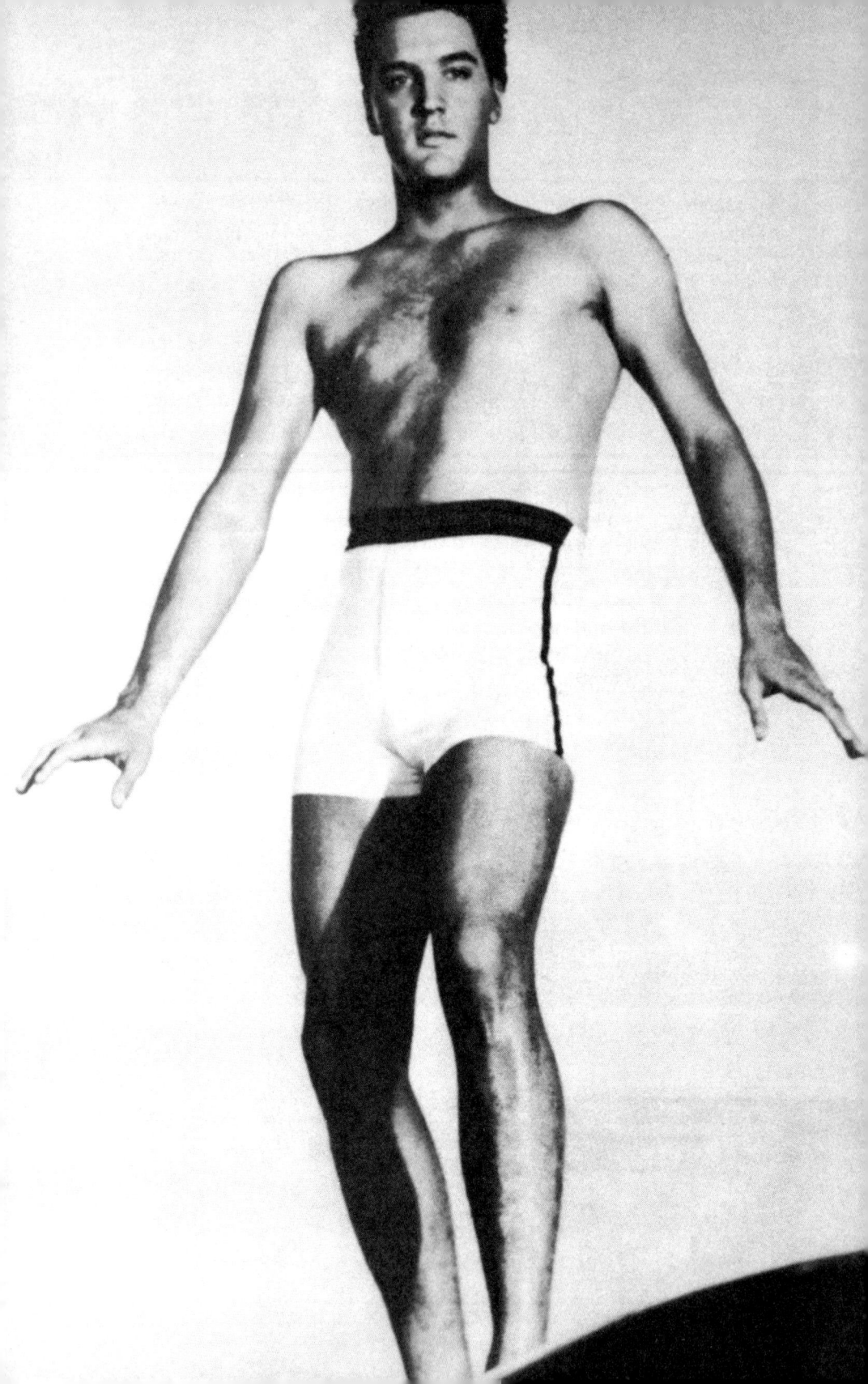

"ingratiated himself with [Jimmy] Dean precisely as he was to do a year later with Elvis Presley. He offered himself as a friend, a guide, a boon companion, a homosexual lover—whatever role or service Dean required." Adams, who died of an O.D. in 1968 at about 37, was one of Hollywood's most interesting lays in that he looked and acted less gay than did most of the officially straight actors. Goldman's use of the word "precisely," if taken literally, suggests that Adams offered Elvis sexual gratification, but we shall perhaps never know whether he did and, if so, whether Elvis took advantage of the offer (he'd have been a fool not to). Goldman's nearly 600-page biography, like almost all books that long, is sloppy and not everything he says is to be taken literally, or even seriously. (The present writer tries to avoid this sort of sloppiness by writing as little as possible, in the belief that the less I write, the better.) The literature gives every reason to believe that offscreen, Elvis's sex life was as ordinary as it was on-screen, and that instead of taking advantage of Nick Adams and trying to take advantage of the adoring Ricky Nelson, he remained a sexual yo-yo (i.e., heterosexual). Certainly a sex episode portrayed in *Elvis* is typically "straight"—he jacked off with a buddy in his bedroom whilst watching two young girls in white bikini underpants wrestle on the bed. The glamorous greaseball Elvis married testified during divorce litigation that he was not well hung. (The writer makes it a policy never to identify by name any of his men who are not well hung.)

Goldman does not complain, as did Elvis's wife, about the size of his meat, but does make some unkind cuts about his foreskin. Even heterosexual reviewers of *Elvis* attacked Goldman's circumcision fetish, and I regard his complaints about Elvis's physique in *Blue Hawaii* (1961), made when Elvis was about 26, as being equally subjective and more revealing of Goldman's personal tastes than of the flesh he pretended to portray. The reader may decide for himself; a still from *Blue Hawaii* accompanies this study. Characterizing Elvis's body as in general "disappointing," Goldman goes on to single out Elvis's "flat chest, skinny legs, weak arms." He can apparently be pleased only by a muscle queen, circumcised.

Debra Paget was also unimpressed by Elvis, but probably not for the same reason as Goldman; there is nothing in the literature to suggest that, like Goldman, she required circumcised gymnasts. But for some reason, during the shooting of *Love Me Tender*, when Elvis, as is the custom among co-stars in pictures, tried to court her, she wouldn't put out. I very frankly don't see how Debra off-screen, or Egan on-screen, could resist Elvis, or how Elvis off-screen could resist both Ricky and Nick. I'm afraid Hollywood isn't always as sexual as its historians, especially me, would like to think.

There were two Elvis Presleys onscreen (and undoubtedly in life). The one is lovable, the other merely desirable. So much has been written about the desirable Elvis—Elvis the Pelvis, the jaded, sneering bumps 'n' grinds artist—that I shan't add my two cents' worth. Less has been said about the lovable Elvis. It is a rare type, the sweet heterosexual, the man who doesn't beat women and children, but obviously genuinely enjoys them. In *It Happened at the World's Fair* (1963), Elvis is obviously amused by the tot, Ginny Tiu, and in his first scene in his first picture, *Love Me Tender*, he shows what is widely regarded as the most beautiful, most untheatrical smile ever recorded on film. I've seen only two comparable portrayals of this rare heterosexual type (rarer in life than on screen): David Nelson in *Peyton Place* (1957) and Tom Drake in *Words and Music* (1948). My search for this rare type is one reason I escape into old movies. There is no personal reason why I should care what today's heterosexual men are like, but for the sake of women, I wish their men could be a little less shitty. It's reached the point where I hate to think of the young girls I know growing up and having to deal with "straight" boys and men. A typical one, President Kennedy, demonstrated the horrible irony they're caught in: he injured himself in the secondary heterosexual activities, football and war, so that his back hurt when he carried out the primary heterosexual act in bed and he wasn't able to give a fullblast, flat-out fuck. Homosexuals and sluts, because they have sex with enough straight males to know that nothing is to be expected of them, are less disappointed in them than are women who want to be nice and have a romance with a nice "straight" man. Such women might as well forget it; I'm sorry. The only thing in this culture capable of awakening a "straight" male's full love and respect is a football player.

LOVING YOU

Loving You (1957), seen in October, 1983, is a superb introduction to Elvis Presley's groin, for those who wonder what all that furor was about in the 1950s.

This was only his second picture and it shows his body language in its full early clarity, years before he became fat-assed. He had an undeniable gift for communicating with his thighs; at times he approaches a representation of a fast stand-up fuck, seemingly shooting his wad at the end of the number. Anyone who thinks this was a minor skill or an easy one should try duplicating in a full-length mirror Presley's thigh movements in *Loving You*.

Aged around 22, he plays a gas station attendant who creates a sensation as a pop singer by flapping his thighs, only to find that decent citizens scorn him as a bumps 'n' grinds artist. He wins them over with a sickeningly wholesome Judeo-Christian number which combines all the worst elements of religion and patriotism, then regresses at once back to his original cocky style, this time getting away with it.

The picture also gives an inspiring example of how a man—namely, Wendell Corey—can be alluring despite the fact that he is 43 years old and, worse, a Republican, as Corey was off-screen. Apart from the allure of his pale, sun-struck eyes and his commanding, even dictatorial thighs, Corey appears to be well hung; it is probable that he was not wearing Jockey shorts in this picture.

The dialogue is characteristic of what could be called the trash metaphor school of screenwriting. Here is Corey quarreling with Lizabeth Scott, who was around 35 when she made this picture and near the end of her career, but still breathtakingly beautiful:

> **Scott:** You're playing a tune that's new to me.
> **Corey:** I'll give you the lyrics.

MACAO

Macao (1952), seen on Channel 9 at 1 p.m. on January 27, 1984, is, arguably, perfect. It may have one or two slight imperfections, but they would be distressing only to the rising middle class (the *Times*, for instance, calls it "melodramatic junk"). I knew that satisfaction was guaranteed the minute I read its *dramatis personae*: Jane Russell (about 31 years of age when she knocked out this picture), Robert Mitchum (about 35), and the beguiling Gloria Grahame (about 27), who can, at least in *Macao*, shoot six sixes in a row. They are three seminal figures in picture history (but without, of course, any semen showing in their pictures).

The artificial Chinese music which accompanied the opening credits gave me what I have learned to expect even of pictures that have only one of the three *Macao* principals: instant gratification. As soon as I heard the menacing gongs and screaming violins, I applauded loudly even though I was alone in my lodgings. (There are some feelings that seek expression even when you are alone; hence, the shocking amount of jacking off that goes on in this country.) At the end of the picture, I applauded even more loudly, this time rising to give the cast a standing ovation 32 years late. My neighbors by now know that I am composing an encyclopedia of "oldies" on TV for readers who cannot be sated by *Times* verdicts that pictures from the 1930s are "dated" (so is Shakespeare).

Out of habit rather than anything in the script, the stars of *Macao*—and under their spell, the supporting players and extras— loiter about leering and sneering at each other, giving attitude. The attitude is one of contempt mixed with lust—an insolent craving, a concupiscent scorn. *Macao* is like an Everard Baths with beaded curtains, wicker furniture, and women; the players look as though

they can't stand the sight of each other, yet want to suck each other off. Everyone is absolutely available but temporarily hard to "get." It is all, for all its conscientious menace, harmless; though they are extraordinarily shitty to each other, there is never a doubt that Russell and Mitchum will end up in each other's powerful arms, and their overwhelming warmth glows through their professional sneers (Russell, gifted with articulate nostrils and some slight imperfection in the nerves or muscles about her lips, is especially good at competitive sneering). The three stars are the very opposite of such lessser players as Ronnie and Nancy Reagan, who, beneath their misleading smiles, have hearts of pig iron, which find expression these days in bullying the minorities, the poor, the sick, the hungry, the old, and, for all I know, the lame, the halt, and the blind; the electorate has voted a couple of depraved old sadists into power when it could, if it had any brains, have people like Jane Russell and Robert Mitchum in the White House.

Like huge stars in general, Russell, Grahame, and Mitchum play themselves rather than bothering with some writer's or director's conceit. The three not only do not especially need such things as shooting scripts and directors; it is even an impertinence to assign someone to "direct" them. They themselves make charming spectacles out of the most tedious nuts-and-bolts scenes; when Russell applies for a job as a nightclub singer (or, as Grahame calls it, "canary"), she swaggers insolently into the boss's office, swinging her purse and casing the joint ceiling to floor with an appalled sneer. Only a few players—certainly Mae West and probably Bette Davis—could, and would, make so spectacularly irrelevant an entrance; any director with a high school equivalency certificate could say, "Jane, there's no need to act so contemptuously in this scene; remember, the character you're playing *needs* the job." But Russell is beyond such mere professional coherence, and it's more fun her way. The dialogue goes thusly:

"Shall we say one hundred dollars a week?"
"I can sing better for one-fifty. "
"Think it over. "
"I just did. When do we start?"

In her attempt to get more money and her immediate and realistic acceptance of the fact that she can't, Russell supplies an inspiring role model for the job applicant (but I can't recommend the rudeness with which she habitually treats cops and customs clerks in the picture; they can "get" you on technicalities if they feel like it).

The whole picture moves as fast as Russell's job application—too fast in the version edited for TV; apparently a song by Russell was cut to make time for commercials. This is a pity, for she is a strong singer who makes Frank Sinatra seem half-assed in comparison; but Channel 9 transmits such a lucid signal that even watching its commercials is an aesthetic experience. My favorite is a corrective for "cottage cheese thighs," an ailment that has not yet been entered in the *Physician's Desk Reference*, but doctors normally lag behind the laity by ten to twenty years.

The stars of *Macao* respond to all frightening and embarrassing crises, as everyone should, merely by making a cool wisecrack. When Mitchum, held captive in a locked room, whistles for help through an open window, his guard, Gloria Grahame, floats in and murmurs, "Aren't you afraid someone will hear you?" Mitchum swims from one boat to another, wearing, as was the custom at all times in those days, a necktie (in *Black Angel* six years earlier, the alluring Dan Duryea, a kind of "straight" Dick Cavett, had worn a necktie even while strapped to a hospital bed for withdrawal from alcohol); when he climbs aboard to embrace Russell she says, "You're all wet." Mitchum: "You better start getting used to me fresh out of the shower." They kiss. It is a rare and touching display of authentic heterosexual passion; Mitchum and Russell were among a minority of players capable of it even in the Fifties, and in today's post-heterosexual era most players look like conscientious but unconvincing students in a school for heterosexual training.

It is clear in *Macao* that Russell and Mitchum want a piece of one another's ass, if I have that imprecise heterosexual locution right, and their first meeting, in which Mitchum, the minute he lays eyes on Russell, grabs her without so much as a hello and kisses her, is thus unnecessarily, excessively heterosexual. But the meeting, absurd though it is, escapes burlesque; Russell and Mitchum are both so comprehensively and consistently outrageous that such an introduction seems not only possible but probable.

During Mitchum's forced embrace, Russell, in a feminist gesture that is prescient but not likely to win the endorsement of more legalistic feminists like Betty Friedan and Gloria Steinem, boosts his wallet. That she had the speed and presence to accomplish this gracefully and unobtrusively while undergoing a surprise assault on her beautifully painted lips is inspiring. That we could all be this resourceful when men try to kiss us.

She removes the cash and, in a movement admirable for its ease and economy if not necessarily its morality (the wallet contains Mitchum's I.D.), tosses the wallet overboard.

Mitchum goes to her wicker-clogged hotel room to retrieve his cash. With enviable force, grace, and rapidity, Russell snatches back the wad of money from him. The whole scene, in which this beautiful tough so easily has her way with a goon, is more heartwarming than those in which pimp types take women's earnings. Anyone who treasures cool virility cannot fail to be favorably impressed by Russell; her easy masculine style is more admirable than the more showy machismo of men, for, unlike them, she does not prey upon the vulnerable but merely counter-attacks when men prey upon her. She stole Mitchum's wallet, after all, while he was trying to steal something that is also worth money, especially in the "straight" world: a kiss. In that world, a kiss can sometimes lead—and does so lead in *Macao*—to half a man's income for life.

When a cop threatens to arrest the penniless Mitchum on a vag charge, Russell saves him by returning his cash warm from her cleavage, where, inevitably, she had stashed it. Some viewers might miss these complex financial transactions while distracted by preposterous Frederick's of Hollywood-type fuck clothes slit up to a fraction of an inch from Miss Russell's pussy, which was one of the most sought-after in the film capital. The scene doubtless required more than one take, since it includes a struggle in bed between Mitchum and Russell in her perilously-cut gown. That Mitchum may not have objected to doing the scene repeatedly is suggested by his reputation for unorthodox behavior, a reputation which culminated in a recent incident aboard a TWA flight when, as recorded in the flight log and soon thereafter in the *New York Post*, he demonstrated disapproval of a fellow passenger by bending over in front of her and farting loudly. That's show biz.

No such incorrect behavior mars Russell's record. Despite her screen persona, offscreen she is more Christian than pagan, and she is an important worker in children's causes. The only shocking fact in her bio is that she is from Bemidji, Minnesota.

Her first meeting with Mitchum in *Macao* had been prefaced by an even more sensual, but less direct, encounter. Russell, on the lam, needs new nylons, OK? Without any effort, she acquires a pair from a convenient salesman aboard ship, OK? She dons them on deck, deep-sixing the pair she's wearing (the only incredible detail in the whole picture is that the carefully groomed star is supposedly wearing dirty stockings). They land a deck below on a face that looks made for them (Mitchum's). It is a stroke of genius, one that shows how fine art can out-porn pornography. The nylons on Mitchum's face do not seem tasteless; on the contrary, since Russell had established that they needed changing, they were probably tasteful, but not too tasteful, as dirty underpants, had she removed them in a porn pic and dropped them on his face, might have seemed to the queasy.

MR. DEEDS GOES TO TOWN

I have been trying to think why the sight of Gary Cooper wearing lipstick is so interesting. Lipstick was, as the bar scene shows, optional, and in submitting to it (or did he apply it himself?) Cooper looks abandoned in the best sense: desirable, available. A man who wears lipstick will do a lot of things. I cannot agree with Carole Lombard that Cooper was "effeminate." In fact it is his masculinity which makes his lipstick more fascinating, more abandoned than it would be on a babyfaced man. Lombard's evaluation of Cooper was ironic in light of the fact that one of her husbands, Clark Gable, was a former gay male whore and thus not 100% butch in the classical sense. (His most alluring feature to me, but not of course to her, was his prematurely false teeth; I wonder if he made those little clicking sounds with them.)

For what other surrender than lipstick was young Cooper, fresh out of Helena, Montana (a city which also gave us the incomparable Howard Freeman), available in the fancy world of Hollywood? The official line on how he got into pictures—always the single most interesting detail in a star's biography—is that "in 1925 he was introduced by friends to Hollywood casting directors." Sadly, the official line is often true; but who were these "friends"? Was one of them the "young tobacco heir" with whom Cooper, according to Shirley Sealy's *Celebrity Sex Register*, shacked up? The same book—literally a seminal work—says that Cooper was "famously endowed" (well hung); did his big and, to judge from his sexual record, juicy dick enter into the decision to hire him (even into the "casting directors")? The only time I saw "Coop" (a man who spends as much time on the streets as I do naturally sees a lot of celebrities), he seemed to have that immense dignity which comes only from being well sucked. Certainly his dick did not hold him back in his

career, nor did Cooper hold it back: "In his dressing room," Shirl writes, "he was a nudist, a totally uninhibited exhibitionist." I like the use of "totally." Can this mean that he displayed his butthole too? I doubt it.

My best thought on these stills is that there is something more important than thought: instinct. Trust your instincts (unless you're a Republican). My instinct is that the stills of Cooper wearing lipstick are fascinating, never mind why, and that they will seem fascinating to other men. I first saw their like in an Eighth Avenue bar which had a life-sized, hand-colored blow-up of an old black and white print of Cooper wearing lipstick. I returned to the bar once in awhile for that reason alone; it was not a gay bar, except in the sense that all athletic bars are (this one was next to the old Madison Square Garden). In 1984, while preparing this book, I thought of the photograph again and made enquiries of the Museum of Modern Art. Its Film Stills Archive supplied the bar scene shown here from *The Legion of the Condemned* (1928) and a corroborating still of Cooper with Colleen Moore from *Lilac Time* (also 1928). Cooper was about 27 when the stills shown here were made; he had been in pictures two or three years. I didn't know when I visited

Colleen Moore in her vast apartment years ago that she had worked with Cooper. She had been a huge star, before even my time, but she didn't mention her career in pictures; I was seeing her on a more sordid matter (brokerage).

Anyway, she was not the sort of woman I could have asked for confirmation of the data on Cooper's dick in *Celebrity Sex Register*; she was ladylike, all smiles and hospitality, with none of the foul-mouthed show biz slut in her personality. She clung affectionately to her husband, a rich old invalid with an ailment no amount of money could cure. As I look back upon my visit, I can't help but think that had I to choose between mere love, such as that displayed by Colleen or today by Nancy and Ronnie Reagan, and sex, I'd choose the latter.

Cooper's earliest pictures were not available as oldies on TV, but *Mr. Deeds Goes to Town* (1936) is; I saw it at 1:15 a.m. January 27, 1985 on channel 5. Cooper was about 35 when he made this picture with the beloved Jean Arthur. He had bags under his eyes but his face was still breathtakingly beautiful. He didn't have a nice butt and didn't need one, not with a face like that. He'd not have needed an extraordinary dick either; the fact that he did have one, and displayed it in his dressing room, was an unnecessarily generous bonus. I doubt that Franklin Pangborn, the Central Casting gay stereotype, objected to having his face only a few inches away from Cooper's succulent meat when, as a tailor in *Mr. Deeds*, he abruptly kneels and, with the absurd efficiency of a minority man who wants to display expertise even in the most menial act, quickly unzips Cooper's pants and pulls them down. The visual pun of the act, which would be appropriate both for a clothes fitting and a blow job, was defused by Cooper's long boxer shorts—at least for the audience, if not for Pangborn (for in light of the star's dressing room displays, Pangborn might well have seen the naked piece of meat now poignantly concealed by voluminous, pre-Jockey shorts era underpants).

Pangborn's role as Mr. Deeds's tailor is perhaps his most homosexual one; after he has done a fantastic amount of intricate fussing over Cooper's body while fitting a suit, Cooper smiles and says, "You go to an awful lot of work to keep a fellow warm, don't you." Pangborn gives an accommodating laugh in acknowledgement of

the possibility that by "warm" Cooper could mean both "clothed" and "horny," and the two shake hands a little longer than, as tailor and customer, they ought.

Pangborn is not the only player to kneel before the handsome Cooper in *Mr. Deeds*. Twice, Cooper has to tell his valet, the adorable Raymond Walburn, to get up off his knees—once when he's helping Cooper with his pants and once when he's helping him with his shoes. In fact, there is sufficient kneeling before Cooper in the picture, and sufficient embarrassment and comment from Cooper, to constitute a virtual comic sub-theme of cocksucking.

Pang, as he was called, appeared in 27 pictures in one year alone (1937), bringing to them his own fully-developed gay caricature, which required little directing. He could be depended upon to do such things as suck on a pencil when appearing with a handsome actor, but for being able to afford to let himself be used as a gay scapegoat, he had the biggest balls in Hollywood. It is not even faintly surprising to anyone who knows the truth about the military, as opposed to the Pentagon version, that Pangborn was wounded in the Argonne in World War I, while such he-men as John Wayne and Ronnie Reagan performed their heroic military acts exclusively on camera, in "A" and "B" pictures, respectively.

Pangborn's best friends were not, as I'd have assumed, Clifton Webb, Vincent Price, Henry Daniell, and Basil Rathbone, but rather those two grand old cookies, May Robson and Edna May Oliver. He lost them both to the Pale Rider within a three-week period in 1942.

Cooper's most publicized lays were the blatantly available Clara Bow and Lupe Velez. Velez committed suicide and Bow ended up in sanitoria (or, as Ephraim Katz calls them, sanitoriums; Katz also reports that Billy Halop, the handsome Dead End Kid, became a "male" nurse). Bow's and Velez's tragic endings were not caused by Cooper; men like him help make life worth living but are hardly worth dying for.

MY FAVORITE WIFE

I protest the abuse given to Gail Patrick in *My Favorite Wife* (1940), seen at 1 p.m. July 29, 1983 on channel 9. Early in the picture, a judge denounces her for pulling out her compact during a legal proceeding and even threatens to charge her with contempt of court.

A face like Patrick's, flashing a ferocious full-blast glamour, is no mere accident, but the result of prolonged and frequent treatment and maintenance by a large variety of beauticians and, when none is at hand, by herself. In a business where most of the workers projected a high degree of glamour, she was one of the elite who went beyond that and always, in all of her pictures, beamed forth a total, 100% glamour. For a full half century, she has been an icon for millions; even the great Lamparski, who usually describes the players in his *Whatever Became Of...* books with jaded understatement, gives her the rare rating of "sheer delight."

Though the judge's objection to her compact is irrelevant, incompetent, immaterial, an abuse of his juridical power, and shitty, Patrick apologizes: "I'm sorry." To do so was out of character for Patrick the woman, who offscreen had once had the intention of becoming Governor of Alabama and, even more charming, never looked, during her inspiring career, at the countless pictures she made. But what could even Gail Patrick do when the director in charge was the sexually inadequate Garson Kanin? (His sexual problem still showed 40 years later when he used the word "fag" on television, showing contempt not merely for homosexuals but for a whole audience which, he assumed, was not aware of his motives.)

The judge was not only unjust in the way judges can be but also in the way many laymen are: he projected onto women a trait (vanity) that men share equally with them. "Straight" males, who are the greatest highway killers, contemptuously use the phrase "women

drivers," and I once dropped on the spot the acqaintance of a comparatively interesting and attractive jazz musician when he said "women are so emotional." The absurdity of the "straight" male attitude that it is women and homosexuals who are narcissistic is well known to anyone who has spent any time in men's rooms, where the wash basins are frequently inaccessible because so many "straight" men and boys are using all available mirror space to examine their hairstyles, faces and, when the mirrors are large enough, the profiles of their hind ends. Numerous men's rooms in corporate headquarters buildings resemble the Rockettes' dressing room at the call of "Curtain in 10 minutes." Once at Citicorp as I entered a men's room a blatantly heterosexual youth from the computer room was testing his face at different angles in the mirror to see how it "took the light," as they say in Hollywood. He moved his head up and down, sideways, this way and that to see which angle produced the image of maximum allure in the mirror. I went into a booth and gave (I don't use the word "took" here on the ground that it is as inaccurate as the male heterosexual attitude that only women and homosexuals are vain) a shit. When I left the men's room the same youth, by now bent over the wash basin with his face up against the mirror for a tight close-up, was touching up his lovely but overdressed hair. I have seen thousands of other "straight" youths primping and preening in a way that few homosexuals dare; they would be baited for doing so. (Nor is this the only way in which heterosexuals dare to be more homosexual than homosexuals, as anyone who has ever seen men with wedding rings openly eating cock in public men's rooms can testify.)

MY PAL GUS

Richard Widmark has the kind of clear, clean face that makes men wonder what, *inter alia*, his peter is like. The writer examined hundreds of cuttings from "straight" periodicals at the gay branch of the public library in Lincoln Center, but found nary a clue; the "straight" press are famously shallow and none of the writers, male or female, who interviewed Widmark over the years touched upon his dick or raised the questions of how many inches he has, how fat it is, whether it's juicy, and so on and so forth.

My Pal Gus (1952) at least gives a prolonged display of this big butch blond in heat. Even though he is fully dressed, it is the most engrossing image I've seen on film. When I saw the title, *My Pal Gus*, on the TV schedule for 1 p.m. February 1 6, 1984 on channel 9, I hoped it would be an early version of those Paul Newman-Robert Redford pictures of the "buddy-buddy" genre; homo if not sexual. Newman and Redford are too lovely to be interesting, but I wouldn't mind seeing Widmark busily bonding and buddying; in his first picture, *Kiss of Death*, he confided to Victor Mature after he got rid of his doxie and the two of them were alone that, "dames are no good if you want to have some fun." This was in 1947, years before Newman and Redford made the discovery. But it turned out in *My Pal Gus* that Gus is not Widmark's asshole buddy but rather his child, and that Joanne Dru LaCock—who (wisely, I think) dropped her last name for her career in pictures—is Widmark's sex object.

O.K., so he's driving her home, she won't fool around in the car, she won't let him in the house. It's insane not to let Richard Widmark feel you up, but what can I tell you; she closes the door in his face, that face with those high cheek bones and those fat, sharply-outlined lips. Right away the bell rings. It's him—he. He

just stands there leering at her, saying nothing. He walks in slowly, still staring at her, still not speaking. The look on his face suggests that his thoughts are unspeakable, but that she knows what they are. He looks both in need of help and determined to get it—both tender and tough.

It's a fantastic way of seducing someone. Don't say anything, just leer; just watch Widmark in *My Pal Gus* and look at someone the way he looks at Joanne Dru. I have seen it. It works. It embarrasses and thrills them, makes them laugh sheepishly and try to talk and eventually give up. It is red hot.

Even babies enjoy being stared at in that way. They know that by withholding speech you are teasing them and they like to be teased. I assumed everyone would enjoy having Widmark leer at him like that

but almost half of the men I polled say they have never wanted to suck Richard Widmark off; it's incredible. Gregory McVay, an authority on flaws of the stars—he finds, for example, Guy Madison's nose too long and Rossano Brazzi's arms too short—says Widmark looks "skinned, like those animal heads in the Paris butcher shops."

Still, Widmark's face is so effective that it does not matter that he has no body to speak of. In fact it would be infuriating if he did. But fortunately his waistline is perhaps as much as 4" too big in relation to his legs, which are inconsequential, and what in *My Pal Gus* he calls his "keister" is nondescript. Serves him right, the devil. But it is thrilling just to hear him say in *My Pal Gus* anything as personal as the words, "my keister." It is as intimate as almost all of us can ever be with Richard Widmark.

NORTH DALLAS FORTY

North Dallas Forty (1979), seen on NBC's "Sunday Night at the Movies" in 1983, marks a turning point in Nick Nolte's career, assuming the same harshly sexist and ageist standards that are applied to women in pictures. When Nolte got out of bed wearing Jockey shorts in this picture and wandered around long enough for the viewer to subject his body to analysis, he ended his era as a piece of eating stuff and entered a new, lower rank as just a plain fuck (and a rather plump one at that). In other words, in 1979 Nolte was kicked upstairs from tits 'n' ass work; henceforth he could play only coach roles (the Vince Lombardi story?) rather than, as in *North Dallas Forty*, a player on the team. His butt had swollen almost closed, to the point where it lacked that all-important cleavage so vital in tits 'n' ass roles; his hips had lost their flatness and taken on the beginnings of an unmanly voluptuousness; he had the beginnings also of a soft belly and his ankles were far too thin in relation to his full thighs—which, left unchecked, will one day rub audibly against one another when he walks.

By now he is embarrassingly close to fifty years of age and almost lardy enough to play Pope John Paul II; the Holy Father's body, in all probability, is dreadfully soft and white. Nolte's face is still worth a small fortune, but it is a fortune that should be garnered quickly, before it is too late; it lacks the bones of a durable star like Gary Cooper, who remained quite handsome of face (but not, as we shall see, of body) until the end. Nolte's jaw line is beginning to show a double chin and the rest of his face, even in sharp focus has begun to blur with age; it is in danger of becoming, like that of Jack Paar, the former TV comedian, a "face pissed in snow." Indeed, the only characteristic which made Nolte still alluring in *North*

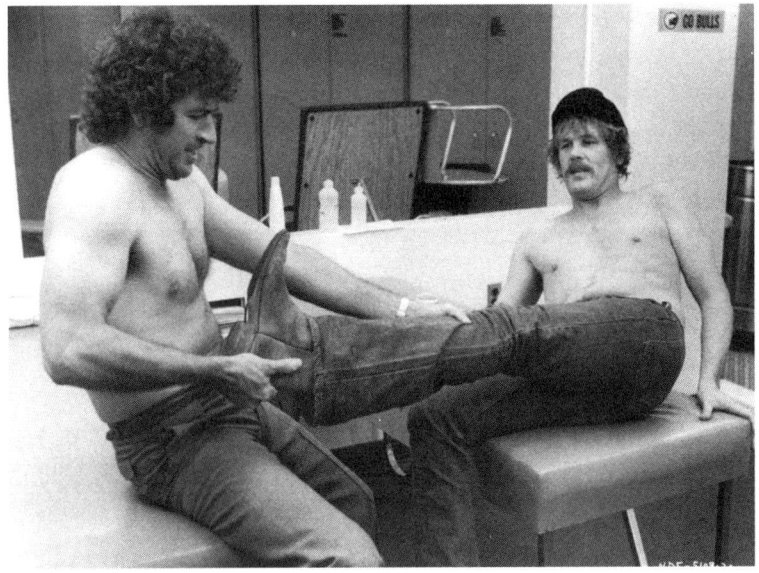

Dallas Forty was the fact that he either had little body hair or body hair that doesn't photograph. The same can hardly be said for Cooper, who displayed his puny, naked torso only the evening before on Channel 13 in an antique from 1932 called *A Farewell to Arms*, which is undoubtedly inferior to *Farewell to Manzanar* (1976), starring Yuki Shimoda, Akemi Kikiumura, Clyde Kasatu, and, simply, Mako. With a cast of hairless Japanese like that, who could go wrong? Unhappily, I haven't seen it. If I do I'll report on it.

PEYTON PLACE

Except when David Nelson, who has the kind of face and flesh men can easily get interested in, was on the screen, *Peyton Place* (1957), seen at 3 p.m. December 2, 1984 on channel 7, didn't hold my attention. I did keep watching the thing but only to watch for David, and in between his takes my mind wandered; when the superintendent of schools visits Lana Turner, sees a photograph on her mantle, and asks, "This your husband?," I thought how charming it would be if the photograph were not the standard portrait of a man in a suit but rather a juicy young AMG model holding his dick. The thought, especially in light of the fact that Lana was playing a respectable shopkeeper, made me laugh uncontrollably. There are few things more debasing than laughing when you are all alone, but I couldn't help it; I'm sorry. At least it was better than laughing alone in a crowd, which can happen too, when something funny comes to mind. People look down on you for doing it, even though you're of course better off than they are, just as they sneer at you if they see you turning your head to examine a piece of ass, even though here again your lust is better than their scorn.

Although Lana was already about 37 when she made this picture, had been married four times (with three more marriages to come), was in the midst of her most ferociously heterosexual years (the year after *Peyton Place* her daughter killed Lana's battering boyfriend), and, most hardening of all, had been educated in a San Francisco convent, she was still a softie. She seemed to have inexhaustible reserves of weakness. I like her better now (1985) when she's 65, is post-sexual (or as she calls it "celibate"), and is hard finally. At least she looked hard when I saw her in "Night of 100 Stars" at Radio City Music Hall—hard, glittering, in command, and nobody's patsy. Only the

previous year, she had publicly called the editor of her memoirs a "cocksucker," and while this of course is shitty, it illustrates the moxie that is missing in her movies. The opposite of Johnny Carson, who is frequently said to be a zombie off camera, Lana put her heat into her life and saved her insipidity for her pictures.

I was thus more impressed by her triumphant P.A. in "Night of 100 Stars" than by her workmanlike emoting in *Peyton Place*, even though all she did at the charity fundraiser was saunter out and take an ovation. But she did it well. Taking an ovation is apparently not as easy as it seems—at least some of the other stars, such as Olivia DeHavilland, Robert DeNiro, Dustin Hoffman, and Sir Laurence Olivier, didn't do it well. (But Esther Williams, Lucille Ball, Robert Preston, Danny Kaye, and Sidney Poitier, in addition to Lana, did.)

David was about 21, and bursting with cream, when he made *Peyton Place*. Inexplicably, he remains fully clothed throughout the picture—a poignant waste of one of Hollywood's most edible slabs of meat. As the stills show, he had the potential for growing out of his natural sweetness into an alluring slob. There is no reason why he could not at least have been shown in latex swimming briefs; millions of men would pay millions of dollars just for a glimpse of his nipples, belly button, and thighs, and some input from his bulge that would enable them to estimate the length and plumpness of his prick. If anyone—a former girl friend, wife, long-necked occupant of an adjacent urinal, or co-worker on any of his pictures or on his family's TV show—knows how many inches David has, the writer would like to hear from him or her at once. I assume David himself would not release this measurement unless he has eight inches or better, in which case he might; normally men who have eight inches or better manage in one way or another to make it known.

When, in the picture, David is drafted into the Army, not only is the requisite examination of his dick, nuts, and butt hole not even alluded to, there is not even a bare-chested scene in which the medics check out such lesser organs as his heart and lungs. Either the people who made the picture were blind to his beauty, or else all too aware of it and anxious to hide their hunger by hiding his beauty. The picture was a commercial success, but some representation of David undergoing an Army physical could have added as much as $50 million or even $75 million to gross receipts and have been a boost to Army recruiting as well. Too often the military draws young men from the wrong set, but millions of higher quality men, seeing David examined, could have been inspired to rush out and join the service.

I don't want to seem unreasonable; I don't expect, for example, that in 1957 a director could have shown David's pink butt hole in a tight close-up when the Army doctor says "Bend over and spread your cheeks" for the examination for hemorrhoids (a word which, because of its affected spelling, is one of my favorites, as is diarrhea, even better in its alternate spelling, diarrhoea). I do not know that David's asshole is pink; some assholes, I deduce from the barrage of butt brochures I receive in the mail possibly as a result of my subscription to *The New York Review of Books* (for some publishers sell their sub-scription lists to others), are brown. But such an examination could at least be shown in profile. Nor do I expect the picture to show David's dick; but he could be photographed from behind as he stands bareass before the doctor and with his right hand obeys the order to "skin it back and milk it down" in the test for dick drip. The same shot could include the doctor reaching forward and telling David to "cough," without actually showing the doctor's hand holding David's balls in a check for hernia. A sound effect, easily reproduced by pouring water into a glass, could effectively simulate David giving a sample of his piss. It would not, finally, be difficult to find a chaste angle to photograph David as he sits on his bare butt for the psychiatric examination:

Q. Do you like girls?
A. Yes.

My "yes" put me into the Army and David's would be even more credible.

The sensitive reader, looking at the selection of stills from David's movies supplied by The Museum of Modern Art, can imagine, as I was forced to, the physical examination that *Peyton Place* failed to show. The movie does include some tender romantic scenes between David and I believe Hope Lange; it was made in the days before heterosexuals communicated such sentiments as that which I recently overheard a young girl express to her boyfriend: "Why the fuck not, asshole?"

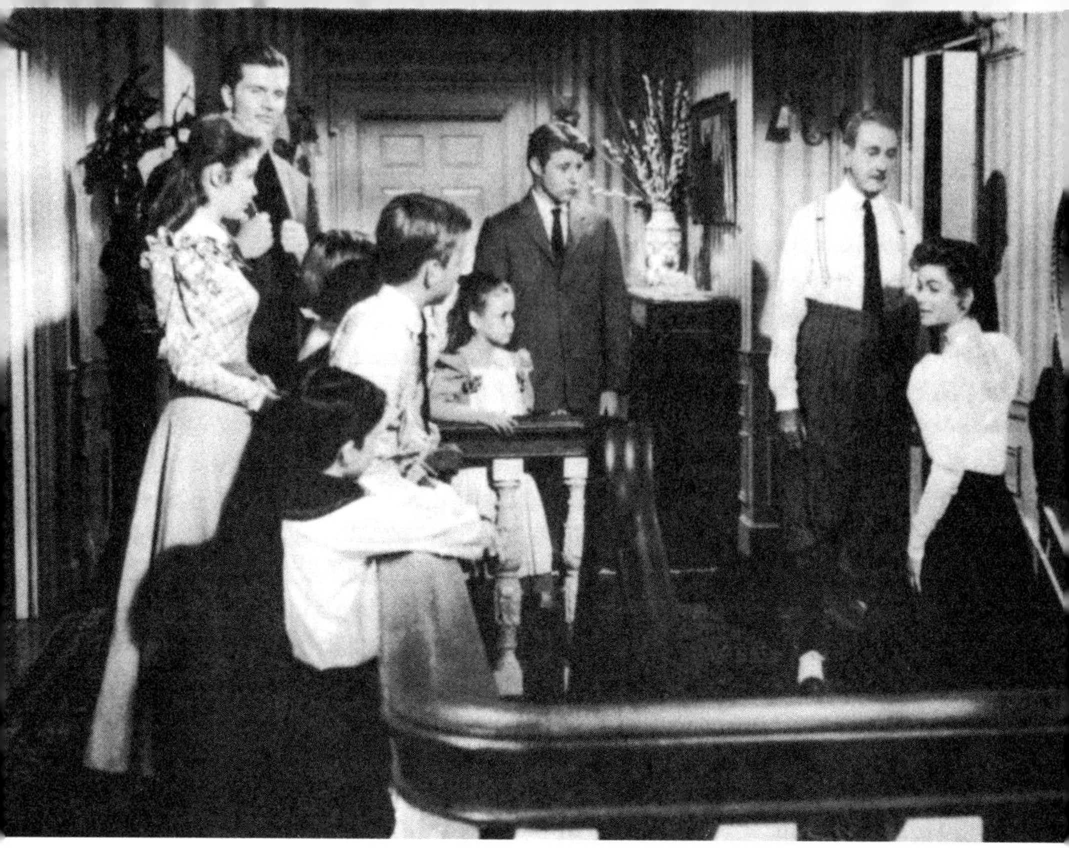

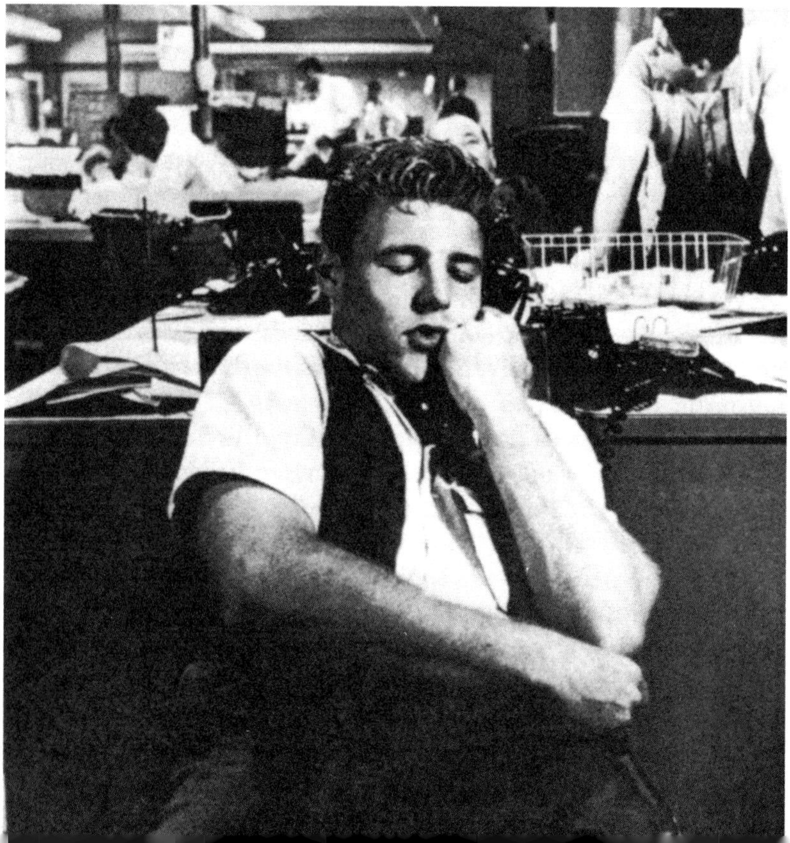

RUN FOR THE SUN

The look of wholesome obscenity which Widmark gave in full force only once in *My Pal Gus* is on display more frequently in a picture he made four years later: *Run for the Sun* (1956), seen at 2 a.m. March 15, 1984 on channel 5. The plot requires that he spend a lot of time alone with Jane Greer and he spends a lot of that time constructively, leering at her. His leer helped keep alive the concept of hot sex in an era when there were few direct representations of it. The only people who might be prudish enough to object to his leer are those ineligible to receive it.

You can say or do anything to a man who looks like that; you can feel of his fly and, a little later, unzip it. In fact he wants you to (he thinks it's good for you).

About 28 years after they made *Run for the Sun*, Greer, at the age of about 60, and Widmark, about 70, worked together again in *Against All Odds* (1984); how extraordinary. Both got good notices as supporting players.

Probably because so many men today seem merely non-homosexual rather than positively heterosexual, today's actors swaggering about bareass or in their underpants lack the sexual authority of Widmark fully clothed. For it is a question of the face (the eyes, the mouth) and personality, not the body and not the underpants. Widmark's face cannot be directed or scripted (or even described). Thus his work is strictly a personal triumph for him alone. He demonstrates the importance of the movie star over the movie and thus the importance of star reviews over mere movie reviews, with their constant complaints about plot. A movie is the last place in the world to look for literary distinction. But there are hundreds of players, men and women, whose work I find worth watching in any picture they make (plus many, such as Warren Beatty and Katherine Hepburn, that I skip). Thus the only "input" (as I believe they call it in business) I need to decide which "oldies" to watch on TV is the cast list, and I remain unmoved by any praise or complaint that may be made about acting, writing or directing, by Pauline Kael, the *Times*, Leonard Maltin, and so on. I often watch pictures whose supporting players are bigger stars, personally or anatomically, than the billed stars who have mere mass appeal, like Ronnie Reagan.

By the time of *Run for the Sun* Widmark has gotten so confidently alluring that it does not particularly matter that he has also gotten a little old (about 42) and, when not lit properly, a little wrinkled; he obviously doesn't use night cream, as does Robert Redford (according to Cindy Adams in the *New York Post*). But no man is so attractive as he who doesn't give a shit how he looks, but only about how other people look; and it is refreshing to watch Widmark in this age of primping, preening, posing heterosexual males. He presents a stronger case (but of course still not a very convincing one) for heterosexuality than does Tom Cruise in the heterosexual training film, *All the Right Moves* (1983), in which Cruise, as a rather elderly high school student, achieves heterosexuality through, by order of importance, football and fucking. It may be Widmark's strength that he was born in a little town in Minnesota and raised in little towns in South Dakota and Missouri, where few men use night cream and he was safe from the influences of Manhattan and L.A.; both cities have disastrous effects upon the eroticism of the American male, whether homosexual or heterosexual.

Redford is from L.A., the night cream capital of the world; I suppose even the cops there use night cream.

SIDE BY SIDE

Marie Osmond's gum tissue, the dominant feature of her stills in the supermarket magazines, is for some reason not displayed as prominently in *Side by Side* (1982), seen at 11:45 p.m. October 16, 1983 on channel 2, and that is not the only good news about this picture. When Joseph Bottoms complains about her housekeeping, she slaps his face. It was her first screen slap—the first, it is to be hoped, of many. Slapping men will not stop them from slapping women. Nor will it, in life, produce the beneficial results it does in *Side by Side* (immediately upon being slapped, Bottoms began helping with the cooking, laundry, and house-cleaning). But slapping men makes the individual abused woman feel better. That is the sole purpose of revenge therapy: not to improve anyone's behavior but to make the individual victim feel better.

Osmond's screen slap would have been *avant-garde* coming from any actress; it was especially so coming from her. She is a member of The Church of Christ of Latter-day Saints, vulgarly known as the Mormons—a church which treats women as mere waitresses for men. She is an unlikely source of leadership in sexual politics but in striking Joseph Bottoms she escaped the constrictions of her religion and of her image.

The same cannot be said for her father nor for her brother, Donny, who remain offensively Christian. Her father and mother appear in this picture for a brief reminiscence about their courtship. Mrs. Osmond seems appropriately earthy when she says she fell in love with Mr. Osmond the minute she laid eyes on him, but Mr. Osmond even at this late stage of his life is far, far too heartwarming when he says it was that double scoop of ice cream she served that got him. Donny, mercifully, is not in the picture; tops in taps but

bottoms in balls, he opposes equal rights for women (how else could a male like him manage a relationship with a woman if she were not kept in a waitress role).

In addition to the reason for which Osmond slapped him, Bottoms deserves a slap for another reason, and that is that while courting her he would knock on her door without warning. Had she struck him the first time he pulled this she might have slapped a little sense into him. How would Joseph Bottoms like it if Marie Osmond knocked on his door unexpectedly while he was taking a shit or beating his meat?

But even sexual politicians may find it hard to stay mad at anyone who has a rear end as alluring as his. There are fairly frequent views of it in this picture. It is always fully clothed; this is an Osmond Productions picture and it would be asking too much that the Osmonds show his bare ass. It is gratifying enough that they show Marie slapping him. Anyway, his butt is of that insistent, determined type that shows itself even through ordinary pants and does not need pants especially tailored for butt display, like Levis. If anyone in Hollywood has the brains they could make this butt a powerful and profitable property; it could become one of the legendary bare asses of this part of the century. But they'd better get on it fast; Joseph is now almost 30 (the other Bottoms, Timothy, is about 34) and the butt is among the first parts to "go."

STAGE DOOR CANTEEN

Hail to the extras! Many are more fun than the stars. The extras look like people, not actors, and the sailor shown here in *Stage Door Canteen* (1943) could have stolen scenes from such familiar beauties as Tyrone Power and from such actorish creatures as Charlton Heston.

I don't know whether the sailor is a civilian dress extra or a real sailor (insofar as any player of that legendary role can be real), but he has the kind of face that makes men in trains, buses, and theaters want to reach over and feel of his dick. Unless he has some sexual illness that is not apparent in his face, more hands than his own

have played with his meat. How many would be an interesting statistic, one which I hope he will send in a letter to the Editor should he see these words, along with his opinion of his dick and butt, a résumé of their experience (he'd be around 60 by now), what any other men have said about them, how many inches he has, and whether he likes his balls licked. I've always assumed that all men like their balls licked but my next door neighbor told me recently that his are not sensitive. I feel sorry for him.

Distracted by some 50 stars who made brief appearances in *Stage Door Canteen*, I didn't even notice the sailor when I saw the picture at 11:05 p.m. March 17, 1984 on channel 13. I discovered him only later when The Museum of Modem Art sent stills to illustrate my study of the film. The next time it turns up on TV, I'll watch it again in hopes of catching a glimpse of him dancing, talking, or smiling; with luck, I might get some idea of how he moves the cheeks of his butt. It already seems clear in the still that he has hanging between his legs a piece of eating stuff ("seafood," as Navy meat of this grade is called); it would not be surprising, or even unusual, if it turns out upon further examination that his butt also is eating stuff.

Meanwhile, the still is even better than the film in one way: it gives the cineaste a chance to study such details as are available at length. His dreamy, lidded eyes raise the possibility that he is Jewish, and even the veins of his left hand suggest that he is well wired and capable of squirting a mouthful of cream when properly aroused out of his alluring complacency. Attractive as his tranquil, almost entranced, face is, it is the kind of cool face that men want to see contorted by sexual heat.

Stage Door Canteen is a valuable historical record not only of the young men of the 1940s but also of the stage (and some movie) stars of the day. Tallulah Bankhead makes a brief visit, and though they don't give her anything interesting to say or do, they don't have to. Just seeing her is enough. Just seeing her. Merle Oberon is stunning as ever though all she does is greet some service men and give them sweet little smiles, making sure to look each in the eye. Sophie Tucker makes a rare film appearance. I'd never seen her. Her charm is indescribable; it may be simply that she is heavily painted and overdressed and blatantly flaunts the tricks of feminine allure even though she is not alluring, she is fat. There is something defiant and valiant in this and these qualities—defiance and valor—are rarer than mere allure. Sophie uses a handkerchief so vast as to constitute a virtual partner in her act; along with Gail Patrick's, it is undoubtedly one of the biggest handkerchiefs in show biz. (Elsewhere in this book, accompanying the study of Gail in *My Favorite Wife*, is a glamour portrait of the two of them, Gail and her handkerchief. The proprietor of a movie still store told me that he knows of a man who killed himself when Gail died. I suppose I ought to've too, but I just couldn't; I'm sorry. We don't have to do without her, for she's still alive on film, some of which is available on TV.) Katherine Hepburn hideously overdoes her number but it is not as overdone as the fake *noblesse oblige* she displayed years later on the Dick Cavett TV show when, with Cavett's full cooperation, she acted as though she were going through this unpleasant sacrifice as a favor to the peasantry. The name of the business Miss Hepburn is in is show business; she is in the business of showing herself; she doesn't have to, she wants to; she was promoting one of her shows and attendance at her shows, and thus her income, depends on promotion; it is never a coup, as Cavett seems to think, to get a show person to show himself; it is sometimes a coup to get him to stop and get off the stage.

A song rendered by Freddy Martin's orchestra and containing the lyric,

> In a place they call Don't Worry Island
> We can lease a piece of paradise for two,

overstates, as do many lyrics of the period (and so many today), the joy of heterosexuality, at least the heterosexuality displayed by the sailor and his dancing partner in the still. (In fairness to her it should be said that she undoubtedly was programmed to want more than just a brief fling with a transient sailor and was forbidden to enjoy mere sexual pleasure. Many homosexuals, by contrast, would not expect, or want, anything more than a good taste of the sailor's meat.) The other big bands in the picture, especially Benny

Goodman, with Peggy Lee singing *Why Don't You Do Right*, are less schmaltzy.

The picture regards homosexuals and women as amusing creatures. Lon McCallister begins in the picture as a sweet, pretty youth who has "never kissed a girl," and before long one of his fellow soldiers says Lon can be the "bridesmaid" at a forthcoming wedding. Ray Bolger gayly debases himself in a song-and-dance which makes the troops feel big by ridiculing his own lack of virility and ridiculing women as well. A soldier named "Dakota" is similarly unimpressed by women; he says just thinking about them is cheaper than going with them, and almost as fun, and anyway it's hard to find a nice one. I was reminded of Ralph, a glamorous 18-year-old airman who invited me to his hotel room for a drink when I was a teenager; he told me he couldn't find a girl and sucked me off twice.

But the picture is not sufficiently misogynous to account for Ina Claire's astonishing but casual reminder to a group of sailors that they can't dance with each other. What can the scriptwriter, Delmer Daves, and the director, Frank Borzage, whose last name was as glamorous as his pictures, possibly have had in mind? The sailors were not about to dance with each other; the *Stage Door Canteen* was a free club which provided "hostesses" for servicemen to dance with. Still, Ina's advice was as sound as it was gratuitous, for two sailors dancing with each other might well develop hard-ons rubbing against each other and this, along with the intoxicating smell of each other's Vitalis or Wildroot Creme Oil, could well make the sailors lose control of themselves. The sensitive viewer can almost smell Vitalis in the hair of the sailor in the still. It is the kind of hair that leaves a cheap, powerful perfume on your pillow the next day. Whatever the intent of Ina's remark, it has the effect, undoubtedly unintended, of raising the question: which form of dancing (or sexual intercourse) is more instinctive and more thrilling, the kind which must be forbidden or the kind which must be enforced?

Today the closest thing to a *Stage Door Canteen* in Times Square is a U.S.O. center named after Francis Cardinal Spellman. For years there have been constant rumors from a variety of sources that, as happens so often in the clergy, His Eminence was a cock-sucker. In an *Advocate* interview, Gore Vidal gave his information about the matter, but it was not until 1984 that Francis's homo-sexuality was addressed for the first time in the big "straight" media. A group of *New York Times* editors, the highest ranking of whom was Abe Rosenthal, succeeded in getting material about Francis's sex life reduced from several pages in John Cooney's *The American Pope* to a mere footnote. The Rosenthal group claimed that the rumors do not constitute conclusive evidence. But the evidence that Francis was homosexual is at least as good as the evi-dence that Abe Rosenthal is heterosexual; in neither case are there depositions from eyewitnesses. I am willing to believe that Abe is heterosexual—in fact eager. It is mysterious in the extreme that he represents himself as being unable to believe that Francis was homosexual. It could be simply that, unlike so many of us, he has never been sucked off by a priest and thus lacks our strange belief in the clergy.

STALLION ROAD

Stallion Road (1947) is perhaps the best picture in the veterinarian genre—its particular disease is *Bacillus anthracis,* vulgarly known as anthrax—but the genre itself is so remote from the standard tits 'n' ass genres, both male and female, that the picture failed to hold the attention even of its cast, as the still of Alexis Smith, supplied by The Museum of Modern Art, shows.

Inevitably, the reviewers, including the *Times* TV guide, were unable to resist the temptation to make obvious cracks about the superiority of the horses to the actors; Steven H. Scheuer's comment in *Movies on TV* that the picture "offers nothing more than some good looking horses" is typical. It is not good to be typical, yet Scheuer's biographical note in his book seems calculated to establish his credentials as a typical heterosexual more than as a film authority. "Mr. Scheuer," the note reads, "participates in many sports, and is a nationally ranked squash tennis player." Being a nationally ranked squash tennis player is not germane to the question of whether his writing is on the ball, and such people are in danger of favoring pictures that have a sporting amount of aggression and blood, like those cranked out by the "Hollywood Mafia" (Messrs. Scorcese, Cimino, DePalma, and Coppola). The heavy coincidence of vowels in that roster does not mean that I regard Italians in general as bloody; one of the swishiest men in Hollywood history is Vincente Minnelli. Nor am I saying that Minnelli is homosexual; it is heterosexuals who equate effeminacy and homosexuality, even though some of the nelliest men in the nation, such as William F. Buckley, Jr. and Dick Cavett, are married and thus officially heterosexual. Minnelli himself was husband to Judy Garland and father to the excessively energetic Liza.

A producer embarking upon an anthrax picture naturally thinks of Ronnie Reagan for the role of the "vet"; he is more concerned about horses than people. Ronnie was about 36, and already sloppy-assed, when he made this picture; later he had even more reason to be fond of horses, for they helped him avoid paying income taxes by serving as a tax shelter for him. Ronnie and Nancy love America, but also money (not necessarily in that order).

Ronnie's romance with Alexis Smith in *Stallion Road*, seen at 2 a.m. November 15, 1984 on channel 5, is perhaps the coldest ever filmed, but the picture does have one image well worth watching and waiting for. The horse Ronnie is riding wanders close to the camera; Ronnie, photographed from behind, rears up in the stirrups; the screen is filled with two vast asses (Ronnie's and, just beneath it and approximately the same width, the horse's). It is incredible that this routine mishap in filming was left in the final cut.

"My God Almighty!" I cried over the 'phone to a friend when I saw Reagan stick his big butt in the camera, and my friend, watching the picture on his own receiver 60 blocks to the south of

me, released a simultaneous cry of astonishment. *Stallion Road*, like most pictures, is not complete in itself and requires audience participation—additional dialogue supplied by the viewers. This is best done at home; it would annoy patrons in a theater. *Stallion Road* is so bleak that my friend and I, connected by telephone as we watched it, supplied not only additional dialogue (all of it unprintable) but also imaginary conversations among the cast and crew between camera set-ups. Alexis Smith, for example, appears throughout the picture in men's clothes, and in our fancy the director, James V. Kern, a former lawyer who turned out what Ephraim Katz, the film encyclopaedist, characterized as "mediocre" pictures, was not forceful enough to get her to wear dresses. "Shit," she tells him in our fantasy, "I'm not going to wear drag for this fucking picture. If you want a fluff get Loretta; she *likes* to wear veils and all that shit."

It seemed probable to us that Zachary Scott would discuss with Alexis their co-star: "That's some butt Ronnie's got on him isn't it. I've seen better on a fucking elephant. Shit, he's not a piece of meat, he's only Spam."

Had it been Bobby Jordan, the Dead End Kid, who stuck his butt in the camera, the image would have incited positive comments about his butt's primary functions as a beautiful and erotic part of his body. But Reagan's rotten rear forced my friend and I to imagine the secondary function, as an outlet for faeces: Ronnie's taking a shit; the 'phone rings; there's no one around to answer it; he doesn't have time to wipe his ass and he doesn't want to get embarrassing faecal stains on his underpants. So he hurries to the 'phone with his legs spread, holding his pants around his knees.

Even though we were still watching *Stallion Road*, my friend slipped into his impression of Mae West as she might have been while watching an old Elvis Presley picture on TV:

Mmm. That's nice. Mmm. That "love me tender" he's singing—that's his trouble, he's too tender. If I had him here I could toughen him up, make a man out of him. The little shit-ass.

"Tiffany," I cried in the rigid accent of the Social Register women I used to work with at a small electronics magazine (Nina Auchincloss, for example, was the receptionist), "is shit-ass one word, two words, or hyphenated?"

In these ways, we got through *Stallion Road*.

APPENDICES

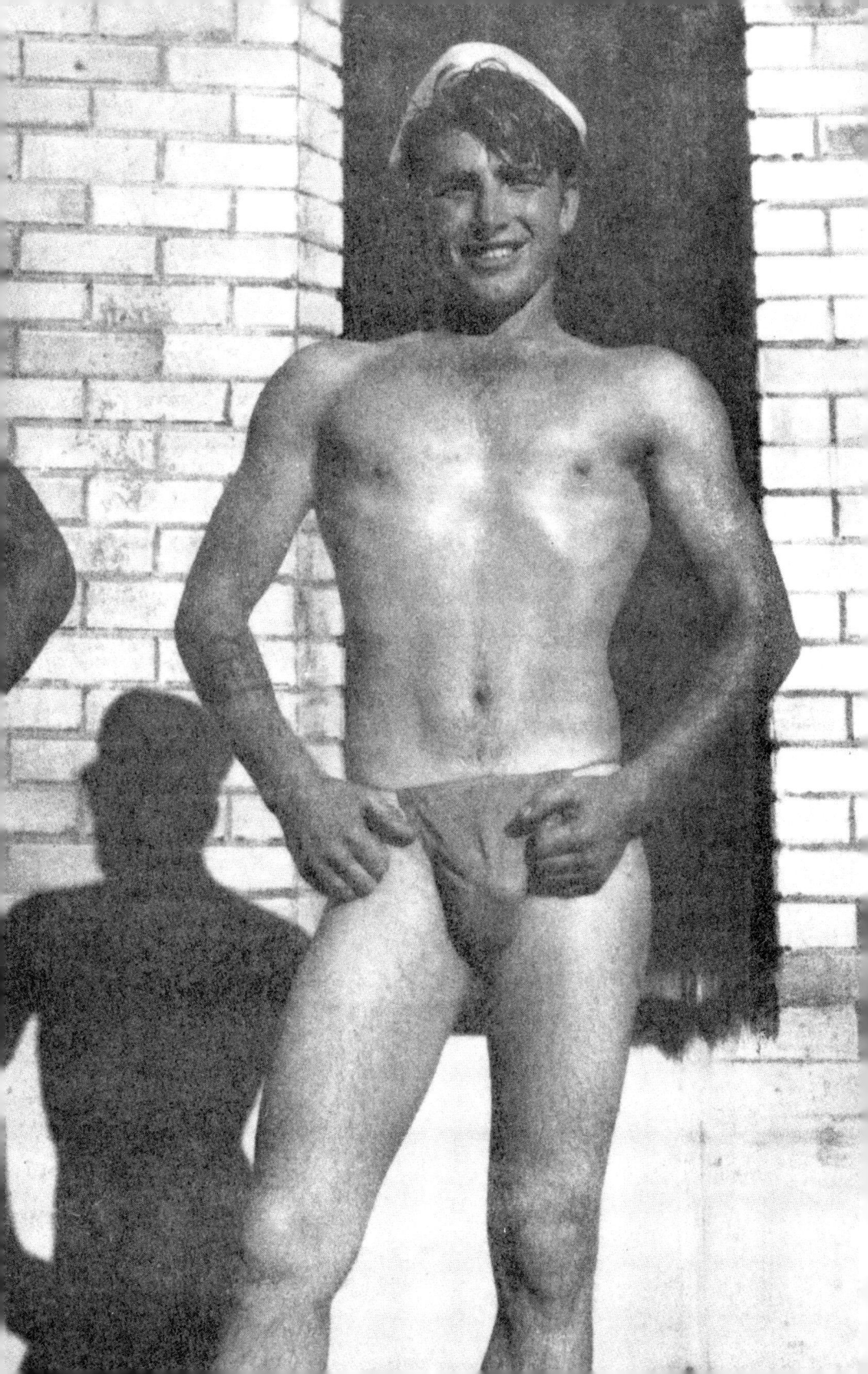

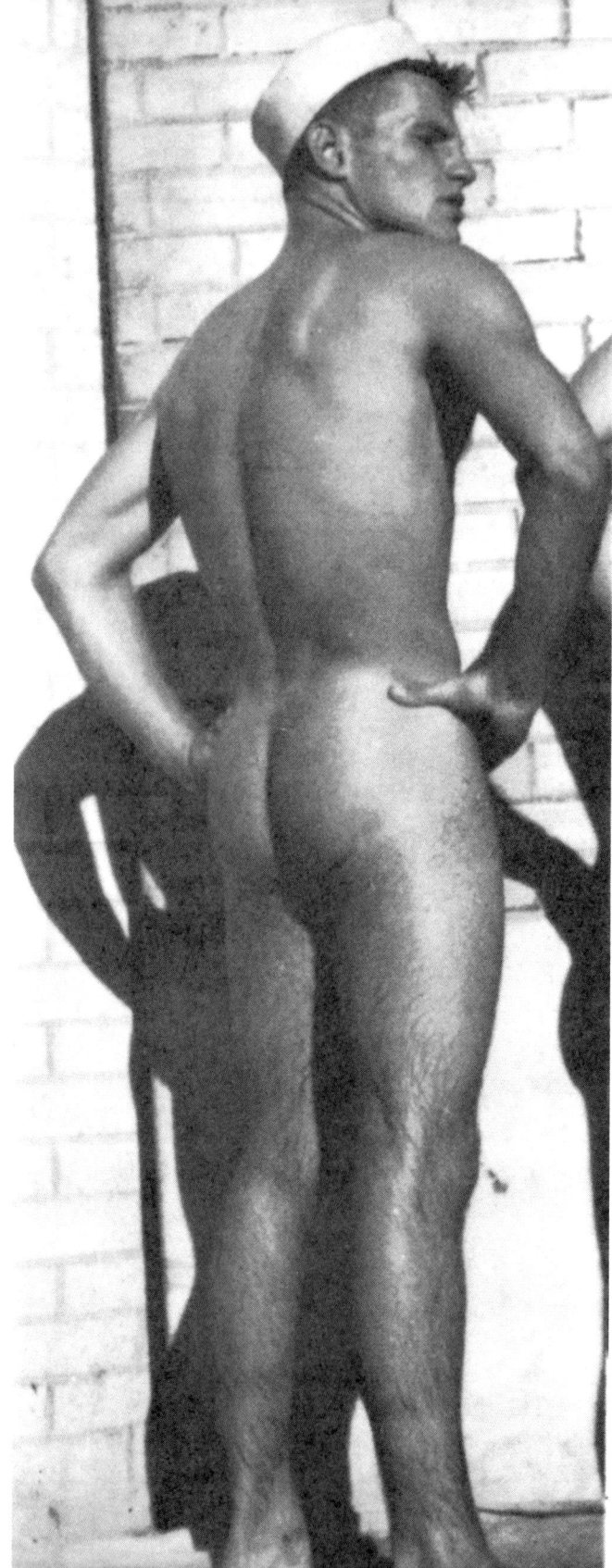

STAR OF STARS

As shown here, Jim Lassiter has just enough leg hairs to establish that he is a human being rather than, as some might think at first glance, a god. Lassiter, of course, was a star in the 50s and 60s at AMG, which most well-bred men rank as immeasurably superior to MGM. In portraying sailors, for example, Lassiter was far more credible than such famous players as Frank Sinatra, Gene Kelly, and Fred Astaire. Paradoxically, the three bigger stars lived the "straight" life but seemed too queer on screen as sailors, while Lassiter, who did sailor parts superbly, undoubtedly had, as what he calls a "hustler," more homosexual experience than Sinatra, Kelly, and Astaire put together.

Bob Mizer, founder of AMG (Athletic Model Guild), was, and remains, the DeMille of posing strap pictures. Lassiter and the other AMG models wore posing straps until recent years, when AMG has been turning out bareass pictures. Shown here is a rare still of Lassiter without a posing strap. It would have been pleasant to see him step out of his strap, but I not only have not seen that, I have not seen him in a motion picture at all. But I don't have to. I can see in his stills that he's a star. Doubtless Lassiter found a ready market for his posing strap when he pulled it off; Mizer allowed fans of his models on the set, which was usually the back-yard of his house in L.A., and Lassiter reports, in correspondence with the writer, that some of what he calls his clients "wanted me to come in them [underpants] often and save them in a plastic bag for them."

The other still of Lassiter in this issue has a spot on his left nate which I assume is just drool from one of the boys in the back room at the photo house which machines prints for me. I doubt

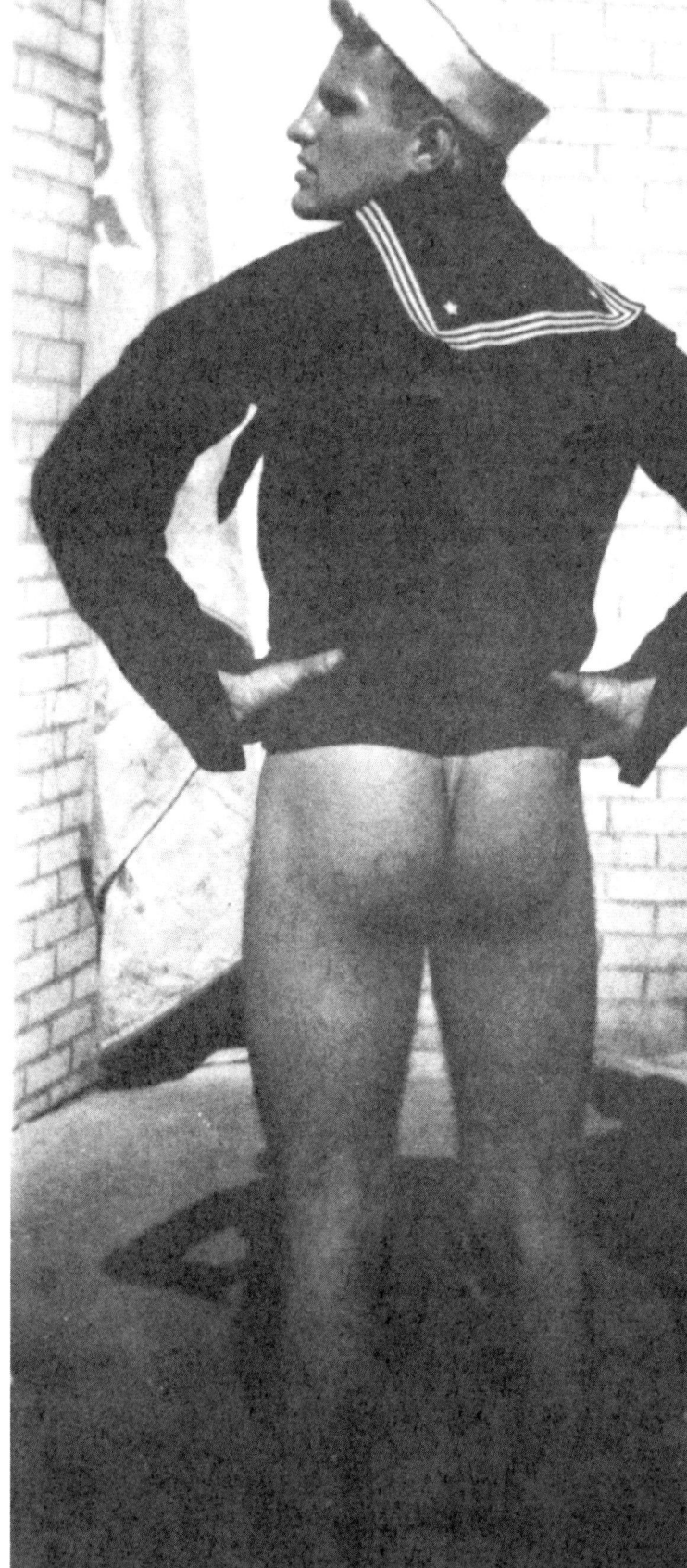

that it is saliva from the manager, a big, beautiful blond who wears his shirt unbuttoned to display a hairless, tanned torso and who is the most undoubtedly heterosexual man I've ever met; he is absolutely untroubled by the pieces of AMG ass I bring him for machining, in the same way that I am untroubled about seeming to be, or becoming, a Lithuanian or a Lesbian.

By contrast, a male at another photo house wore a crew cut before they became fashionable again, which is suspect to begin with, and feels a need to show contempt for the work I bring him. If he were authentically heterosexual, like the blond, he would have no more need to show contempt for my dick and butt art than I have to display contempt for Lithuanians or Lesbians. If I had a young daughter, I'd hope she turned out to be a Lesbian. Lesbians worship women; "straight" males despise them, and love only ballplayers.

Today, Mizer reports, Lassiter is hairier than he was in the stills shown here. Lassiter, a carpenter now, lives near AMG, still visits the studio, and still, understandably, likes to look at his body in the mirror. Through Mizer, I arranged to have Lassiter answer a questionnaire. I knew from experience that this type of man is terse; I tried to compose questions that would elicit informative answers even if the answer were only one word:

Q.: Have you ever sucked dick?
Lassiter: Yes.
Q.: Have you ever taken it up the ass?
Lassiter: Yes.

I thus have more data on Lassiter than on the more famous stars I write about; Ryan O'Neal, for example, has never told me what is the biggest number of times he has jacked off in a single day (Lassiter's answer is five), nor have Chevy Chase and Eddie Murphy told me whether they take it in the ass (I merely assume they do).

Before he was "discovered" by AMG while hitchhiking, Lassiter "hustled around," in his words, in Manhattan. Normally he was stationed outside the Astor Bar in Times Square, a maddeningly glamorous bar, especially during World War II, when a combination of "tomorrow we may die" attitude and the fact that it was not the custom then, as it is now, for women to put out, made the nation's handsomest soldiers, sailors, and airmen readily available for sex with each other and with their civilian male swains. Lassiter had first been sucked off at age 13 in his native Midwest by some fantastically fortunate boy or man, and when he came to New York he soon learned, from a kindly stranger who took him to a coffee shop when he was "broke and hungry," that his dick and ass were worth money. The stranger told him about a bar where his meat would be welcome. He hustled for about seven years, working a seven-day week from one to seven hours per day, averaging "two big spenders" per day. Thus as many as 5,110 men may have "had" him during this seven-year period. Many of them would still be alive today, and I hope any who see these words will write a letter to the Editor giving precise data on the various parts of Lassiter's body as well as on his character.

Meanwhile I can report, from his questionnaire, that he "played the part of a passive gay hustler, enticing men with my good looks. Having a passive nature, I allowed them to do what they wanted while I relaxed and enjoyed it." He had "many married clients."

"I always kept myself clean," he writes. He was thus what is clinically called sweet-assed. He enjoyed having his balls and asshole licked, but this happened "not as often as I would like." I was surprised to read this; in my innocence I had assumed that it would be a routine, almost daily, occurrence. He operated thusly: "We would go to a coffee shop. I would say I was hustling around, he would ask what I did, then the price was set." It is almost painful for men who like the stills shown here to imagine what Lassiter was like earlier when he was one of Manhattan's principal pieces of eating stuff and could be rented for other gratifications as well. It seems certain this his flesh was the finest money could buy.

For me, his most interesting response was to a question about compliments from his customers: "One stands in my mind by a sculpture [sic], he said, I have the most perfectly proportioned body he ever measured." The sentence contains two incorrect punctuation marks and one incorrect word, and thus enhances a charm that didn't really need enhancing; studies conducted privately by the writer show that men who write incorrectly are more fun in bed than those who do. I have for my next book letters from semi-literate heterosexual Englishmen whose use of "to" for "too", as in "to [sic] much," and of "of" for "off," as in "it turned me of [sic]," increase the allure of their sexual secrets. Men who mistakenly use commas for periods are unusually erotic, as are those who use periods for question marks.

The only big budget actor that I find comparable to Lassiter is Mel Gibson, but in *Mad Max* (1980) he had the excessively lovely walk of a dancer. Still, millions worship the ground he minces on. That he is trying to make his image more butch is suggested by his announcement, in the garment industry's gay magazine, *Andy Warhol's Interview*, that he wears dirty socks. But just wearing dirty socks is not enough; I'm sorry. Probably the city's most intelligent, and therefore most confident, editor regards William Hurt (*Body Heat*) as fully competitive with Lassiter. The editor has seen Hurt's bare butt in two pictures and has followed him into a men's room in a Manhattan restaurant, where the star failed to wash his hands after taking a leak. (The same editor reports that Doubleday's most publicized editrix, Jackie Kennedy Onassis, does not wash her hands when she emerges from her booth in the ladies' piss-house. This may be all right if she only took a leak and may not be all right if she actually took—don't you see?—a shit.) The *New York Times* described a rehearsal in which Sigourney Weaver straddles Hurt's lap, facing him in a fucking position. After the scene, Hurt told Weaver, "You're very brave," and the director, Mike Nichols, said to Hurt, "You're brave, too." Of all the adjectives that might describe the simulated taking of Hurt's pecker in Weaver's twat, "brave" seems the least appropriate; we don't call IBM computers brave for performing as programmed, and that, after all, is all Hurt, Weaver, and Nichols are doing. But to compensate for the fact that they are common, ordinary robots: heterosexuals like to heap honors upon each other; just as Hurt, Weaver, and Nichols were congratulatory toward each other, so the United States Government, again according to the *Times*, awarded more medals after its invasion of Grenada than there were troops in the invasion.

If the word brave is to be used for any sexual activity, it should be saved for people like Jim Lassiter; Hurt has turned down a homosexual role but Lassiter isn't afraid of what people think of him. They think highly of him; I have used his photo on my stationery and it has won favorable comments. His simple, strong statement that "I don't think homosexuality is wrong" and his easy discussion of his sexual experience are as inspiring as the stills of his butt; someone who casually admits to doing what is forbidden is more honest and braver than someone who can only do what he is supposed to do—or act as though he does.

STAR FUCKS FAN

A friend of mine has just now told me that forty years ago, when he bent over one day to tie his shoe lace, the sight of his butt was not lost on Henry Wilcoxon.

"Sailor," Wilcoxon said, "I heard you say you're trying to get transportation to L.A." "Yes, sir." The "sir" was in recognition of Wilcoxon's rank, not an invitation to play sexual master; but my friend claims that, as Wilcoxon drove him from San Francisco to L.A., it became clear, without either of them saying so, he was to be the officer's piece of ass.

Wilcoxon (1905–1984) was a rare type of movie star, both beautiful and tough, and his British accent gave him an added aura.

He married, and divorced, Joan Woodbury, a glamorous but minor actress, and was a friend of Cecil B. DeMille. He appeared with Claudette Colbert in DeMille's *Cleopatra* (1934) and with Loretta Young in *The Crusades* (1935).

En route to L.A., Wilcoxon and his passenger made a pit stop at a motel (called "tourist cabins" in those days). After they showered and hit the sack, Wilcoxon kissed the sailor. Wilcoxon took off his "very unglamorous" boxer shorts, the sailor his Jockey shorts. My friend reports that Wilcoxon squirted several loads of cum in his butt hole during the night, that he was short and normally hung, that he didn't talk much but expressed himself in "animal groans," but that he did, as they finished their trip to L.A. next day, show an interest in my friend's life. Wilcoxon dropped him at the gardenia-scented Biltmore, sore-assed but satisfied; Wilcoxon was one of his favorite movie stars. He's one of mine too; thanks to TV, pictures he made 50 years ago are still providing unspeakable inspiration.

AN ORIENTAL IN SCANTY UNDERPANTS

Most American men, especially "straight" men, probably have a secret yearning to be slapped around by hairless, hot-tempered, half-naked Oriental men, and on Saturdays in New York they can at least see kung fu pictures on the blue collar channels. These stations transmit to my receiver signals of museum quality; always have. The white collar network outlets—WNBC, WCBS, and WABC—have never been able to send images of comparable quality. The viewer who is interested, as I am, in the precise bulge and curve of a butt, a thigh, a nipple, a belly button, or a jock pouch naturally discriminates against network attractions in favor of re-runs on the independent outlets. A lucid groin on a blue collar station is preferable to a blurred butt on a white collar one.

Clear as these blue collar transmissions are, I still was unable to determine whether the scanty briefs a certain Oriental wore in a certain kung fu picture seen in November, 1983 were made of cotton or of synthetic fabric. Whatever they were they looked fine on him as, laying on his Oriental butt, he enacted a prolonged death agony, giving exquisite bumps and grinds and the impression that he knew how to act while getting a blow job. It was the finest acting I've seen in a picture, far superior to anything Cary Grant, for example, was ever capable of doing. In my own agony over the Oriental's death (mixed, I admit, with ecstasy), it did not occur to me to jot down the name of the picture and cash in on it by writing about it. But it doesn't matter; there are kung fu pictures on every Saturday with, I assume, their own opportunities to see Japanese jockey shorts. These pictures anyway are meant to be seen, not written about, and this particular picture is especially hard to write about because while I am composing this study I am trying also to catch Eve Arden's takes in *One Touch of Venus* (1950), shown at 8 p.m. December 10, 1983 on channel 5. (The scenes with Ava Gardner and Robert Walker, even though they are interesting players, do not warrant watching because of the picture's barbaric script and infantile direction; but Arden never let little things like that stand in her way.)

In some ways that are too obscene to list here, Oriental men can be more interesting than white men. Many white men crave Oriental meat and so do many Orientals prefer white men; no wonder bars and bath houses provide a meeting place for these two racial types who are so hungry for each other.

GRAND LARCENY: LANA TURNER STEALS "NIGHT OF STARS"

Just as for sex I find a hot piece of meat preferable to a wonderful human being, so in show biz I enjoy a star more than someone who's merely a great actor. Actors work to get what stars get without trying: attention. It was Lana Turner who held mine at "Night of 100 Stars," not the others who formed a line with her on stage: Olivia de Havilland, Robert De Niro, Dustin Hoffman, Danny Kaye, Laurence Olivier, Sidney Poitier, and Robert Preston. The show was taped at Radio City Music Hall February 17, 1985 and telecast March 10.

Some stars, in addition to being stars, can also act, but not Lana; but it doesn't matter. Nor did it matter that Esther Williams is not a great actress. At her best she made bathing suit pictures, and her best was 30 years ago, but she came on with a group of athletes like a great current star and got treated like one. In a sense it's like taking a bow for having a 12-inch dick, but Michael Caine liked Esther too. He'd never met her before they did the show and talked about her to interviewers afterwards.

Lana looks hard at 65 but she's had to be; she's had to put up with something the softer, 69-year-old Olivia never had—a general attitude among reviewers that her work isn't very good. But when it came time for the movie people to join hands and leave the stage, Lana walked over and took Sir Laurence's hand as one of his peers (something the more respected Olivia didn't, and I think wouldn't, do); and when someone in the audience cried "Bravo!" it was Lana, not Sir Laurence, who acknowledged it with a slight wave.

After her film clips were shown, Lana, who, like most of the women in the show and in the audience, was wearing a glitter gown,

strolled casually onstage and took her ovation without surprise or gratitude, without even a full smile (how refreshing after all the jaw-breaking smiles the TV stars give). Without quite touching her lips, she blew a kiss with both hands to the $1,000 seats. It was a gesture as stylized and unreal as ballet. But I think she felt the ovation more than she showed; from my seat in the colored section I could see the right wing and when she left the stage a man in a tuxedo (was it the hairdresser she traveled with last year when she publicly called the editor of her autobiography a cocksucker?) came up and held her. They just stood there while she reentered the earth's atmosphere. It was a nicer anti-climax than in the old days, when she came home from an Academy Awards show and got beaten up by her boyfriend, Johnny Stompanato. Lana's 15-year-old daughter, Cheryl, took Johnny off with a knife in 1958. In so doing, Cheryl demonstrated that she literally (for Johnny died) has executive talent; she was later to make a killing in real estate.

Lana has been tough enough to stay thin. Olivia de Havilland has put on some pounds. It was she, with all her prestige as an actress, who overdid her entrance to receive her ovation. Olivia tried to please; Lana didn't. Olivia came on like Loretta Young, manipulating veils with both hands. While such a gesture might be justified in a crowd scene to obliterate a hated rival, Olivia, like each of the other movie people honored, had the stage to herself before all of them came on together for last call. Olivia came down a lot of steps not exactly with difficulty, but at least with noticeable care. It's not easy to descend stairs with no railing (working without a railing is like working without a net). Lana made it easy for herself by just sauntering in from the right wing. The way to descend steps is the way Elizabeth R. does it—not, like Olivia, trying to do a difficult move gracefully, but blatantly watching your step. In doing so, Elizabeth shows that she's valuable and that she knows it.

Esther Williams, 61, made the stair entrance beautifully. She has Lana's confidence but also a pot belly. Lana is ready as is, without dieting, for a comeback; she will be 10 years from now. But just staying thin, as the tedious Nancy Reagan demonstrates almost daily, is not enough; you've got to be something besides thin, and Nancy just isn't.

Ginger Rogers would look great at 74 with less makeup. It is sad to think that in light of her important place in film history, both as a dancer and as an actress, she still feels she must look young. She came on at the climax of a huge dance number. She participated only in a limited way, appeared winded, and seemed to rely on her partner's memory for the next move. But she got her arm up in unison with the rest of the dancers for an ovation at the end. It was such vigorous dancers as Gregory and Maurice Hines who were the immediate cause of this ovation, but Ginger deserved it too for her glorious past. Word came in from the director's trailer outside the Hall that the number required a second take for the TV tape, and this is one number that the audience was glad to see repeated. Both times it gave a standing ovation.

But in general the taping was a debasing experience for some stars, even such huge ones as Joan Collins. They were not announced (announcements were spliced on later for the TV show) and sometimes got little applause. Once when my eyes swept a stageful of California TV people, I was astonished to see among them Anne Baxter, once an Academy Award movie star. She looked great, as did another big star almost hidden in a crowd, Raquel Welch. Lucille Ball is the only star who got a big ovation when she walked on unannounced; she remains, from her *I Love Lucy* days on TV, one of America's most beloved propagandists for heterosexuality. But while she was making those shows, which presented heterosexuality as cute, fun, and affectionate, she and her husband, Desi Arnaz, were fighting off camera on such issues as drinking and adultery.

Danny Kaye, Sidney Poitier, and Dinah Shore still look great. Dinah gave the audience an additional chance to see how good she looks by walking down an aisle of the orchestra en route to backstage while the show was on. Even I know less ostentatious ways to get backstage. Mark Gastineau has a Mae West figure that only a football fan could love. Sarah Vaughn, Robert Klein, and Robert Preston have put on pounds. Sir Laurence and Jimmy Stewart, as befits their age, look ghastly. Apart from the gymnasts, the only good-looking boy ass was on some of those California TV women, mean-looking women who keep whipping themselves into shape.

Even the blue collar class—the stagehands—failed me. None of them had the legendary lure of the lower classes. But the cops may be getting better. New York cops have tended to be a fat-assed, pot-bellied lot, but on Sixth Avenue after the show I saw a dozen young cops who would look great in a chorus line wearing sequined posing straps and kicking their legs up. And my cab driver, a black man in a brilliant red turtleneck, was of high quality. He was No. 309—the show had 308 "stars," not the 100 advertised. Some were young—Drew Barrymore, aged 10, and Brooke Shields and Matt Dillon, twice that age. One had to be wheeled onstage—one of the actresses from silent films. Even in a wheelchair she wore a glitter gown. As the beloved Estelle Winwood, who died in 1984 at age 101, rasped on a TV drama years ago, "My dear, if you have it you never lose it."

BETTY HUTTON SAID "SHIT-ASS"

The Jack Wrangler Story by Jack Wrangler and Carl Johnes
St. Martin's Press, $ 13.95

Jack Wrangler (*né* Stillman) lacks the nasty, rotten quality that is so alluring in most sex stars. At his publishing party he wore a suit and necktie and could have passed for an IBM junior executive, but he was recognizable even in his clothes. He has dimples and he is nice. Indeed, the subtitle of his memoir is "What's A Nice Boy Like You *Doing*?" and his caption under one of the 30 photographs reads, "Looking at that sensitive face, it's hard to believe I could be into so many nasties."

Despite these handicaps, he has climbed completely bareass to the top in the sexual performing arts. From the very start, he has been a dependable performer in person and on the screen; his first job, one rainy day in L.A., required making an entrance on stage with a big fat hard on. Since then he has been producing hard ons and loads of thick, photogenic cum on cue. In one torture scene, he had to take a corn cob in his ass. I'd have asked for a stunt man.

In stills and movies, the cameraman can wait if an actor has trouble getting a hard on or shooting his wad, but there is no such flexibility in the more lucrative PA's. Still, thousands of men have seen him beat his meat on stage.

Apart from the fact that he did this most difficult of acting chores, unloading cum, superbly, he is admirable for doing it at all. Someone has to, to counteract the propaganda of unattractive prudes, both "straight" and gay. He's had to take a lot of scorn from them. But I regard prudery as a synonym for envy.

He's still in great shape at age 38—he apparently goes to gymnasia—and his career has been a triumph over a sexually

disadvantaged childhood which included attendance along with Greer Garson, the Meryl Streep of her day, at the Beverly Hills Community Presbyterian Church and, even worse, work as a child actor in *Faith of Our Children*, the 1950s TV series which presaged today's rabid Reaganism with its slogan, "The family that prays together stays together. "

Incredibly, Wrangler was a virgin until college, despite the fact that he went to Black Foxe Military School and St. George's. At Black Foxe, to which he was bused with the sons of Robert Cummings, Dean Martin, Jerry Lewis, and Alan Ladd, he did photograph his own hard on with a Polaroid, a promising sign of the healthy sexuality he was later to enjoy.

At Northwestern University he "couldn't wait to run back to my room, open up my physique magazines of half-nude football jocks, and jack off." The school also provided, as all good schools do, hot sex; Professor Charley Shively has just reported to me from Cambridge, for example, that the most divine feature of Harvard Divinity School is its cocksuckers. College gave Wrangler experience in acting as well; he was a local fill-in player for such visiting stars as the immortal Joan Blondell and that tough cookie, Ruth Roman. After graduation, he directed Jane Russell, Gale Storm, and Betty Hutton at a dinner theater in Lubbock, Texas, which Hutton, traveling with a manager who was 15, black, and "very girlish," characterized as a "shit-ass town." Wrangler didn't like St. Petersburg, at whose Country Dinner Theatre he directed Yvonne DeCarlo and Mamie Van Doren. Most people would find work of such extreme glamour fully satisfying, but Wrangler sought relief by going to Tampa and picking up men at Lucille's; his taste was for plain men, rather than the fancy ones he encountered in show biz. Andy Devine objected to one trick who would sit on the floor during conferences in St. Petersburg with his arms wrapped around Wrangler's legs, but Devine claimed that he was otherwise sexually tolerant: "Remember, George Cukor is one of my best friends."

Russell's gig in Lubbock alone warrants a full-length book; a star that huge should have her every comment, every plane ride, every registration at a motel, every call to room service, every activity backstage recorded. But in Wrangler's book she is merely listed along with others in one sentence. Paradoxically, men who have little experience seem to be the most intense writers about it; Wrangler has had a lot of experience. Certainly he has turned out better than that other celebrated Northwestern alumnus, Charlton Heston, who made sordid Judeo-Christian pictures in Hollywood while Wrangler went into the more inspiring sex field.

"I have never worked with an actor who didn't have impeccable personal hygiene," Wrangler writes. Can Heston make the same claim? In light of the shooting scripts for Wrangler's pictures, which normally called, *inter alia*, for cocksucking, ass licking, and butt fucking, the cleanliness of his co-stars was a valuable fringe benefit. Most men, I find, prefer men, movies, and books that are completely tasteless. The perfect tasteless man is one who wears just a jock strap to a bar or disco and who (because of the shocking amount of ass licking going on) has just showered carefully. I suspect that the men who turn out tasteful books and pictures have armpits and assholes as tasteful as their filmic and literary styles.

Wrangler graduated from all-male sex pictures to "straight" ones—e.g., such scenes as that classic favorite of the heterosexual male, having a woman stick a dildo in his ass. His first blow job from a woman was done on camera. He discovered that "Girls don't do it like guys. I found myself going limp." He does not elaborate; I assume he means merely that men, especially "straight" men, are more cock-crazy than women, and eat it like pigs.

Among numerous beneficial results of the pioneering work done by Wrangler and others, when he went to Roosevelt Hospital for surgery "Dr. Rothemel… in consideration of my profession refused to let anyone shave my pubic hair." Wrangler can also claim some of the credit for the balmy atmosphere of utter sexual integration at his publishing party, where, now that Wrangler's pictures are established artifacts of the culture, men and women both "straight" and gay blended with no problems. Held on a Friday night in August, the party drew only the confident, the utterly "in" people; the less confident go out of town on a summer Friday. Margaret Whiting, to whom Wrangler has been informally married for seven years, was the star entertainer. Dazzling as she was in an almost preposterously glamorous gown, her arrival with Wrangler at the Red

Parrot created less of a commotion than did that of Tom Steele, the editor, composer, performer, and so on, who had run part of Wrangler's book in *Christopher Street* and who made a tickertape parade entrance, alternately sending kisses with his hand and using it to give that faint wave to the masses that the Pope also does so well. Steele was dressed, as usual, in what looked like an ensemble picked up at a studio wardrobe auction; I believe I remember the top he was wearing from an old Jack Palance picture, *The Big Knife* (1955), which I saw recently on TV, but it could also have been, as some of his other tops seem to be, from *Goodbye, My Fancy* (1951), also on TV recently.

Because of the usual high volume of sound at the disco, kisses and gropes were used in place of words to greet existing friends and make new ones. At ringside, as Whiting, backed by a full band, gave full-blast high-voltage renditions of standards from the big band era, including her famous *Moonlight in Vermont*, Michael Denneny, the St. Martin's editor handling Wrangler, left his charge long enough to exchange a passionate kiss with Steele. Kevin Smith, the photographer, came up and greeted Steele with a comprehensive and prolonged examination of his butt. Ethan Mordden, glamorous in sun glasses, and Steele took to the dance floor with fluid grace (specifically, vodka). In the men's room a petit Hispanic was stationed with a vast slab of meat dangling out of his fly. A youth in a UCLA T-shirt and black shorts scantier than Kevin Smith's green ones wiggled his butt on the dance floor with astonishing rapidity; two small clusters of husky, hairless Orientals lurked sullenly yet enticingly in the darkness.

The evening was a tribute in more ways than one to Wrangler and Whiting, whose careers have helped make possible such a scene. Perhaps a thousand young men with flat bellies and aesthetic keisters, born after the big band era which Whiting represents, were enthralled by her, and all intelligent men with well functioning bodies admire Wrangler. There was no one with a sexual problem, none of the Norman Mailers and William F. Buckley, Juniors of tomorrow, no real drunks or junkies—I counted only one pool of vomit all evening, which may be a record. The whole thing was so glamorous I could only stand about five hours of it; then I left.

BING CROSBY HAD BAD BREATH

Past Imperfect by Joan Collins
Simon and Schuster, $16.95

"Don't wear pants" was the instruction over the 'phone; so it was to be just a quickie. Warren Beatty's enthusiasm for the abortion was depressing (men who don't want babies are creepy) and to make matters worse the abortionist's office was in Newark, in a *maroon* building with a *green* elevator.

Collins discusses this and other chores without whining. Recent material has been added to the 1978 English edition, but some material from that edition has been excised. She's taken a bad rap from "straight" males on such papers as *Rolling Stone* and the *Washington Post* who act above sex rather than merely out of it. She hadn't had all that much sex. In fact she's proof that you can survive in Hollywood without sucking off Spyros Skouras, Darryl Zanuck, and other men who tried unsuccessfully to "make" her, Zanuck with the boast that "I've got the biggest." It was his pecker he was talking about, not, as some might think, what Collins calls his "protruding, gray-haired belly." Collins wasn't a size queen and nowhere does she tell the main thing the public doesn't know about her famous lays: how many inches they have.

She's more interested in romance; she refused to do career fucking in order to get parts from "fat, ugly, old" producers and also turned down a huge offer for more direct prostitution. She didn't have recreational sex; what she recounts here are marriages and love affairs, one at a time but with some overlap, so that once or twice there was some danger of a traffic jam in her tunnel of love.

JOAN COLLINS

Past Imperfect

IN HER OWN WORDS — THE FRANK AND FUNNY INSIDE STORY OF A SENSATIONAL SHOW BIZ CAREER

She has a neat style: "My voice was quite good but weak (rather like my character)." A more sensitive editor than Michael Korda would have excised such things as the exclamation point after "I had probably blown the part—if not the producer!" There is some horseshit ("It felt good. Too good."). But in general she has surprisingly good taste ("My hatred of football also extended to other active sports"), except, of course, in men. Warren Beatty had pimples, as did Richard Burton. But at least Burton was a drunk—you have to give him that—while Beatty ate wheat germ. Men who eat wheat germ are bad news. Even with wheat germ he remained pale. He complained about a visit from Collins's mother, even though it was Collins's house, and he would characterize a script as "crap," thus betraying a hopelessly middle class mind. The upper classes, especially in England, use "shit" for such things as movie scripts and even the producers have a standard phrase, "piece of shit," for certain types of pictures.

Collins watched TV from the couch while having sex with her first husband, a bit of a poof named Maxwell Reed; he had Shinola hair and wore mascara, gold chains, and sandals laced up his calves.

Harry Belafonte said of the moon, "Two hundred billion years or more it's been there—what does it matter about us?" He has a good point there.

Rafael Trujillo, characterized by Zsa Zsa Gabor as "the Caligula of the Caribbean," gave Collins a diamond necklace which George Englund, a minor director, jealously ripped off in a second-story party room at Romanoff's. Collins suffered even deeper humilation when she appeared with Henry Kissinger in *Dynasty* on TV. This is the only *Dynasty* I've seen; I know everything I want to know about Collins from her perfume commersh (she's great).

Her second husband, Anthony Newley, is the only man who ever slept with her in PJs. Worse, he wore "large wads of pink waxy substance in his ears," a "black eye mask," and an "old camel-colored scarf around his neck." Still, they had two children; she had a third with a third husband, a Mr. Kass.

"Joanie, I just can't watch this—it's too disgusting," Sue Mengers, the agent, said when Collins began nursing her baby, even though "disgusting" could be more accurately applied to Mengers's big fat ass. What a charming, childless couple she and Warren Beatty would make.

Marilyn Monroe went unrecognized without her makeup, something that probably never happened to Natalie Wood, who, at a formal dinner party, seized a knife and used it as a mirror to check her lipstick.

Collins found it "extraordinary."

Bing Crosby had "rancid" breath in their kissing scenes and kept clearing his throat off camera and spitting "giant wads" on the floor.

Orson Welles, who is to sex as he is to the pole vault, thus had reason to tell a minor actor, "You read that just like a goddam faggot."

But you have to watch out for little people too; June Allyson, only "about five feet two in heels," socked Collins so hard in one scene her earrings flew off.

On location for the swamp picture, *Empire of the Ants*, cast and crew had to take a motorboat to the mainland to use a toilet. Finally a porta-pot was put on the camera barge, where even the stars had to piss like common hard hats.

A producer said, "Twenty-six… hmmm… you know, that's not young in this business anymore, dear." Collins says in the book, as she should have said to him, that he is "an elderly asshole." She speaks for all of us when she says she is "physically intact, if not even better than when I was younger." She doing well now, but there is at least one sign—not in the book but in a *Playboy* interview in which she made some shitty remarks about homosexuals—that even when you win the rat race you're still a rat.

LUCILLE TESTICLE FACES HER FANS

It was Johnny Carson, not I, who gave her that name.

"No cameras permitted" always sounds suspect. A young woman on the escalator to Lucille Ball's P.A. explained, helpfully, "She doesn't look good."

But she looked good enough. She looked better than a man her age (73) who appeared on screen in a filmed tribute, even though he seemed to be wearing more makeup than she was: President Reagan.

But after her Q. and A. session, as she walked to an elevator being held for her, she looked down, avoiding eye contact with the fans who clogged the corridors. She was surrounded by four guards and one husband (Gary Morton), but a blond youth tried to get in her elevator anyway. They didn't let him. He took it well; he laughed. A woman yelled, "We love you, Lucy," and from the elevator came a deep, flat "Thank you."

She wasn't well dressed; like most stars, she's too short to look right in a basketball warmup jacket. Secondly, why do women wear boots with dresses when it isn't—as it wasn't at 5:30 p.m. April 10, 1984—raining or snowing. The warmup jacket was of course fancy and it matched the Beverly Hills beige of her dress, but it was merely fashionable, not stylish. Anyway she took it off once she got into the game of Q. and A.

Appropriately, the P.A. was held in a bank—Citicorp's auditorium on Park Avenue. It commemorated the summer-long showing at the nearby Museum of Broadcasting of about 60 programs from the four Lucy series on TV: *I Love Lucy* (1951–1957), *Desilu Playhouse: The Lucille Ball and Desi Arnaz Show* (1957–1960), *The Lucy Show* (1962–1968), and *Here's Lucy* (1968–1974). During the first two series, Desi Arnaz was part of the deal; he married Ball in 1941.

They divorced in 1960. In 1961 she married Morton, a nightclub comedian who did not appear on her shows.

After she was introduced, she waited longer than anyone except Dick Cavett before coming on. Then she came on in a hurry, with a business-like walk rather than a theatrical carriage. I found the really loud standing ovation more thrilling than she evidently did. I hadn't known she's so beloved. She clearly does know; she did not show pleasure at the ovation, but quieted the audience easily and got the Q. and A. off to a smashing start by abruptly turning into a burnt-out sports announcer and saying flatly, "Well, that's about it for tonight." [Laughter.] But she stayed on longer than scheduled and there were still many hands in the air when it came time to say, "They tell me we have to go," and to walk off, sending kisses to fans.

They were youngish and conventional. Some of the men wore "topcoats" (semi-formal, calf-length garments from the 1950s). There was virtually no ass in the crowd. I saw only one youth wearing the Arabian shit-catchers which are so popular. Say what you will against the middle class, these people were preferable to the dead-eyed goons and alcoholic trainees who piss all over the Madison Square Garden neighborhood on hockey nights.

I was more surprised than Ball at the fanatic quality of the questions from the audience, such as how many eggs had she used in such-and-such an episode (the answer is five dozen). Ball had more moxie than her audience, possibly because she hadn't had to stand in line for days to get a ticket (I had a press pass). In fact she was pretty swift; when a nice youth from a Catholic high school in Utica said he'd been trying to reach her by mail for seven years, she said, "The mail is slow from Utica."

A man asked if the reason she didn't want to do a Broadway show is that it would separate her from her grandchildren.

BALL: No—that would be a reason for *doing* a Broadway show.

A man said he'd come all the way from Washington to see her.

BALL: Give my love to the President.

It was a shocking sentiment, considering who's president; in First Century Rome, entertainers didn't tell fans to give their love to Nero.

A young woman described some of her difficulties in getting started as a comedienne.

BALL: How can you be dried up at 20?

A man gave a little sermonette about how special she'd been in his life, with all her warmth and so on, and asked if she'd ever, under any circumstances, do one more Lucy show.

BALL: No. [Laughter.]

A man said, "You mentioned that *I Love Lucy* was sort of the forerunner of situation comedies—" Ball interrupted: "Not sort of, it *was*."

A question at an audience mike was too loud for her. She said, "You blew my brains out" and, her timing off for once, held her hands on her ears too long; I have always felt stars should be kind to those who aren't stars.

During one long question from an abject fan, Ball pulled out a compact, whose ornaments sparkled in the spotlight, and carefully painted her lips. It might have been shtick; it was as though she didn't want to encourage all these people to regard her as a more laughable, more loveable mother than their own. But her lips might actually have needed re-painting; she smoked two cigs during the session. This was more than the audience did. I suspect many of them jog and eat at Amy's. There are few things more offensive than being trapped in a room with hundreds of non-smokers for two hours, and I was glad enough finally to get out and get a breath of stale air; I like the smell of tobacco, whiskey, and so on.

Some stars don't smoke on occasions like this; it looks bad to consume a known poison. Tallulah Bankhead died of emphysema in St. Luke's in 1968; her name was the only one that produced sighs when Ball listed her guest stars. She described Bankhead as "no lady." Who is—Irene Dunne? Irene Dunne is a Republican, for Christ's sake. They're hard; hard. A woman can be a lady when a man's a gentleman, O.K.?

At rehearsal, Bankhead claimed an inability to remember her lines, and Ball was worried. But on camera Bankhead not only bellowed out all the lines in the script but added one of her own; noticing Ball's tension, she said, "What's the matter darling, can't you remember your lines?" [Laughter.]

John Wayne didn't want to do the Lucy show; he said he didn't know how to do TV, but was strictly for pictures. But he did finally do it. What impressed the business-like Ball (who wouldn't accept flowers from several fans on the ground that it would take too long) was that Wayne got to work at 9:30, although he wasn't due in till 10.

In her early days in pictures, before TV got going, Ball was what she calls a "stock girl." Apparently a stock of girls was kept on hand, like a stock of light bulbs, to brighten up scenes as needed. She learned how to deal with directors and assistant directors by watching Katherine Hepburn, Ginger Rogers, Jean Arthur, Carole Lombard, and Irene Dunne.

BALL: Do you know who Irene Dunne is? [Applause.]

A man asked her if she's ever boring. [Sounds of audience disapproval.]

BALL: I'll tell you if I was ever *bored* and get you off the hook that way.

Pretty swift. She was bored—she didn't use the word depressed—when her mother died. "She was something." Again when her co-star, Vivian Vance, died. "She was something." Again when she divorced Arnaz, even though it was a nice "one lawyer" divorce. They had "two wonderful children." [Applause.]

Finally, she was bored after she quit work. She said she misses it. It was the kind of work that was fun, especially with Vance, "and it shows." I haven't seen the Lucy shows, but it must be true.

On top of all this, Lucille Ball discovered Ann Miller, whose bullet-proof smile has thrilled millions; this alone would have guaranteed Ball a place in show biz history.

THE JOY OF HETEROSEXUALITY

Howard Hughes, the handsome heir to a drilling tool fortune, used to take his wife, Terry Moore, the actress, into an unused men's terlet at the old Goldwyn Studios in Hollywood, where he would wash off her lipstick with paper towels, wash her hands, sterilize a needle in the flame of a match and lance what Terry, in her autobiography, *The Beauty and the Billionaire*, calls her "blemishes."

ASSES OF THE STARS

Sylvester Stallone is not quite the "Italian Stallion" he is billed to be but he does have a nice butt, according to a correspondent who teaches the classics in London. The teacher has not had sex with Stallone but he has just seen him nude on video. He writes:

I have now acquired a video machine and I put the stars through the most degrading explorations. For example, Roger Daltrey bares his magnificent globes in *McVicar* when he jumps out of bed and slips on his trousers. After viewing the sequence in slow motion, stopping at a point where the buttocks are parted just enough to hint at a sweaty crack, I then ran it forward and backward repeatedly so that Daltrey was like a prick-teasing hooker, lowering his pants off his buttocks a split second after pulling them up. I had him doing this for me while I played with myself and came. While I've studied Richard Gere, William Hurt (truly wonderful), and Sean Connery (in loin cloth, alas), by far the most exciting discovery has been Sylvester Stallone's rear end turning up in an early soft-porn masterpiece called *Italian Stallion*. His arse looks great but his cock is soft throughout and not too big. He doesn't just fuck but dances in the nude and admires himself in a mirror. I found these sequences of hoochykooch burlesque-queen style wildly arousing. And he does have a great ass.

THE FIRST LADY'S HOLES

In an interview with Rudy Kikel published in *Philadephia Gay News*, Kenneth Anger, author of the two "Hollywood Babylon" books, claims that he has a photo of Nancy Reagan's twat, made when she was Nancy Davis, a Hollywood actress. While most of what Anger says in his books and interviews seems to be true, some of his statements have been challenged. In the case of Nancy's photo, I don't especially care whether it's really her or not. However, since she is at this writing the wife of the President of the United States, the writer would like to hear from anyone who may have a photo showing the First Lady displaying her butt-hole.

CRUISING BROADWAY

Paradoxically, the most intelligent presentation currently on Broadway is also the cheapest. A mere six dollars given to a friendly woman at the turnstile of a theater in the Times Square district entitles you to male sex films, a stage show featuring four male strippers, and, all night if necessary, all the sex you can eat (or all the mouths you can fill). The sex is with two types of men: the audience and the strippers.

Theatergoers who are undecided whether they want one or more of the strippers have an opportunity to appraise them carefully after the stage show; the strippers come and stand, completely bareass except for sneakers and sweat socks, with one foot on the arm of the patron's chair. While the dancer is thus poised, the patron can examine his dick, nuts, and asshole. Indeed, the dancers are so frequently pawed that I should think their sexual parts would be worn smooth, like pebbles in a brook.

The dancers keep their meat at its maximum state of stiffness and allure by caressing and pulling on it, during and after their act.

I shan't mention the name of the theater. Catholicism is still the dominant religion of the New York gestapo and since the Catholic church only recently gave official recognition that the earth is round rather than, as it has traditionally maintained, flat, I do not expect an intelligent Catholic attitude toward sex in the foreseeable centuries. As long as the official Catholic position on sex is still at the flat-earth level, I do not wish to remind the New York cops of any sexual ambience that departs in significant respects from their own. I doubt that the theater I went to is much different from several other "all-male" theaters which advertise strip shows in the papers. I recommend that theatergoers look these places up in the papers and

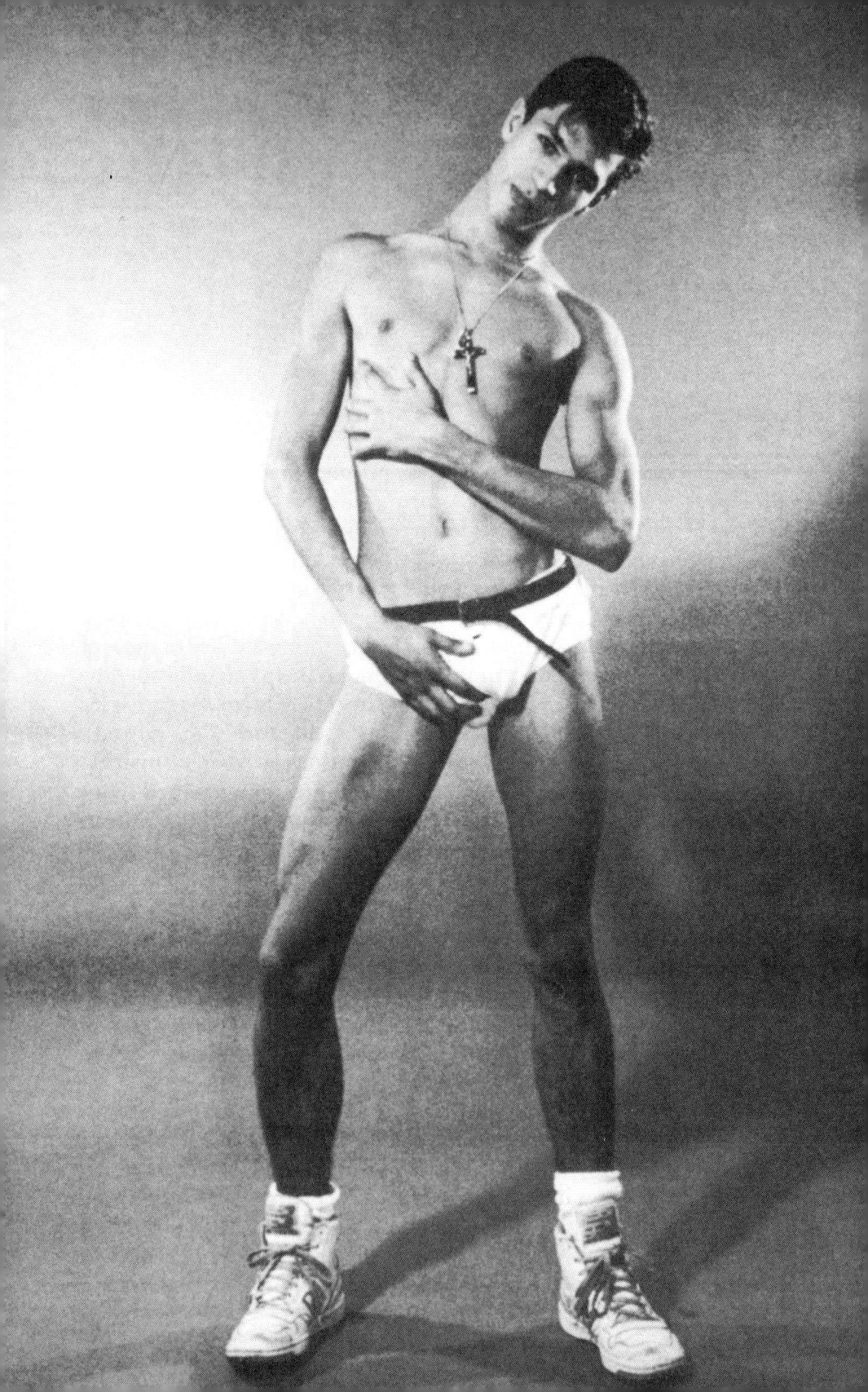

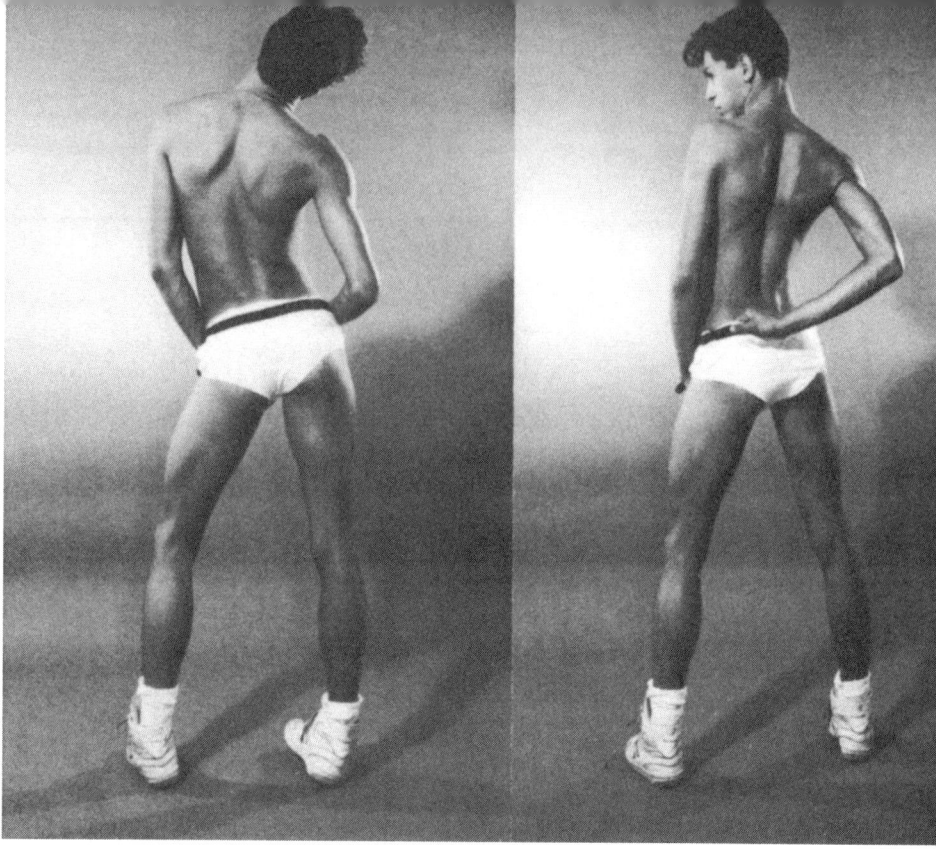

check them out. I have not seen a theatrical attraction as dramatic since the golden days of Tallulah Bankhead and Lynn Fontanne. The advantage the male strippers have over the women, of course, is a big one; it can be as big as 12 inches, but it is more likely to be 8 inches and on up. It is of course their pricks, which, under their own and the audience's expert handling, reach a state of clearly visible excitement that no woman, be she a stripper or an actress of Bankhead's genius, can duplicate. May I say that I like women better than men, but not for cock.

The theater I attended is the only one I know of (but there may be others) in which the naked youths come right into the audience, holding their dicks and waving them at interested spectators. This is the reason I went to the theater and this is what gives it its extraordinary charm. Nudity itself is no big deal in appropriate settings, such as bedrooms, bathrooms, lockerrooms, showers, bathhouses, and so on; even in films and stage shows. But nudity gains in value when it is displayed in settings in which its only purpose can be sex: outdoors, in automobiles, in office buildings, among the seats of a

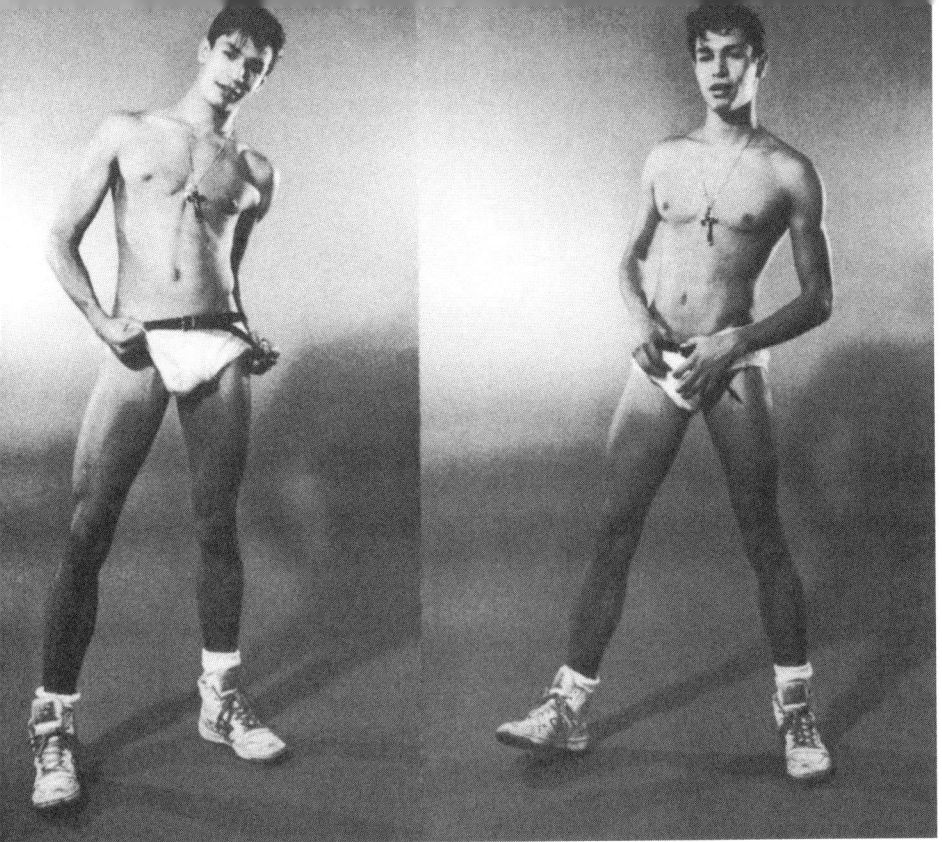

theater, among men who are fully dressed (except for those theater-goers who habitually leave their dicks hanging out of their pants).

During the live show, there is no sex activity in the audience. But after the show, during the movies, members of the audience can get sucked off in the comfort, safety, and convenience of their own chairs. By wandering around other areas of the theater, they can have sex with other prowlers and with stars of the show.

I admire—greatly—both the strippers and the audience. They were directly, honestly, fearlessly, wholesomely, powerfully homosexual. It is a kind of homosexuality I have always enjoyed ever since I came to New York, a kind that neither the prissy queens of the Gay Liberation Movement nor the threat of disease have managed to kill, or even noticeably reduce. I often regret these days that I did not, in the days when I was eligible, become a stripper and whore, rather than prostituting my mind. In what I see as a conflict within the gay life between queens and commoners, I take the side of the commoners, and not because it is clearly the winning side, but because it is more attractive. I am drawn to the dancers and their

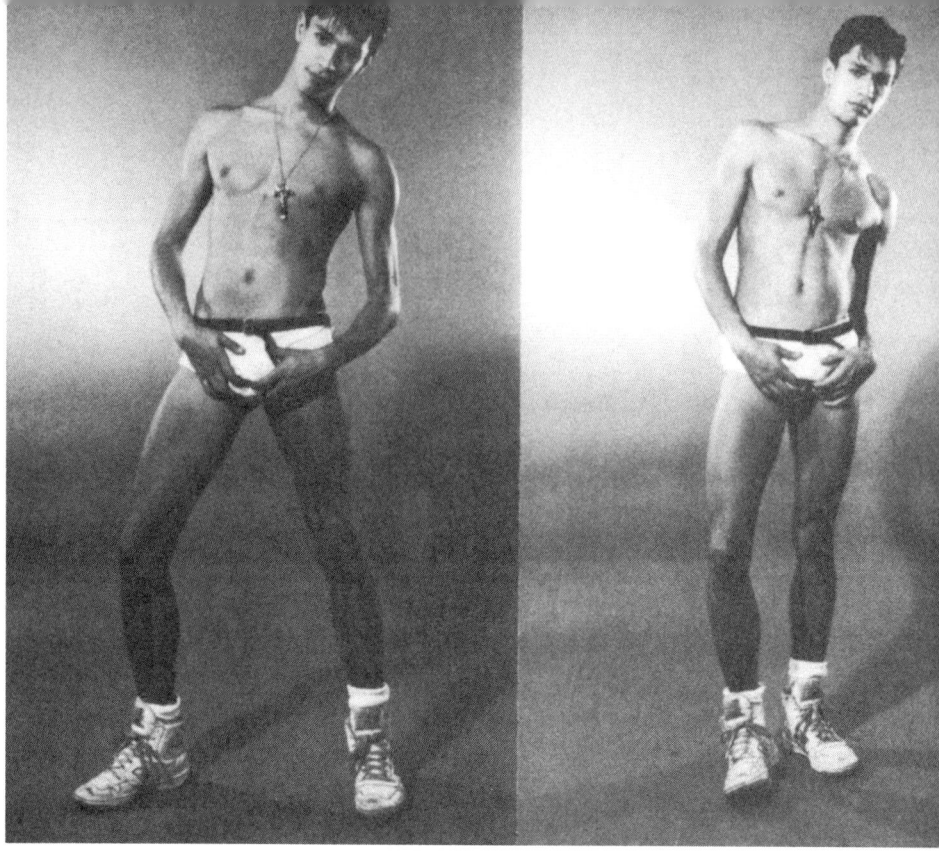

audience more than I am to the queens. Apart from the aesthetics, we know, do we not, who is more intelligent: men who have sex or queens who represent themselves as being above it. A one-second glance at them shows whether they are above it, or just out of it. Homosexuality is the only culture I know of whose queens are middle-class and whose commoners are upper-class as well as lower-class. The man I attended the strip show with is one of the city's most original intellectuals, a man whose intelligence gives him confidence to do what he thinks best both in his literary career and in his private life. The audience also included some alluringly coarse members of the blue collar class, who can be as coarse, when they want to, as we are. The middle class are not coarse, merely common. It takes a higher degree of intelligence than that possessed by the wax fruits and artificial flowers of the middle class, including the educated middle class (for education has nothing to do with intelligence), to know that the Judeo-Christian culture, and the ways in which men achieve dignity and respect in it, are, in a word, shitty. In the long run, the only real dignity and respect come from the

simple truth, including truth of sex. In light of the numerous queens who can easily put them down, to say nothing of put-downs from the "straight" world, the strippers I saw seem like sexual heroes, with bigger balls than "straight" men who are all boast and no action.

I wonder if any impresario in this branch of the theater has ever thought of just putting his boys on stage, one after another, and having them strip and play with themselves in silence instead of copying the traditional female format of dancing to music. If the boys would simply undress and play with their dicks, balls and assholes, as they do at home alone, it would reduce the artistic interference of the theater and enhance both the audience's and the performer's experience of, respectively, voyeurism and exhibitionism. Such a format could simulate the experience—one of the most enjoyable available in cities with cluttered housing like Manhattan—of looking into a boy's or a man's bedroom when he undresses. Both voyeurs and exhibitionists are admirable, and need each other, and give each other great pleasure. Indeed, the terms "voyeur" and "exhibitionist" are not really necessary; all men are one or the other and most men are both.

Another gimmick that might enhance the presentation would be to have the boys, once naked, piss into a bucket onstage. This could be a real crowd-pleaser and would require only a little strength of character on the part of the boys; they could simply drink a lot between shows and hold their water until they are on stage. To my knowledge, the closest the theater has come to a piss scene is the night Noel Coward stood backstage during a performance and fiendishly poured a kettle of water into a bucket, creating an unmistakeable sound which could be heard by most of the audience.

Finally, the strippers might sniff and lick the annpits of their T-shirts and the pouches of their underpants or jock straps when they remove them, or even sniff and lick their finger after rubbing it on their piss-holes or assholes, in this way demonstrating their allure.

But these are petty details in relation to the main point, which is that the mere fact that the youths stripped at all, and the audience went to applaud them, was theater of overwhelming valor and beauty.

A GOLDEN TREASURY OF GREAT AMERICAN RE-WRITING

From the entry on Henry Hathaway in *The Film Encyclopedia* by Ephraim Katz, 1982: "... a skilled craftsman who handles his material straightforwardly with few complications or pretensions."

From the *New York Times* obituary of Hathaway, February 13, 1984: "... a skilled craftsman who handled his material straight-forwardly, with little fuss and less pretension."

ARTHUR

God this place is cold.
—JANE RUSSELL

"Hey Arthur," the autograph hounds would shout, "Arthur!" He had interviewed so many stars he was almost one himself. Once just a fan, he was welcome inside the velvet ropes now as a writer, sought after by the stars; Bette Davis called him. He no longer had to invent acceptable identities in order to get in to ask for a star's signature, no longer had to say he was "Miss Bankhead's agent" (this worked), or "Gene Tierney's nephew" (she said she didn't have one but wanted him brought in anyway), or a war veteran whose hands had been shot off in combat. This worked by mail and got sympathetic letters from patriotic stars, but when Sophie Tucker, who recorded "Make It Legal Mr. Segal," called and heard his boyish whisper on the 'phone, she put the post office on his case; and Kitty Carlisle called the house detective when Arthur hit her room. But he ran and escaped.

While still a boy, he had to leave the beloved movie palaces of Brooklyn and move to Montreal. He was "heartbroken"; children under 16 were not admitted to theaters there. He subsisted on movie fan magazines. They were no phonier than *Rolling Stone* today and a billion times more beautiful.

But his family moved back to New York and he became one of the city's most distinguished autograph hounds. They were stationed at spots like Sardi's and 21 and they quickly spread word through the hound network about who was where; Arthur claimed they knew more than Walter Winchell.

"Dietrich," he said, "was strange." He got her at *House of Flowers* (1951), which she attended under escort of Harold Arlen, composer of "That Old Black Magic" and "Over the Rainbow." Without once taking her eyes off her face in her compact mirror, she put an M and a D in the autograph book Arthur held under hand.

"Barbara Stanwyck was wonderful," he said. "She always signed. She was so beautiful and so nice." Tierney was " the most beautiful." Maria Montez alone was as glamorous as anyone could stand but she hung out with two glamorous sisters and the three of them, in "drop dead theatrical clothes, gloves up to their armpits, ostrich feathers, and so on," comprised a virtual circus of advanced feats of glamour. They would ask Arthur how he liked the way they looked.

"God this place is cold," Jane Russell said when she entered a West 52nd Street restaurant for lunch with Arthur and a "very effeminate" young man who had dyed blond hair (he was Russell's, not Arthur's). "She was dressed for the hot weather," Arthur explained, "but not for air-conditioning." She removed a tablecloth and draped it around her kissy but cold shoulders. Where Shirley MacLaine struck Arthur as "a foul-mouthed fraud" and "a phony from the word go," he found "not a hint of phoniness" about Russell. He liked her "tremendously"; unlike Pauline Kael and her sniggering male counterparts, Arthur had no heterosexual reason for making fun of Russell's big fat tits. He was not jealous of them, nor was he a titsucker, nor did they make him feel bad for not being "up" to such a piece of hot stuff as Russell. He was able to ignore her tits and give her a fair hearing as a woman and an actress. His articles in the *Voice* and elsewhere gave a unique perspective not only on Russell but on players in general, even on American life; if there were more movie fans like Arthur and fewer boxing fans like the *New York Times* the world would be more peaceful. The goal of boxing, after all, is to inflict brain damage; how much more inspiring were Arthur's tastes. But in this perverse culture sports lovers are more respected than movie lovers (especially by homosexuals).

He met the cinematic love of his life, Gloria Grahame, outside 21. He told her she looked sultry and she asked what that means. He asked for her autograph and told her how much he'd liked her in *In a Lonely Place* (1950). "She laid a speech on me from the picture," he said, and did so again later when Arthur, who by now had naturally expanded his autograph operations to interviewing the stars for the *Voice*, did a column on her. "Gloria Grahame," he said, "was my favorite actress and I wrote about her extensively and about that lower lip and that voice and the way she looked at people—incredible. I got to know her and she was very shy and couldn't believe that people knew of her and liked her."

He was also fond of Paul Douglas, Jan Sterling, Judy Holliday, and Vivian Blaine; he didn't like June Allyson (too icky) or Paul Newman (too snotty). He liked Richard Gere at first but was upset when Gere spread his thighs during an interview; it made Arthur feel used. He came to despise Gere, and did so in print after *American Gigolo* (1979), which had some anti-homosexual dialogue; Gere called and said, "How could you?" It seemed easy for Arthur; he publicly attacked fagbaiters, booing Frank Sinatra at Madison Square Garden and shouting insults to the director of *Cruising* (1980) at a press conference. He had balls.

Crazy as he was for Gloria Grahame, for some reason he mentioned her death only briefly in his *Voice* column. Perhaps he felt, as I do, that by then it's no use. I haven't wanted to do a memoriam on Arthur; what good would that do now. It's just Arthur Bell, 1932–1984; apart from that, I wanted only to mention some of the stars in his life. I knew him just well enough to believe that he would have deemed this appropriate; what could be more serious or more important than movie stars.

WHEN WORDS FAIL

Nick Adams. Eve Arden. Henry Armetta. Jean Arthur. Mary Astor. Lionell Atwill. Mischa Auer.

Hermione Baddeley. Tallulah Bankhead. Lynn Bari. Binnie Barnes. Wendy Barrie. Richard Basehart. Anne Baxter. Louise Beavers. Jean-Paul Belmondo. Robert Benchley. Bruce Bennett. Constance Bennett. Joan Bennett. Jack Benny. Milton Berle. Betty Boop. Joan Blondell. Ben Blue. Mary Boland. Marlon Brando. Lloyd Bridges. Helen Broderick. Hillary Brooke. Tom Brown. Nigel Bruce. Virginia Bruce. Victor Buono. Billie Burke. Raymond Burr.

Bruce Cabot. James Cagney. Louis Calhern. Joseph Calleia. Keith Carradine. Madeleine Carroll. Jack Cassidy. Paul Cavanagh. Ilka Chase. Eduardo Ciannelli. Dane Clark. Montgomery Clift. Charles Coburn. Steve Cochran. Contance Collier. Jerry Colonna. Joyce Compton. Richard Conte. Tom Conway. Elisha Cook, Jr. Gary Cooper. Jackie Cooper. Rita (also Paula) Corday. Wendell Corey. Joseph Cotton. Jerome Cowan. Broderick Crawford. Laird Cregar. Laura Hope Crews. Richard Cromwell. Bing Crosby. Alan Curtis.

Arlene Dahl. Dan Dailey. Henry Daniell. Marion Davies. Bette Davis. Gloria DeHaven. Gerard Depardieu. Bruce Dern. Marlene Dietrich. Phyllis Diller. Ruth Donnelly. Paul Douglas. Johnny Downs. Tom Drake. Marie Dressler. Margaret Dumont. Faye Dunaway. June Duprez. Dan Duryea.

Sally Eilers. Denholm Elliott. Hope Emerson. Dame Edith Evans. Douglas Fairbanks, Jr. Peter Falk. Glenda Farrell. Frank Faylen. W.C. Fields. Barry Fitzgerald. Geraldine Fitzgerald. Errol Flynn. Nina Foch. Joan Fontaine. Lynn Fontanne. Harrison Ford. Anne Francis. Kay Francis. William Frawley. Howard Freeman. Annette Funicello. Betty Furness.

Martin Gabel. Greta Garbo. John Garfield. William Gargan. Marjorie Gateson. Gladys George. Richard Gere. Mel Gibson. Wynne Gibson. Billy Gilbert. Hermione Gingold. Jackie Gleason. James Gleason. Paulette Goddard. Thomas Gomez. Leo Gorcey. Gloria Grahame. Margot Grahame. Farley Granger. Sydney Greenstreet. Joan Greenwood. Joyce Grenfell. Tito Guizar.

Huntz Hall. Billy Halop. Jean Harlow. Julie Harris. Laurence Harvey. Jack Hawkins. Sterling Hayden. Richard Haydn. George ("Gabby") Hayes. Louis Hayward. Darryl Hickman. Valerie Hobson. William Holden. Sterling Holloway. Mirian Hopkins. Edward Everett Horton. Esther Howard. Trevor Howard. Rochelle Hudson. Kim Hunter. William Hurt. Ruth Hussey. Walter Huston. Betty Hutton. Lauren Hulton. Robert Hutton. Wilfrid Hyde-White.

Frieda Inescort.

Allen Jenkins. Adele Jergens. Rita Johnson. Bobby Jordan. Allyn Joslyn. Arline Judge.

Madeline Kahn. Boris Karloff. Nancy Kelly. Patsy Kelly. Pert Kelton. Kay Kendall. Arthur Kennedy. Edgar Kennedy. Percey Kilbride.

Alan Ladd. Veronica Lake. Elsa Lanchester. Jessie Royce Landis. Charles Lane. Jack LaRue. Louise Lasser. Charles Laughton. Piper Laurie. Marc Lawrence. Vivien Leigh. Margaret Leighton. Sheldon Leonard. Oscar Levant. Sam Levene. Beatrice Lillie. Herbert Lorn. Carole Lombard. Peter Lorre. Myrna Loy. Bela Lugosi. Paul Lucas. Ida Lupino. Jimmy Lydon. Paul Lynde. Diana Lynn.

James MacArthur. Lon McAllister. Mercedes McCambridge. Joel McCrea. Hattie McDaniel. Roddy McDowell. Frank McHugh. Victor McLaglen. Fred MacMurray. Butterfly McQueen. Gordon MacRae. George Macready. Anna Magnani. Marjorie Main. Mona Maris. Herbert Marshall. Lee Marvin. Groucho Marx. Victor Mature. Marilyn Maxwell. Donald Meek. Ralph Meeker. Dina Merrill. Mayo Methot. Sylvia Miles. John Miljan. Ray Milland. Ann Miller. Martin Milner. Thomas Mitchell. Robert Mitchum. George Montgomery. Constance Moore. Dickie Moore. Roger Moore. Victor Moore. Agnes Moorehead. Frank Morgan. Wayne Morris. Robert Morse. Alan Mobray. Ona Munson. Audie Murphy.

J. Carroll Naish. Mildred Natwick. Hildegarde Neff. Barry Nelson. David Nelson. Ricky Nelson. Cathleen Nesbitt. Jack Nicholson. Lloyd Nolan. Nick Nolte. Kim Novak.

Jack Oakie. Merle Oberon. Edmond O'Brien. Donald O'Connor. Una O'Connor. Warner Oland.

Jack Palance. Eugene Pallette. Franklin Pangborn. Jean Parker. Gail Patrick. Lee Patrick. Katina Paxinou. Joe Penner. Gerard Philipe. ZaSu Pitts. Donald Pleasance. Eric Portman. Dick Powell. William Powell. Elvis Presley. Vincent Price.

Basil Radford. George Raft. Claude Rains. Jessie Ralph. Vera Hruba Ralston. Marjorie Rambeau. Basil Rathbone. Gregory Ratoff. Martha Raye. Beryl Reid. Anne Revere. Thelma Ritter. Edward G. Robinson. May Robson. Roy Rogers. "Slapsie" Maxie Rosenbloom. Shirley Ross. Jane Russell. Robert Ryan.

Sabu. George Sanders. Olga San Juan. Joe Sawyer. Lizabeth Scott. Randolph Scott. Zachary Scott. Jackie Searle. Norma Shearer. Johnny Sheffield. Ann Sheridan. Penny Singleton. Alison Skipworth. Walter Slezak. Gale Sondergaard. Ann Sothern. Ned Sparks. Robert Stack. Kim Stanley. Barbara Stanwyck. Maureen Stapleton. Rod Steiger. Henry Stephenson. Jan Sterling. The Three Stooges. Gale Storm. Erich von Stroheim. Grady Sutton.

Akim Tamiroff. Kent Taylor. Rod Taylor. Ingrid Thulin. Thelma Todd. Sidney Toler. Regis Toomey. Audrey Totter. Claire Trevor. Sonny Tufts.

Lupe Velez. Helen Vinson.

Anton Walbrook. Raymond Walburn. Robert Walker. Lucille Watson. Clifton Webb. Johnny Weissmuller. Raquel Welch. Mae West. Dame May Whitty. Richard Widmark. Henry Wilcoxon. Marie Wilson. Marie Windsor. Toby Wing. Jonathan Winters. Shelley Winters. Estelle Winwood. Cora Witherspoon. Anna May Wong. Fay Wray. Jane Wyatt.

Michael York. Gig Young.

George Zucco.

GREAT MOMENTS IN MOVIES

WHEN EVE ARDEN CRUISES KENNY BAKER

This particular great moment is indescribable; there is very little I can add to the heading. It happened in *At the Circus* (1939), seen on Channel 9 at 3 a.m. an April 21, 1983. Eve Arden, engaged in conversation with a menacingly Christian Kenny Baker, gave him a fast but total once-over, head to toe, sizing him up and obviously, from the look on her face, finding him too small. What made it astonishing was that there was no reason for it in the plot of the picture or in the character Arden was playing. She had no interest in him whatsoever. How could she? How could anyone be interested in this prudish castrato, the poor man's Dennis Day, with that high voice so many cops and football coaches have. I can only assume that she did it for the sheer hell of it, to have a little fun in a generally tedious picture. But it did serve to illustrate the absurdity of casting her as a villainess. She is too adorable—much too. I felt closer than ever to understanding why so many homosexuals like certain actresses, including, of course, Eve Arden. But I still don't quite get it. No one seems to. It is not that homosexuals "identify with" women, for Arden, in this role, was anything but a woman. She was the sex subject, not the object; the predator was out prowling for meat and finding Kenny Baker too stale a male ingenue. But it doesn't matter; I like her so I watch her.

WHEN NICK NOLTE AND PETER STRAUSS SMELL EACH OTHER

"You smell like a wild animal," Peter Strauss tells his bed mate, Nick Nolte, in *Rich Man, Poor Man* (1976). This is not a compliment, as it would be coming from the mouths of some men; Strauss plays a fastidious youth.

In light of the character Nolte plays, that of a gorgeous slob, it is likely that Strauss's simile is accurate and that Nolte's reply is the truth: "I like the way I smell."

His evaluation of Strauss's smell is also no compliment. "You smell so nice," he says, ironically, "like Pepsodent toothpaste." The next step is, "My friends think you're some kind of a fruit." The extraordinary charm and seductiveness of this conversation, however, leads nowhere; Strauss is as "straight" in the picture as Nolte. The mere fact that you're clean doesn't necessarily mean that you're gay, even some heterosexuals are clean. Not many, perhaps, but some, and Strauss is one.

The two men are brothers and they are not, as in an "adult movie" (a classification I like for its implication that Shakespeare and so on are kid stuff), sniffing out each other's underpants, pubic hairs, cocks, balls, and butt holes. Strauss is wearing pajamas, as befits his chaste character, and Nolte, boxer shorts (but his chest is bare). He might at least have pulled off his underpants under the bed covers and tossed them onto the floor; he is by no means above that sort of thing, and he could easily have forced Strauss, as so many husky boys force their weaker brothers, to take care of his hard on. But he doesn't. Nonetheless, the sight of the two in bed and their dialogue about the so-called "body perfumes" does give the sensitive viewer a good idea of what it would be like to sleep with the naturally fragrant Nolte and the artificially scented Strauss, separately or together. Each is alluring in his own way.

Rich Man, Poor Man was not released to theaters but was made for television (as were Nolte's nipples). I saw it (and them) on channel 9 at 4 p.m. in November 1984.

The late Arthur Bell told me that Nolte was never without a can of beer when Bell visited him on location for a picture he was making, but this, I suppose, would be of interest only to the minority of men who would like to swallow an abnormally large amount of Nolte's piss.

WHEN FIVE BROTHERS DIE
IN THE NAVY

The Fighting Sullivans (1944), a.k.a. *The Sullivans*, seen at 8 p.m., March 2, 1985, on channel 5, is an unintentional masterpiece of heterosexual camp, with satisfaction guaranteed for fans of heterosexual excess. The particular excess depicted here is the joy of dying in war.

The five Sullivan brothers are in the Navy in World War II. Ward Bond comes to the Sullivan house with what he calls "very bad news."

> WOMAN: Which one?
> 2nd WOMAN: Is it Al?
> BOND: All five.

What makes the death of all five brothers even shittier is the fact that the surviving family members scarcely express remorse. After all, that's what boys are for (dying in combat), and the father, Thomas Mitchell, simply goes off to his job on the railroad without a word. The Sullivans are not sissies, merely sheep.

Obedience to authority, however unjust, is established early in the picture. One of the boys reports to his mother that his father "hit me and I didn't do a single thing." His mother, just as rotten, says, "That's his right." It's one of the most Irish Catholic pictures ever made.

The death of the five brothers is called "glorious" at the christening of a ship named after them and, even sicker, the TV station's lead-in for the running of the film called it "heart-warming." Pray, whose heart could be warmed by the death of all five boys in a family? The only surviving Sullivan sibling, a girl, joins the Navy.

To make the picture totally campy, she'd have gotten killed too. But for some reason she doesn't (not that it matters much to the parents). But the picture does end with one of the great camp images in film history: the five Sullivan boys, in Navy costume, walking on clouds in heaven. They're photographed from behind and as they walk briskly in their Navy spray-on pants they show, all five of them, nicely-moving butt cheeks.

WHEN LOUISE BEAVERS
AWAKENS JEAN HARLOW

Louise Beavers (1902–1962), the Central Casting Cook-Maid, was quietly overwhelming; she held attention even in competition with such dazzling creatures as Mae West and Jean Harlow. In *Blonde Bombshell* (1933), a.k.a. *Bombshell*, Beavers, normally confined to a servant's costume, is given a chance to compete with her mistress, Jean Harlow, in one of Harlow's own preposterously ornate costumes: a fur-trimmed satin evening coat. What makes the thing especially effective on Beavers is that under it, she's wearing bed clothes, and she wears it into Harlow's bedroom in the morning to awaken her. It is in keeping with Beavers's screen persona that she would wear such an absurdly elegant wrap for a night on the town, but as Harlow points out, "I gave that to you as an evening wrap, not a bedroom robe." Beavers explains that her bathrobe got torn to pieces yesterday; Harlow makes a crack about Beavers's sex life on her day off.

The scene, like many others in the picture, is a triumph of an imagination that is hardly characteristic of Catholicism, and *Blonde Bombshell* was indeed made at the end of a period in Hollywood history which gave the Jews who ran the studios a chance to show what splendid work they could do before the Catholics started bullying them. The year after *Bombshell*, the sexually inadequate Catholic Legion of Decency, which could more accurately be called the Legion of Jealousy, put the heat on Hollywood and by threats of boycotts managed to establish a more spiteful attitude toward sex. No more Louise Beavers getting rough fucks on their days off; there followed the era of sweet nuns in artificial eyelashes and sweet priests like Bing Crosby (who off-screen was a mean, effeminate old drunk). Apart from the Legion of Decency's fundamental flaw—it assumes

that sex is wrong but never explains why—the Legion was intolerable in that it sought to impose a specifically Catholic sexual cruelty upon the general population of non-Catholics. This is simply against the law, but the Legion was tolerated for more than 30 years.

To return to a more intelligent creature, Beavers: she had a problem with Mae West, who, perfect in performance, was imperfect offstage. When Beavers was playing the maid in West's Las Vegas act, West sent word complaining about her private life. Beavers sent word back that West could "kiss my big black ass." That's the way to be, and Beavers's big black ass does indeed deserve a kiss for her inspiring behavior, which could serve as a role model for anyone who has to deal with oppression, suppression, or aggression.

WHEN ZACHARY SCOTT'S WHEELCHAIR GETS HIT BY TWO TAXICABS

Whiplash (1948) has probably the best wheelchair death ever filmed, better, even, than that in *Kiss of Death* (1947), in which the succulent creep, Richard Widmark, shoves Mildred Dunnock's wheelchair down the stairs. The *Whiplash* death of the neat and nasty Zachary Scott is completely satisfying for fans of this form of death.

I did not enjoy seeing Zachary die; I never enjoy seeing Zachary die, for he is one of my favorite people—superbly sleazy, a male Mary Astor. My editor's remark, early in my composition of these studies, that he was fond of Zachary was one of the first indications that he too has good taste. Indeed, in years of working with him, I have "caught" him in only one lapse of taste (his fondness for Audrey Hepburn, whom I've always regarded as eligible only for anorexia roles).

But enough of life; back to death (I hope readers will not suspect, because of my emphasis on death, that I'm a Catholic; I'm not). Zachary's attendant shoots Jeffrey Lynn, who is able, nonetheless, to shoot him too. Then Zach's wheelchair slides down a ramp. He is unable to stop it. When the wheelchair rolls onto the street, two (2) taxicabs hit it. Satisfying though the scene be, I'd rather have seen Zachary survive.

The putative stars of the picture are Dane Clark and Alexis Smith, but both are too tense and self-conscious. Clark's strain is that of an actor trying too hard, Smith's that of one who doesn't give a shit. The real stars are Zach and, as in all of her pictures, Eve Arden, the American Dame Edith Evans. "I may not be beautiful," Eve says in a line that accounts for the sexual triumphs of a large percentage of the population, "but I'm available." Extreme availability

has always been a more attractive quality in the sexual marketplace than mere beauty.

Zachary Scott was born in Austin, Texas, in 1914 and he died there, in his mother's house, of a brain tumor in 1965. In addition to his exquisitely rotten characterizations on screen, his offscreen accomplishments include the acquisition of what Ward Morehouse called "a spacious, high-ceilinged apartment" on West 72nd Street in Manhattan; even more important, in 1959 he was still wearing, according to Morehouse, the same clothing size he wore in 1934—this despite the fact that he and his last wife, Ruth Ford, were arrested for drinking in "a Negro saloon" (I cite this strictly because such drinking, if indulged in routinely, would have increased his clothing size). Moreover, Zach was one of the first American men to wear an earring; he was seen in one as early as 1955. Now, of course, many urban toughs wear them as part of their attempt to show that they can wear long hair and other feminine lures and still look butch. Indeed, today's youths have appropriated virtually all items of feminine apparel except Kotex belts and they soon will be wearing them if they follow the precedent set years ago by Joe Namath, the quarterback, when he posed in panty hose.

Zachary's widow, Ruth Ford, a minor actress, went on to become one of Manhattan's most publicized fruit flies (that is, fag hags) as companion to Dotson Rader.

STEVE COCHRAN

Before I became privy to certain information about their off-screen lives, I evaluated Virginia Mayo and Steve Cochran strictly by what they managed to get on film. They were paired in at least two pictures—*White Heat* (1949) and *She's Back on Broadway* (1953)—and my evaluation was that they are both just common, ordinary movie stars. Cochran (1917–1965) is only almost, and not quite, sucky (but I can see how countless women and perhaps almost as many men might want to get fucked by him), and Mayo (b. 1920) similarly lacks that breathtaking presence that the extraordinary women of Hollywood have—women such as Anne Baxter, Gloria Grahame, Vivien Leigh, Merle Oberon, and Mamie Van Doren.

But Mayo's life, sadly, downgrades her work from ordinary to sub-ordinary, whilst Cochran's promotes him from ordinary to extraordinary. By this I mean that to watch the two with knowledge of their lives in mind detracts from Mayo's and enhances Cochran's performances.

Arthur Bell revealed in the *Village Voice* the appalling news that not only is Mayo a Republican, but one of the worst sort, one who campaigned for Nixon and (in her words) "did some work to support Ronnie." Bell did not present—nor, I think, regard—this as shocking, but I was shocked. I had assumed, watching her in the two pictures under discussion, that she is a humanist and thus unable to embody fully her sub-human roles in them; but it turns out that if she had put her life into her work, had drawn upon the monstrous greed and chill that go into the making of a Republican, she could have been more credibly sluttish as gun moll to both Jimmy Cagney and Steve Cochran in *White Heat*, seen at 2 a.m. on November 30, 1984, on channel 5, and could have represented

more authentically the quintessential shittiness of a celebrity in *She's Back on Broadway*, seen at 3 a.m. on May 21, 1985, on channel 9.

Cochran's life is rich in details which upgrade his allure from medium to maddening; almost every cutting in his file at the Lincoln Center Library of the Performing Arts records exemplary and even inspiring behavior. He displayed aggressive leadership qualities early, getting expelled from school three times (we do not expect original work from boys who "go along" either with their peers or with their professors). On New Year's Day, 1952, he hit Buddy Wright, a former boxer who may well have deserved it, with a baseball bat and was assessed 16 grand in damages. A South African jockey took Cochran to court on an adultery charge. He was arrested not only for reckless driving, but also on the more patrician charge of reckless flying. Sidney Skolsky wrote that Cochran not only slept in the nude but swam in the nude and, even more important, had green eyes and three marriages (one to what the old *New York Herald Tribune* called "a teenage Danish beauty"). He had at least one child (F.) and the sexual ambition of hiring a harem of six teenage domestics (F.).

The circumstances of his death at age 48 revealed that he may finally have achieved this goal at least partially; he died of an acute lung infection aboard his 40-foot schooner, the *Rogue*, in the company of three Mexican women, aged 14, 19, and 25, who survived. He had hand-picked the three from 180 who answered a newspaper ad.

To die with three woman aboard is three times more alluring than to die with just one, and in light of his habit of nudity and his reputation as a cocksman it is breathtaking to imagine the extreme informality that prevailed aboard the *Rogue*.

Herbert Horowitz went considerably above and beyond his duty as U.S. Vice Consul in Guatemala City by reporting that Cochran's "body was horribly swollen and completely unrecognizable." The statement suggests that Horowitz would have recognized Cochran's body had it not been swollen, but I've seen no hint that Cochran had any homosexual impulses that could not be discharged in humor. For example, George Eells and Stanley Musgrove write in their magnificent *Mae West* that when West arrived with Cochran at a rehearsal of *Diamond Lil* and found the assistant stage manager reading her lines, she told him she was favorably impressed by his performance. "So am I," Cochran told the man. "Why don't you come down to my dressing room and see me sometime?" The remark got a laugh, but there is always the possibility, and sometimes the probability, that men who indulge in such homosexual horseplay are not kidding, but don't dare be serious about it either.

A number of women—for instance, Denise Darcel, a French actress who was one of Cochran's friends and who is still alive—could probably reveal how many inches he had, and will I hope before they die. A friend of mine was standing next to Cochran one night in Glennon's, a Third Avenue bar, but reports no abnormally large bulge in the crotch of his (Cochran's) pants. Cochran was with a cunt and they struck up a conversation with my friend, during which the star was quiet, cool, easy, friendly, considerate, and gentlemanly—a man so experienced and established as a lover of women that he had no need to display the fact. This is more than can be said for the Marines outside the Port Authority Bus Terminal and the sports lovers watching football on TV in bars, both of whom feel the need when a homosexual walks by to insist in one way or another that they themselves are not homosexual. Surprisingly, in light of the fact that he'd worked on a railroad and as a cowboy, a store detective (for Macy's), and, even tougher, an actor on Broadway and in pictures, Cochran tried his hand

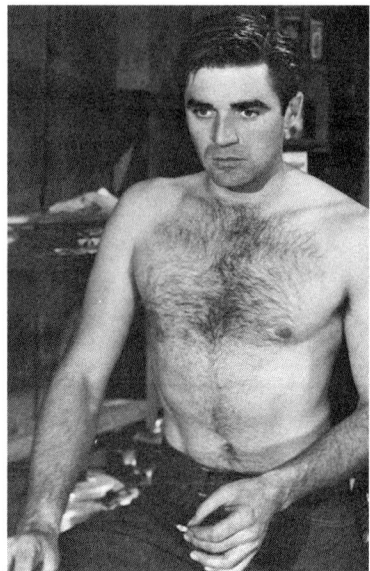

at the less butch occupation of writer near the end of his life. Few writers have his assured masculinity; most, as can be seen in the still of a typical American author, Sylvester Stallone, who wrote his own screen parts, make themselves into bizarre cartoons of men. The stills of Cochran and Stallone present a striking contrast between a natural man and one who has been manufactured in gymnasia, between an understated virility and a stridently insistent one, between the classic movie star and today's "macho" star. Cochran was so confident that he could afford to play a coward in *Storm Warning* (1951), seen on television in New York in 1985. The writer can remember a time when men like Stallone were scornfully called muscle queens. I should add that I do not have any reason to suspect, and especially to hope, that Stallone is gay. He merely has the standard inadequacies all boxing fans have.

But I have digressed form my topic, and digressed so far that it may be necessary to remind the reader what my topic is: the size of Cochran's meat. A classics professor in London claims, in a letter to the writer under the date of October 21, 1984, to have seen Cochran in a swim suit in one of his pictures—a swim suit "revealing the power of his thighs." The professor continues, "Many of my many masturbation sessions centered on fantasies of just what power his swim suit withheld from the high school public. He was an instant hard-on creator when I was in my middle teens and I went out of my way to see the crummy features he was pushed into. When John Wayne announced that he intended to lick the Big C, the director Henry Hathaway is reported to have believed he was referring to the Clap. I prefer to believe he was referring to Cochran." By "C," of course, Wayne, who evidently spoke in a Rona Barrett style, meant cancer.

It would not be safe to deduce from Cochran's big fat fingers alone that his meat was correspondingly worthwhile, but it would, I think, be safe to conclude from the fact that Mae West took him on as a steady lay while he was appearing in her *Diamond Lil* that he was at least normally hung. Throughout her life, as the stunning Eells-Musgrove biography demonstrates, West was frequently curious about the size of a man's dick, and in auditioning men for her shows she would sometimes ask them to show it to her. Cochran was about 31 and West about 56 when she put the make on him. She had the desire, the power, and the balls to hire choice pieces of meat and it is a virtual certainty that Cochran was one.

Thus there is no accounting for the fact that in *White Heat*, *Storm Warning*, and *She's Back on Broadway* the directors did not cash in on his sexual gifts and experience. The only glimpse of his flesh I saw in all three pictures was an inch or two of his calf in *She's Back on Broadway*. Nothing less than an inch or two of his dick could have saved a picture this routinely written and directed. One obvious place for using Cochran's charms in the picture—one of many—is the scene in which he his discovered sleeping off a drunk, fully clothed. It seems incredible that the director would go to the trouble of setting up and lighting this scene without taking advantage of the obvious opportunity to show Cochran lying on his bare butt with his legs spread wide enough to give at least an idea of his butt-hole and his fat fingers resting lightly on a fat piece of meat.

Still, I recommend all three of the Cochran pictures I've seen, not for any specific sexuality but for the general reasons already adumbrated—that they show a quietly authentic man, rare in pictures of that era and rare in fact today, when so many actors seem only that: actors. My dear, if you are already something (for instance, a man), you don't have to try to become it.

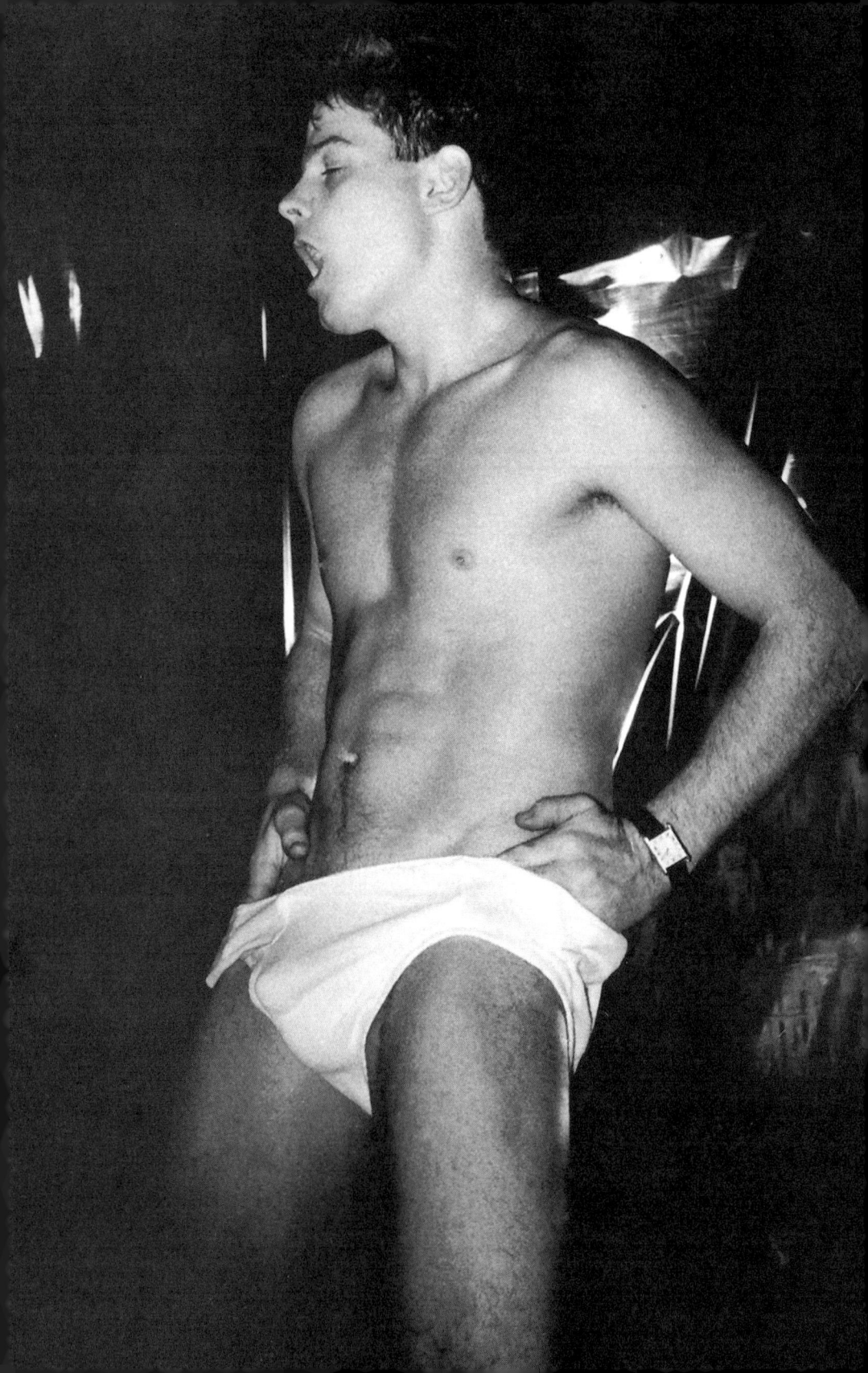

FOR LADIES ONLY

Wisely, I think, the makers of *For Ladies Only* (1981), a picture about male strippers, put an actor with underwear experience in the leading role; Gregory Harrison had emoted in his Jockey shorts four years earlier in *Fraternity Row*, a major picture in the underpants genre, yet not one that has any single scene competitive with the opening of *Fat City* (1972), when Stacy Keach, in his Jockey shorts, wallows in his flesh on a bed for awhile, then throws his legs apart and gets up to look for a match.

Yes, I'm aware that I have already cited three pictures in the first sentence; before I finish, it will be necessary (or at least distracting) to cite five other pictures, one play, and one TV show—I'm sorry.

I'm not trying to seem erudite. On the contrary: to have seen this many shows is something to be ashamed, not proud, of. It's debasing to be a mere member of the audience, not a performer; a voyeur rather than an exhibitionist. But there are satisfactions in being a seer rather than seen; sometimes I even have the thrill of being a spy, discovering information about dangerous heterosexuals in the media and selling to their enemy (the humane press).

One frame near the beginning of *Fat City* displays the ultimate in depersonalized pornography: it doesn't even show Keach's head, just his body in Jockey shorts. It looks good, better than his face (as the director, John Huston, was doubtless aware in thus calling the viewer's attention to this alluring kind of underpants).

For Ladies Only is a logical progression for Harrison from this sort of Jockey shorts work to the scantier groin-wear of the stripper (the one shown here is not, of course, in *For Ladies Only*, but rather in one of Manhattan's strip shows for men, which have a lower level of obscenity, and thus a higher quality, than do the strip shows for women; the shows for men feature manipulation of the sex parts, both front and rear, by both the performers and the audience). The plot requires Harrison to be a bashful stripper at first, but eventually he seems enthusiastic about throwing his groin and butt around, and he puts a satisfying energy into his bumps and grinds.

There is no more dramatic sight in the theater than a man performing bumps and grinds, and *For Ladies Only* is not only a state-of-the-art effort as of 1981, when it was made for TV rather than theatrical release, but even seemed surprisingly and satisfactorily audacious on September 26, 1985, when I saw a re-run at 9 p.m. on channel 9. After all, 1985 was the year Phil Donahue had delays, difficulties, and deletions in his attempt to show a group of male strippers who, at least in the version seen on channel 4 in New York, were no more *avant-garde* than those in *For Ladies Only*, made three years earlier; and 1985 also saw that miserable wretch, Roone Arledge of ABC-TV, "kill," as it were, a *20/20* segment about President Kennedy and his brother Bobby having sex with Marilyn Monroe (not at the same time). Had that show gone on the air it might have inhibited at least a little of the U.S. government's official party line that it is homosexuals who are security risks rather than people like the Kennedys and President Nixon.

In light of the difficulties of getting the truth, reality, actuality, and nature on television (to say nothing of the print media—in 1985, the *New York Times* tried to suppress the fact that Cardinal Spellman was a cocksucker), we should, I suppose, be surprised and grateful that *For Ladies Only* got shown. These are the Reagan Years, and it's easier to show things like *Little House on the Prairie*, which enables President and Mrs. Reagan, sitting on their sloppy asses in expensive chairs, to feel wholesome.

A big blond, Marc Singer, has the Mayo Methot role in *For Ladies Only*. Film scholars will feel as patronized as non-scholars feel grateful when I explain that the beloved Mayo was the aging "hostess" (whore) at the Club Intime in *Marked Woman* (1937) who was losing her looks and thus her income (another whore, Bette Davis, intervened with the executive pimp to try to save Mayo's job). Singer is cast as a Viet Nam vet and star stripper who loses status to the vigorous newcomer, Harrison, partly because Singer is "on" something

(my guess is Horse or Snow). I'd have thought the one who's on dope would be the better—i.e., the more obscene—stripper, but not in this picture. I'd have thought also that Marc could find lasting happiness by returning to the Marine Corps; Marines strip beautifully, many are on junk, and Singer could have displayed his gift for stripping at bedtime in the barracks while his buddies let off homosexual steam (jokingly, of course) by acting like queers. But Singer commits suicide during a police raid at the strip club, and Harrison goes on to the "legitimate" theater.

But what could be more legitimate than stripping, which is, after all, the display and admiration of nature? And what "legitimate" attractions, apart (as we shall see) from *Salonika*, come as close to nature as strippers? Thus, instead of saying that both Harrison and Singer are better strippers than actors, which is true enough in this picture, I'd say that stripping draws on their real talent, while the hack writing and hack directing evident in *For Ladies Only* and in pictures in general only call forth hack acting. I had expected to loathe Patricia Davis, Harrison's co-star, as I loathe

her parents, President Reagan and "the First Lady" (Patricia uses her mother's maiden name). But I'm pleased to report that her personality and performance in this picture are a triumph over the grave handicap of having that dreadful couple as parents. She's wrong, however, when she tells Harrison, who wants to get out of stripping, that no producer would put a stripper into a play which seeks the approval of "serious critics." Number one, "serious critics" is a contradiction-in-terms. There's no such animal. Critics are subjective; if they like something, e.g., tuna on rye, they call it good, and if they envy something, e.g., beauty, they call it bad.

Secondly, in 1985, Maxwell Caulfield, in an important role in *Salonika* at the prestigious Public Theater, gave New Yorkers a taste—or rather, a chance to imagine the taste—of the breathtaking bare butt and dick he exposed to Londoners when he worked as a stripper in a male club there. Throughout the entire first part of *Salonika*, he lay naked on his belly; then he stood and displayed his meat, which, according to one acquaintance who saw the play, is normal sized and, according to another, perhaps slightly plumper than normal. Both went to *Salonika* largely to see Caulfield's flesh, which had been widely publicized; so that I'm not alone in calling bareassed men as legitimate as legitimate theater.

Moreover, the reviewers, even the comparatively "straight" ones, not only did not complain that Caulfield's nudity was unnecessary, but gave rave notices to his body while finding little redeeming value in the play itself.

Sadly, a fascinating actress, Jessica Tandy, was upstaged by Caulfield's rump, a masterwork chiseled by that obscene sculptor, Nature (Caulfield claims he doesn't "work out"; it's unnatural to work out). It is always heartening when the public gets a chance to have butt of this quality in its face, but I didn't like to see an actress of Tandy's quality placed in unfair competition with it. I'd seen Tandy recently in a TV re-run of *A Woman's Vengeance* (1947), and the picture is worth watching for her alone. It's notable also for the relentless sobbing of a dripping Ann Blyth, whose tears and snot drench the picture throughout; she must hold the Hollywood sob record. I remain unmoved, since the man she was crying for—Charles Boyer—does not happen to be one of my 55 or 60 types.

I did sob uncontrollably during recent TV runs of *Men of Boys Town* (1941) and *Pocketful of Miracles* (1961). I was appalled at the ease with which I was manipulated, even victimized, by the cheap tricks of a bunch of hardened Hollywood hacks. The only sensible response to their shameless corn would have been coarse, cynical laughter; instead, I sobbed.

As a rule I try to control my addiction by watching only old movies on TV, never a TV show itself. It's not that I'm a TV snob. On the contrary. I am as susceptible to its sordid charm as I am to old movies. But each day I try to accomplish as much literary composition and jacking off as I can, and it's hard enough to do this between movies, without having TV shows to watch too. I'm not the sort who can jack off while watching TV, unless it's the occasional specialty like Leni Riefenstahl's filthy *Olympia* (1938), with its uninhibited takes of international crotches and bare buns at the 1936 Berlin Olympic Games.

I've broken my rule, however, for Maxwell Caulfield. He's irresistible, and now I watch him on *Dynasty* on TV. I assume the producers, the Shapiros, are hip enough to show him in Jockey shorts, but as of press time, they haven't.

I have been disappointed to discover that, on top of everything else, Caulfield is a competent actor—that is, one who acts like he's not acting. It's infuriating; he has everything, including something not everyone wants, a wife many years his senior. But men who are not quite orthodox men frequently marry women who are out of their peer group and easier, for that reason, to handle. I know nothing about Caulfield, and would like to know anything; he is unorthodox in the sense that the average husband never worked as a stripper in a male club. I don't believe such a job could have been the only sort available in London at the time.

RETURN ENGAGEMENT

Return Engagement by James Watters
Clarkson N. Potter, Inc. 168 pages, $25

I was surprised to discover that many of the 74 actresses in this collection of then-and-now photographs are almost as vain as the men I see primping and preening in office men's rooms.

Dorothy McGuire: "No close-ups, please; no close-ups."

Joan Fontaine: "I've held up well. My hands are bad, but I always had bad hands."

Lynn Fontanne: "Tell me my face doesn't look like those walnut faces I see in the papers." If she hadn't admitted to 92, she could have passed for late 80s.

Ginger Rogers "is a Christian Scientist, hence she has never had a face lift." Of all the cruelties perpetrated by religion, this seems the cruelest.

Katharine Hepburn's cosmetic surgery was a good job, on the evidence of the photograph of her in this book, but Vivienne Segal's was not altogether satisfactory: "I've lost my smile. I have no nose left and I had a cartilage implant over my lip, so there goes the smile."

"Some actresses," Loretta Young says, "had terrible times with their necks. Connie Bennett got two terrible lines by age 45." Yes, Loretta still wears on her arms the indescribably complex yardage of fabric which was the dominant feature of her TV show. I once saw a friend make the Loretta Young entrance into a bar, his arms outstretched, humming her theme song. His entrance was the more effective for being in a "straight" bar; such entrances have been routine in gay bars ever since the *Loretta Young Show*.

Elsa Lanchester offered to "put Vaseline on my cheeks if you think I'm not bright enough." She belongs to the small minority of the sane, but she still has her gift for looking crazy. Since words cannot express my adoration of her, I've decided to act it out by gathering twigs in my neighborhood parks and displaying them in little piles in my studio, as Elsa did in *Ladies in Retirement* (1941), a picture which enabled her to develop fully her gift for insanity.

"I have only one side," Claudette Colbert said, "really I do. I have a terrible nose. My key light was always overhead; it straightened my nose. I have a grey streak right down the middle, but it's all mixed and looks bad. My friends tell me to keep dying it a few more years."

Barbara Stanwyck ought to follow Claudette's example. True, Barbara's cotton-like hair would make her an ideal candidate for *The Babs Bush Story*, should Hollywood decide to do the cotton-haired, foul-mouthed wife of our Vice President. Moreover, it would be a meaty part; Babs Bush, unlike her husband, is an authentic tough, and Stanwyck can play toughs well. But Stanwyck's hair does limit her. She needn't go as far as Vera Hruba Ralston, whose hair is shoe polish black in this book, but she could do something.

The best looker in the book seems to be Frances Dee. The worst is one who started out as one of the most beautiful women in Hollywood: Virginia Bruce. Horst, who did the photographs for the book, got her at the Motion Picture Country House and Hospital not long before her death at 72. She had been in ill health for a long time. She wore her "good pearls," but they didn't help. She is hardly recognizable. She had been widowed twice and, worse, had a daughter on welfare; but at least her third marriage, to a Turk twelve years her junior, sounds like fun. At a certain age women should stop marrying their contemporaries and start marrying "stuff." But her Turk was rather a hood and wound up in jail.

Still, Virginia had compassion for others even worse off. "Do you know," she asked the author, James Watters, "Norma Shearer is just down the hall? She was the biggest of them all and here she is blind and dying."

Mary Astor was also photographed for this book at the country house. She still looked like Mary Astor after a heart attack, two

strokes, and conversion to Catholicism. That Mary, who once confided to her diary that the well-hung playwright, George S. Kaufman, "fucked the living daylights out of me," may still have a good fuck left in her is suggested by her remark to Watters (a remark that departs in significant respects from Catholicism): "If you run into Alan Alda, tell him he can put his shoes under my bed anytime." But by 1985, when the incomparable Joe Franklin, of the indescribable *Joe Franklin Show*, took a TV crew to the Country House, Mary would no longer be photographed.

Someone should form a Committee of Concerned Homosexuals who would visit the Country House regularly: comprised of plastic surgeons, dieticians, druggists, hairdressers, dress designers, shoe salesmen, jewelers, furriers, hatters, dry cleaners, air conditioning and humidity control experts, cosmeticians, aestheticians, beauticians, lighting engineers, and above all photographers, these hordes of homosexuals could swoop down on the Country House periodically and keep its beloved creatures restored like Rembrandts. What could be a more important civic service?

Writers should visit all the stars regularly and record every opinion and memory; even during his sometimes brief conversations with them, Watters accumulated fascinating historic details.

Bette Davis evaluates her fellow Warner's player, Ronnie Reagan, as "lousy."

Joan Bennett was a grandmother at 39. Heather Angel saw her husband stabbed to death by an "intruder."

Marsha Hunt was "suspected of being a Communist sympathizer during the McCarthy era." I would rather hear that than that she was a McCarthy sympathizer.

Fay Wray used to pick Janet Gaynor up in her Model T in the days when Hollywood had dirt roads.

Barbara Stanwyck fell in love with Robert Wagner, 33 years her junior, while making *Titanic* (1953). She really likes weak faces, doesn't she? (Her second husband was Robert Taylor.)

Maureen O'Sullivan "found love," in Watter's phrase, with Robert Ryan, but he died of cancer before they could marry.

Isabel Jewell called Watters from a pay 'phone—she couldn't afford a home 'phone.

Katharine Hepburn "dropped" Garson Kanin, wisely, I think, after he wrote a book about her and Spencer Tracy. Garson Kanin is bad news, and not merely for Katharine Hepburn.

Ginger Rogers and Fred Astaire both had their mothers living with them until their deaths.

Ann Miller listed her occupation on a passport form as "star." A mind that thrilling warrants a more extensive treatment than the mere half-page Ann gets in *Return Engagement* (some stars get several pages).

Claudette Colbert, in just a five-minute sitting, named so many of the wrong kind of people—the Annenbergs, the Reagans, the Pope, Frank Sinatra—as to all but destroy the positive impression her photograph makes.

Myrna Loy and Gary Cooper lived on the same block in Helena, Montana, when they were kids. Cooper was four years her senior. "He told me later," Loy says, "how he remembered my freckles and how I used to go sliding down a hill in our neighborhood."

Shirley Temple "made $10,000 just signing 2,000 limited Shirley Temple posters at $5 each," but she turned down that "What Becomes a Legend Most" series of ads. "I wouldn't feel comfortable," she told Watters, "with the state of our country, by posing in a fur coat and being known as a rich Republican." Shirl thus reveals herself as more sensitive than Lady Di, Prince Charles's wife, who sometimes spends several thou a week on clothes. Moreover, some of her clothes are more suitable for Las Vegas than London; as recently as her November, 1985, tour of Australia, she was photographed getting out of a car in a dress slit almost up to her hole. If I seem disrespectful toward Her Royal Highness, it's because she has a male disease, one that the toughest lower class broads like Anita Bryant have: homophobia. Di let it out via *Time* and *People* that she doesn't want her two sons attended by homosexuals.

Joan Fontaine was "so in love" with Adlai Stevenson. Think: if he'd won the Presidency, we could have had Joan and Adlai instead of Ike 'n' Mamie.

It is sad that Joan has been reduced in recent years to doing commercials and promoting Hummel ware in shopping centers while Broadway is usually starless. The only place to see real stars any more, as opposed to the people in *Cats* and so on, is dinner theaters. Where once people came to New York to see theater, now some airline should offer theater flights for New Yorkers to go to Lubbock, Texas, St. Petersburg, Florida, and so on, to see movie stars at dinner theaters.

Watters is respectful toward the stars; he doesn't mention such things as that two of his stars, Loretta Young and Barbara Stanwyck, have sons, natural and adopted respectively, who were arrested on porn raps. The sons' work was in a way more interesting than their mothers', but only in a way.

The book includes many of the beloved toughs who are homo-sexual cult goddesses. Jane Russell claims that being a sex object has been "a pain in the ass." Iris Adrian's remarks similarly suggest that she could have been a valuable author had she not been so much in demand in show biz. "If an actor gets a pimple on his butt," Iris says, "he thinks he's ruined for life. They are so damned vain, it would be like marrying another dame." Iris solved the problem by marrying a football player named Fido Murphy. Heaven knows many football players are as concerned about their butt pimples and so on as actors are, but evidently Fido was an exception.

The greatest star of all, Lynn Bari, is not in the book; is it possible she wasn't asked?

Irene Dunne was asked but said no; she wants to be remem-bered the way she was in pictures. She must look a sight; decades of Republicanism can really give you a dried-up look. Look at Nancy Reagan.

(The reviewer is indebted to Jim Tamulis for a research grant in the form of a gift copy of the book, which costs $25. No movie writer should be without it. Indeed, no movie writer should be without Jim Tamulis. He knows many of them and is an inspiration to them; when he was seven years old, for instance, he found a huge mud puddle in his native Worcester, Massachusetts, and wallowed in it as a way of duplicating the experience of Nyoka the Jungle Girl in a quicksand sequence. I'm trying to get him to write his "memoirs of a movie lover" for *Christopher Street*.)

PEOPLE WILL TALK

People Will Talk by John Kobal
Knopf, 1986, 728 pages, photographs, $25

People Will Talk is a big fat collection of interviews (or as John Kobal, its author, prefers to call them, conversations) with actresses, one actor, and crew people. It's enchanting, like all movie books, even the worst. Kobal's is one of the best.

Jack Cole is, or was (for many of these interviews date from the 1960s and 1970s), only a choreographer, but he would have made a great writer. He says, "Glenn [Ford] always looked like he was fucking the whole time or he was playing with himself. I mean they really pushed that with Glenn and Rita [Hayworth]; they just stared at each other like they were saying, 'I'm going to eat your ass from here to kingdom come.'"

"Lana Turner," he says, "really liked men; she liked to fuck a lot." Many of the other actresses merely liked to act sexy.

Kim Novak, "when I first saw her… was this tough Polish broad from Chicago; *really* tough lady, really *tough*." It sounds fascinating. What a pity she became what Cole calls "ethereal"; men being what they are, the tougher women are the better.

Marilyn Monroe was confused. Cole told her to "stick a finger up your ass; I think that's quite within the realm of your technical facilities." There is that in Cole's photograph which suggests that a finger up the ass is more his "thing" than Marilyn's.

John Engstead also could have been an important film writer had he not gone into photography. In fact he got his start by interviewing celebrities for his Los Angeles high school paper. (It was a daily; it's fantastic.)

Ann Pennington, he says, was in "a dirty little dressing room—and she was sort of a little crummy herself." I don't know who Ann Pennington is, or was; I'm sorry. But his description of her shows a strong literary gift.

John Barrymore, says Engstead, "was making *Don Juan* and God! His breath! All I remember is this man with those red eyes. He had been drunk the night before, obviously."

Kobal asked Engstead why he stopped photographing Marlene Dietrich, "She was all through, baby... she wanted me to come back and reshoot her because she said she looked like a female impersonator in a session we did." Apparently this was in 1959.

Non-writers are often better writers than writers; another example, not in Kobal's book, but in a letter to the reviewer, is a professor of Greek and Latin in London who gave in one sentence a better comprehension of Ricky Nelson than does an entire section on the subject in a recent *Rolling Stone*. The professor wrote, "I would have loved to sniff his Jockey shorts."

Joan Blondell, on the other hand, wouldn't have made it as a writer. "There are a few outstanding memories," she told Kobal, "but they are *not* to be told on the air, on television, in print, or anywhere." Why not? The stars owe it to us; after all, we made them stars.

Louella O. Parsons wore rubber underpants and had a piss-pot under her table in a cafe scene in *Hollywood Hotel* (1937), says Madison Lacy, a stills photographer at Warner's; "she had kidney troubles."

"Yeah," says his wife, a showgirl in the picture, "she sure did."

Louella's "kidney troubles" were enhanced by the fact that she was a drunk—specifically, on occasion, a wino.

Hedda Hopper, the other great columnist, was the one who seemed like a real pisser to Rita Hayworth; Rita, Cole says, wanted to call Hedda "a dirty cunt and let her have one right in the nose."

Ingrid Bergman distinguished between the two columnists by pointing out that Hedda was "openly nasty and asked direct and nasty questions" while Louella "would be very, very sweet and try to trick you." The reviewer distinguishes between the two writers by weight: Louella, fat, was an old bag, while Hedda, slim, was an old hag. To put in contemporary terms, our President's wife,

Nancy, is an old hag while the Vice President's wife, Babs Bush, is an old bag, if that helps clarify the matter.

Louella's right-wing politics were as unsound as her kidneys, as were the politics of Hedda and, for that matter, Nancy and Babs and their husbands, Ronnie and George, respectively, not to mention the male studio heads, who bullied women but cowered before censors and congressional investigators of political sympathies. "Bully" and "coward" are usually synonyms and it would have been healthier for poor Rita had she followed the lead of some of her sister stars and treated columnists and producers as poorly as they treated actresses. Rita, Cole says, wanted to tell Harry Cohn to "shove it up your Jewish ass"; after all, Cohn had called her "a dumb Latin cunt," according to Cole, and according to Kim Stanley, Cohn "would go and have a pee with the door open while Rita was sitting there where she couldn't miss it."

Cohn call Ann Miller "a dumb broad with large thighs." What kind of thighs did he want, Gary Cooper's?

The way to treat him was the way Kim Stanley says she treated him. Cohn, in her presence, asked Fred Zinnemann, "Why are you bringing me this girlie? She's not even pretty." Kim told Cohn he was "a pig." The stunning precision of the image suggests that she could have been a poet had she not gone into show biz.

Loretta Young also handled men well.

DARRYL ZANUCK: My wife wouldn't wear a dress like that.
LORETTA: Your wife isn't a movie star. I am.

When Zanuck ordered Loretta not to add or subtract from any of her agreed-upon costumes, she says she retaliated by holding up the whole crew while waiting for Zanuck to return from polo so she could get his permission to carry a handkerchief in a scene in *Suez* (1938).

Errol Flynn caused a costume crisis in *Adventures of Don Juan* (1948) by wearing a noticeably built-up crotch. Vincent Sherman, the director, says the cameraman wouldn't photograph it; it was all right from the front, but in profile "it was awful … this thing was sticking out to here." "What did you do," Flynn's wife Nora said when she saw it, "stuff a towel in it?" Flynn, Sherman says, "turned red."

Kobal tells Louise Brooks, "I think it was Carole Lombard who, when somebody asked what it was like being married to the King of Hollywood [Clark Gable], said that if his pecker was one inch shorter he'd be called the Queen of Hollywood."

Loretta Young says she "started smoking when I was eight, stealing them from my uncle." It's surprising and inspiring; if more girls would steal cigarettes at eight they might grow up to handle men as well as Loretta did (but they ought to stop smoking at nine).

Eleanor Powell evidently handled men beautifully.

LOUIS B. MAYER: I'm going to take you to the Mayfair dance this Saturday night.
POWELL: I'm sorry but I can't go.

Mayer couldn't even get her to stop having lunch in the commissary with a friend of hers who was a cutter; Mayer felt she shouldn't be seen with "the lower echelon."

Arletty contributes a brief and enticing picture of Berlin circa 1932–1933: "There were many Frenchmen dressed as women ….There is an erotic climate in Berlin. Even men who were not homosexual would become somewhat homosexual *un peu pédéraste* if they stayed long enough in Berlin."

Fredric March must have been heterosexual; during the groping that is acceptable in dancing, he asked if Eleanor Powell was wearing a girdle.

POWELL: Just dance.

June Duprez fought off assaults from Harry Cohn and David O. Selznick, both of whom tried to break into her apartment (not at the same time; had they combined forces they might have succeeded). Many actresses felt it would be unwise to reject a producer. "Nobody did that in those days," Duprez says. "*Nobody.*"

Kobal himself is, or was years ago in a photograph in the book which was taken while he was talking to Dietrich, almost of star quality. Those lips, those eyebrows, that hat. It was his first hat; a Tyrolean hat. He enhances the impact of the photograph by mentioning his "extreme" height. Mmmm. These days, sadly, he has a moustache; a big one.

Jean Louis, the clothing designer, spoke imperfect English but a remark he made to Kobal in 1977 is a good summary of the way many people feel about the old Hollywood: "Well," Jean Louis said, "we had stars, it was fun; we don't have anybody no more."

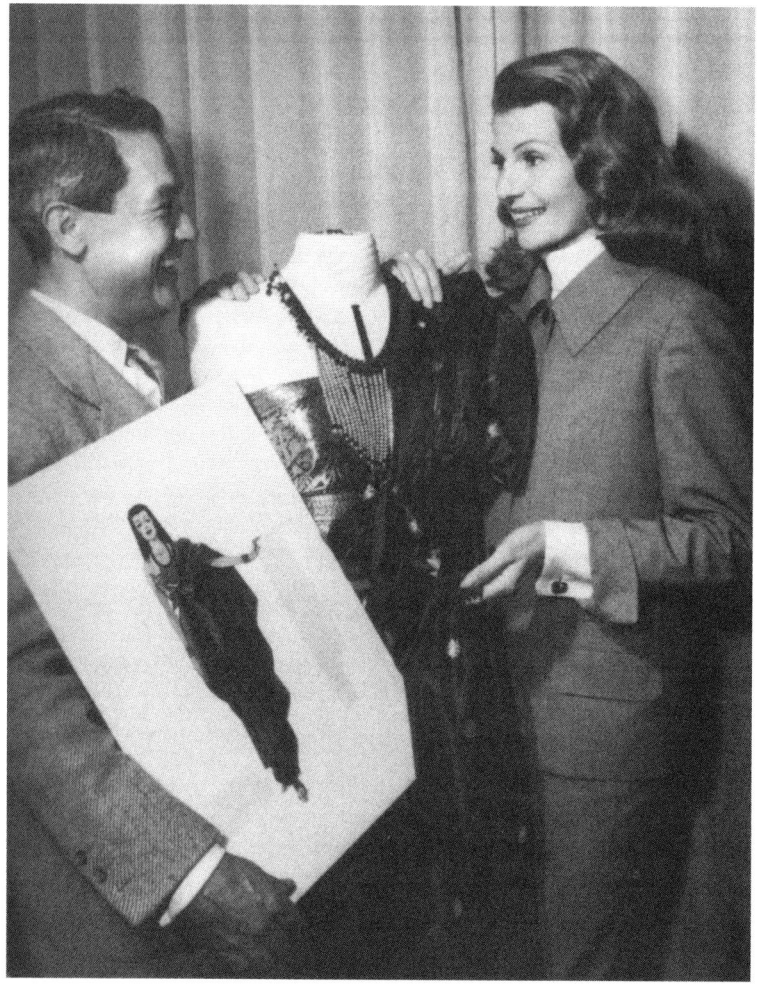

GENE RAYMOND

I never much liked Gene Raymond I until I saw him in underpants. Fully clothed in *Red Dust* (1932), he was, to be sure, breathtakingly blond and clean looking, as were his clothes—a white shirt and khaki pants that were unusually well cleaned and pressed for a jungle setting. In *Sadie McKee* (1934), he remained well-groomed even while on the skids. Still he looked a little *ordinaire* and hardly the sort of man who makes men want to kiss his asshole.

But in his shorts in *Flying Down to Rio* (1933), he abruptly and brazenly established himself as a piece of eating stuff. Most men look better dressed than undressed; Elvis Presley, for instance, could pass for "stuff" in his tight, white pants, but in his Jockey shorts, *forget* it. But while clothes conceal flaws in most men, in Raymond it is his beauty they conceal—and not merely the beauty of his hairless flesh, but his beauty of character. For any man who would appear in 1933 in erotic, rather than comedic, underpants is a courageous pioneer, one who is conscious of his allure and honest in displaying it, and one who raises a question of the most inspiring nature: if he will go that far in public, how far will he go in private?

Men being what they are, I don't think it would be an exaggeration to say that millions, perhaps billions of them would want to kiss, after seeing the surprising Gene Raymond of *Flying Down to Rio*, not only his butt-hole but his balls, dick, pubic hair, armpits, nipples, belly button, fingers, toes, and legs. Men who enjoy acting especially abject, as a way of goading their partner into sexual assertion, would even pick up Raymond's underpants off the floor and kiss *them* while looking in his eyes meaningfully.

During the screening of *Flying Down to Rio* at 2 a.m. December 5, 1985, on Channel 9, the writer had to take a shit and upon my

return I was startled to see the TV screen filled with the beauty of Raymond's nude torso. His arms and chest were fully developed without being vulgarly gymnastic (as Maxwell Caulfield's are becoming since he went to California and began appearing on *The Colbys* and, evidently, going to gymnasia). Raymond arose, revealing tight boxer shorts; put on an athletic undershirt, giving a glimpse of blond armpits, and stepped into his pants, giving a sublime profile of his approximately 25-year-old butt. Raymond's bare chest, with the type of nipples men like to suck on, is considerably more alluring than that of a more acclaimed sex object, Clark Gable, in *Hold Your Man* (1933). Gable's teats, plump for a man, jiggled. But while Gable routinely appeared bare chested in his pictures, he never, unless I'm mistaken, appeared in his underpants. Raymond's underpants, because of the probable beauty of the parts they conceal, are competitive even with underwear displays in today's more permissive climate. For example, the sight of Ron Reagan, the president's son, in his briefs on *Saturday Night Live* in February of 1986 arouses in sensitive men not lust but fear that his crotch—both the crotch of his briefs and his naked crotch proper—might be at best rancid, at worst putrid. It is conceivable that some less fastidious men might want to fuck him, but hardly likely that any would want to suck him off (the only decent Reagan seems to be Patti). By contrast, the natural and normal reaction to the sight of Raymond in *Rio* is a desire to drain a big wad of cream from his dick and even, as we have seen, to see what his asshole tastes like.

Brief though Raymond's semi-nude sequence be—it's even briefer than his underwear—it is still long enough to offer conclusive evidence, beyond the shadow of a doubt, that he belongs in the Eating Stuff Hall of Fame. It is satisfying to make the discovery even at this late date (if it's not too late, for a number of his pictures are available on commercial TV) and to rectify decades of neglect by placing his name on the honor roll of Hollywood "stuff," a list that includes but is not limited to these men arrayed in alphabetical order rather than in the order of the probable taste of their secret parts: Turhan Bey, the aforementioned Caulfield, Alan Curtis, Tom Drake, Dan Duryea, Billy Halop, Darryl Hickman, Robert Hutton, John Kerr, Charles Lane, Gordon MacRae, Martin Milner, Wayne Morris, Audie

Murphy, the Nelson brothers (Ricky and David), Donald O'Connor, Joe Sawyer, and, above all, because men with a potential for nastiness are the best partners in this form of sex, Jackie Searle.

Raymond is still alive at press time (April 1986) and around 78 years of age, but he is said by the renowned Lamparski to be a "conservative" and I doubt that he would answer the questions that inevitably arise from his underpants scene in *Rio*. How anyone who participated in anything as destructive as the Vietnam War can be called "conservative" is also a question (Raymond was a pilot). I've always assumed that the only thing conservatives want to conserve is their own money, and this was confirmed by one of the richest of them, Nelson Rockefeller, who once said, "I'm a conservative; I have a lot to conserve." (Nels, I might add, since we are dealing with underpants, died in his, in the company of a young woman who worked for him.)

Were Raymond's shorts in *Rio* custom-made or just store-bought? Was he wearing anything under them to subdue his dick and to absorb any drops that might leak out of his piss-hole?

Did the crew stare at the crotch of his shorts, searching for encrusted urine deposits?

Did they stare at his crotch, looking for an outline of his meat?

Were the shorts he wore on camera the same pair he put on when he dressed for work that morning, or did he change into a "fresh" pair for the scene (not that any pair he had would be stale)?

Did he, after putting on the shorts shown in the movie, take a shit or a piss, at home or in the studio? How many takes did the scene require?

How long was Raymond working in his underwear?

What comments on his body or his shorts were made by Raymond, the director, or the crew? Whose idea was it to show Raymond in his underpants?

It seems unlikely that it was his own idea, but unlikely also that he resisted. "I like to ride and swim," he told Frederick Russell for an article that ran in *Film Pictorial* under the date of March 23, 1935. "I'd like parts which would give me a chance to do that sort of thing." (He's not the only one. It's especially disappointing that, so far as I know, he did no swimming pictures, for in his shiny, latex swimming briefs in a snapshot taken in Hawaii with his wife, Jeanette MacDonald, and shown in his file at the Lincoln Center library, he looked irresistible. It's unfortunate also that he did no polo or jockey pictures; horseback riding, like bicycle riding, offers a rich opportunity for displaying a man's spread butt, and the end of a horse race, when the jockeys stand in their stirrups, gives unusually good butt views, sometimes even the chance to see the seams of the riders' jockey shorts showing through their tight, white breeches. Raymond's other physical exertions, according to his files, were tennis, golf, hunting, fishing, gym, and fencing; but of these only gym and tennis, because of the costumes, are photogenic.)

It is unlikely also that the scriptwriter specified Raymond's underpants scene in *Rio*. It seems probable that it was the inspiration of the director, Thornton Freeland (b. 1898); Freeland was born in North Dakota and the writer knows from having been born in South Dakota that these states, among the least important in some ways, rank high on the list of lecherous locales and indeed make such places as New York City seem sexually inadequate by contrast. For example, Gov. Janklow of South Dakota has been accused of driving a car in the nude, a distinction no other governor can boast, and an inspiring model for the natives. Freeland's other credits indicate that he turned out a sexual product; *Week-End Marriage* and *They Call It Sin*, both released in 1932, sound especially intelligent, and *Six Cylinder Love* (1931) suggests, but probably does not show, back seat blow jobs. Freeland seems in his entry in Ephraim Katz's *The Film Encyclopedia* to be comparatively heterosexual and thus safe from accusations that a desire to photograph Raymond in his shorts is queer. The credits of Freeland's wife, June Clyde (b. 1908), sound spectacularly heterosexual: *Tanned Legs* (1929), *Her Resale Value* (1933), and *Intimate Relations* and *School for Husbands* (both 1937). The last title contains the suggestion, more widely accepted today than in 1937, that heterosexuality is unnatural and must be learned.

Raymond's file at Lincoln Center yields a treasury of romantic data, but only to the scholar who is blessed with the gift of a dirty mind. "When I first met Gene about four years ago [*circa* 1931],"

Russell writes (*op. cit.*), "he was a somewhat nervy, arrogant, rather smart-aleck young man, too conscious of his appeal to women." The passage suggests that Russell was not homosexual; had he been, he might well have found these "nervy, arrogant, smart-aleck" qualities alluring rather than (as he hints) offensive. Most journalists who want to seem "straight" interview ball players, not movie stars.

It is characteristic of the fan literature of the era that Russell singles out "women" as being fond of Raymond and completely ignores the impact the alluring, full-bodied blond had on men.

Raymond himself could not have been unaware of his effect upon men and boys; he was, Katz writes, "on the stage from age five ... and made his Broadway debut in 1920 [at around age 12]." The atmosphere backstage and off camera, then as now, is so routinely and easily obscene as to shock those of us whose manners were formed at the comparatively chaste Everard Baths, and had any player, man or woman, boy or girl, wanted to check out the pubescent Raymond's sexual development, to see whether he was sprouting dick hair, whether it was blond, how big his meat had grown, even to feel of his asshole; they would in all probability have undone his pants without hesitation and examined him. Raymond Guion, as he was named then, would have been even more succulent in his early years on stage than he was at age 25 in *Rio*, and it is likely that men and boys backstage made this clear to him. Moreover, Hollywood producers, in the days before such non-sex objects as Elliott Gould were put into pictures, used the same aesthetic standards in selecting men as cocksuckers traditionally have in toilets.

"Indifferent to Girls" was the promising title of an article by Charles Grayson published *circa* 1932. "Girls," Raymond says in the article, "take your mind off your work."

The *New York Evening Post* ran a headline in 1936 that confirmed this report:

GENE RAYMOND, A BACHELOR, WILL STAY ONE, HE SAYS.

In 1934, the *New York Sun* recorded his trip to Europe in the company of his mother. The trip, the *Sun* reported, included "dancing and skiing at St. Moritz."

Grayson wrote that Raymond "goes for long rides in his car. He drives at night usually and alone... when he returns he feels much better." The writer can empathize with this pleasure. When I lived in Spuyten Duyvil I used to drive home from Manhattan bareass. There is no hint that Raymond made his night drives in the nude, but certainly he would have constituted a magnificent sight if he had.

The writer, who has seen some fascinating men while prowling around and hanging out in Grand Central Station, Penn Station, and the Port Authority bus terminal, can empathize also with a news clipping from 1933 which reports that Raymond "believes he has discovered a novel method of picking up bits of characterization with which to color his screen portrayals. Once in awhile he passes an afternoon in a Los Angeles railroad station, lounging around in the waiting room...." Mmmmm.

But all reveries of Raymond lounging around railroad stations, prowling around in his fucking car at night, and dancing with Mom at St. Moritz are shattered by the reality, if that is what it is, of the headline over an article by Katherine Hartley in the July 1937 *Movie Mirror*:

WHAT LOVE HAS DONE TO GENE RAYMOND.

His love object was Jeanette MacDonald and, Hartley writes, "As for Gene's new found interest in interior decoration, well, that is some-thing about which he is kidded a great deal today.... When he enters a friend's home now he has the rather unguestly habit of wandering, alone, from room to room, examining the decorations." Two can play that game, and if Raymond could get away with wandering around a host's house, so could other guests. One might run into Raymond in some room upstairs well away from the party and the chances are that the houses he prowled about in were sufficiently large so that such an encounter would provide privacy. A guest who represents himself as admiring the textures and fabrics used in interior decorating could seem sufficiently artistic to admire also the texture of Raymond's pants and could, without undue suspicion, ask, as a man once asked me in my basement laundry, if he might examine it. This in turn could lead, as it did with me, to an examination of the crack of the butt and the bulge hanging between the legs in front.

"Jeanette," Hartley continues, bringing us back to reality, "may be intrigued in a bridge game in the living room, but possible grand slam or no, when Gene calls for her attention from the upstairs den, up the stair she must run ...." Hartley constructs their conversation.

> **GENE:** "See, darling, how they've used pine paneling in here? It's effective, don't you think? Only I'd like a beamed ceiling with it, wouldn't you?"
> **JEANETTE:** "Yes, darling, only there's plenty of time to make up our mind about that."

It seems safe to say that Raymond's conscientious and detailed scrutiny of interior decorations produced a home as lovely as his groin and butt-hole.

It is but fair to mention that the other guides to "oldies" on TV do not specify Raymond's underpants as the great moment in *Flying Down to Rio*. Leonard Maltin in *TV Movies* calls the picture "memorable for... Astaire and Rogers... in their first screen teaming of Astaire and Rogers." Pack journalism establishes a party line for many pictures and the one on *Flying Down to Rio* is that it is the first screen teaming of Rogers and Astaire.

The writer finds dancing offensive, and the sight of Gene Raymond in his underpants lifts the picture above that level.

STATE OF THE UNION

State of the Union (1948), seen at 11:55 p.m. March 15, 1986 on channel 13, is about politics, but its most moving scene is not political but romantic, and not romantic in the usual way of beautiful movie stars kissing but romantic in its mystical suggestion of the enduring trust in each other that a couple of enchanting old sports seem to have.

It is ironic, cruelly ironic, that this couple is not Katharine Hepburn and Spencer Tracy, stars of the picture and asshole buddies offscreen as well, but rather a couple of supporting players who for all I know may never have met before Frank Capra put them in this picture: the beloved Maidel Turner (1881–1953) and the beloved Raymond Walburn (1887–1969).

They are one of only three heartwarming heterosexual couples I've seen in pictures—that is, couples who show any real feeling for each other, as opposed to feeling which is scripted and directed. The others are Myrna Loy and William Powell in the six *Thin Man* pictures (1934–1947), and Jane Russell and Robert Mitchum in *Macao* (1952).

For reasons unknown, or perhaps no reason at all, I have remained immune to the charm of Hollywood's most married couple today, the ever-pregnant Meryl Streep and her husband, even though Meryl confirmed on TV the precision of my impressionism when she told an *Entertainment Tonight* reporter who questioned her about the "pressure" of being an Academy Award nominee that the only "pressure" she felt was to find what she called "a bathroom"; I had written years earlier that she always looks as though she has to take a shit.

Meryl's search for a "bathroom" was at the Dorothy Chandler Pavilion in L.A. on the occasion of the 1986 Academy Awards. The award show itself, like Audrey Hepburn's earrings and Lionel Ritchie's chin, was too long.

And when is the Academy going to give its overall career award to someone really valuable like Sheldon Leonard instead of such creatures as Cary Grant and Charles (Buddy) Rogers?

Maidel Turner and Raymond Walburn have only one scene in *State of the Union*, but it is a long one, at the end, and it is worth waiting for. On top of its warmth it is funny, thanks more to Turner and Walburn than to the script or direction. Walburn always seemed to regard the story as none of his business; his business was to look astonished, outraged, or delighted whenever anyone said anything to him, no matter how trivial it was; even if it was only his secretary saying good morning.

The two have, however, been given a good entrance, either by the writers or by the director. They sail into a big room on Walburn's line, "Anybody home?" It is an enchantingly mindless line in light of the fact that someone very clearly is at home: perhaps a hundred people. There's a party and it's being televised, with the extreme clutter that cameras, lights, cables, and crews make.

This dear old couple (Turner was around 67 and Walburn around 61) exude the impression that they are in tight with each other. They do so without the help of dialogue, simply by bursting with intimacy. There is only one line which suggests their satisfaction with each other and that is Turner's statement to the butler that only Walburn can mix her Sazerac (a Southern drink; she is cast as one of the loud ladies of the South, Lulubelle Alexander, wife to Walburn's Judge Alexander). Since anyone can mix a drink, it is an absurd conceit but an affectionate one, one which puts into words their blatant rapport. Otherwise their relationship goes without saying.

Though Walburn knows the hostess, Katharine Hepburn, he registers his usual pop-eyed, open-mouthed shock when she does the least shocking thing: walks over to receive him. His look is no less eye-catching and scene-stealing for being completely uncalled for by the situation. He looks surprised again when a request that surprises no one, a request he must have heard a thousand times, comes from off camera: a request from Turner that he make another Sazerac for her. In *Christmas in July* (1940), he similarly looks astounded when, standing at a microphone as the sponsor of a radio program, the least astounding thing happens: an announcer walks up to the microphone. It is Walburn's irrelevant but arresting image, not what the announcer said or what Katharine Hepburn said, that is memorable.

I wonder if any director ever told him that it was not necessary to look so startled. I doubt it. A bright director would not only complain that Walburn's look was irrelevant to the story, but would realize that it added value to the story, which was, as often as not, less interesting than Walburn.

In their long scene, Turner has only one line that is out of the ordinary: "I haven't had so much fun since Huey Long [a corrupt Louisiana politician of the era] died." But she doesn't need any lines; her laugh is enough. Her role is to laugh at Hepburn's lines, but it is Turner's laugh, not Hepburn's lines, that is memorable. (This is not the only time Hepburn had a scene stolen from her by a supporting player; in *Adam's Rib* (1949), the overwhelming Hope Emerson, weighing in at 230 pounds, easily made the courtroom scene her own solo *tour de force*, drawing attention away from both Hepburn and Spencer Tracy, whom she lifts.)

Turner had played Mrs. Alexander in 1945 in the Broadway play from which the picture was made, and had also held her ground on stage against such difficult and dazzling players as John Barrymore and the female impersonator, Julian Eltinge. She appears not to have "lowered" her stage style for the camera, which does not need the extreme force that is required to project sights and sounds to the balcony. But her scene in *State of the Union* is so crowded and noisy that nothing less than a stagey performance could command attention. If the long scene required a number of "takes," it must have been exhausting for Turner to deliver such a huge amount of hearty laughter.

Walburn was on the stage for 28 years before he went into pictures and he appears not to have bothered to change his almost vaudevillian style for the movies. Here again it doesn't matter; he was not called in for parts that required subtlety and quietude.

The failure to adapt stage technique to films often does lower the quality of a movie. In *Murder by Death* (1976), for example,

Neil Simon, mainly a playwright rather than a screen writer, handled the revelation that Peter Falk has male physique magazines the way he would in a play, in dialogue between Falk and his secretary, Eileen Brennan; a theater audience could not of course see the magazine photographs. But in the film there is no reason why Brennan, and the camera, could not have discovered the actual photographs.

As a property, *State of the Union*, except for the added value that such players as Turner and Walburn give it, is surprisingly *ordinaire* in light of the fact that it was written by two "names" which in those days were household words, like "shit" and "fuck"— Howard Lindsay and Russel Crouse, authors also of the tedious hit, *Life With Father*.

The picture's basic absurdity—and it is not an amusing absurdity, as are Walburn's—is that its hero, Spencer Tracy, is a contradiction in terms: a compassionate Republican. A politician can be one or the other, but not both. The Republicans, historically and especially today under Ronnie and Nancy Reagan, are not for the little people but the big ones—the banker against the depositor, the landlord against the tenant, the doctor against the patient, the manufacturer of armaments against the accountant who tries to expose corruption, the star against the fan; the Reagans actually had a *Dynasty* person, Catherine Oxenburg, and a heterosexual muscle queen, Sylvester Stallone, in to dinner at the White House (what taste), and President Reagan, normally a friendly and folksy old fart, had just, at this writing, attacked homosexuals again, presumably feeling that if anyone as nellie as his own son can get married we all should.

Nancy, the Imelda Marcos of Pacific Palisades, has never gone as far as Imelda's purchase of 500 black brassieres, but the reason for this may simply be that Nancy, as can be seen in swimming photographs which White House press agents unwisely permitted to be taken and released, shows no need for even one brassiere.

The Reagans, like William F. Buckley, Jr., know all too well that people who have no values of the heart and mind need the added value of jewels and $$$, and the President has shown an obscene concern for the problems of the insanely greedy Marcoses, Imelda and her husband, Ferdinand (whose tightly-stretched face skin suggests that he employs the same cosmetic surgeon Merle Oberon had toward the end).

As the Marcoses were packing their jewels, cash, and negotiable securities and preparing to flee the Philippines after glomming billions of dollars from that poor country, the two first ladies, Nancy and Imelda, were in touch by telephone. I have no reason to suspect that Nancy advised the Marcoses to smuggle their emeralds and rubies through customs by wrapping them in surgical cotton and hiding them in their shit-holes—not in those words, anyway (Nancy would have used "anus"; I doubt that she knows its plural, "ani"). Nonetheless, why hasn't someone conducted an anal search—routine among lesser criminals—of Imelda and Ferdinand as they cross international boundaries in search of a country that will have them?

If this seems farfetched, consider the alcoholic junkie I used to know who stashed his money in his butt-hole. One night when he was literally floored from debauchery, he pulled out a small wad of bills from his hole, washed a ten spot, dried it, and gave it to me for a rum run. It brought to memory the "laundered money" of the Nixon presidency.

Spencer Tracy's concern for the powerless in *State of the Union*, while incredible in light of his Republicanism, has, however, been a traditional concern of the Democrats. But today some say the Democrats could get more votes by copying the Reaganites and supporting only our society's winners. The Democratic chairman, somebody named "Kirk," thinks the party would be more popular if it didn't encourage homosexuals, and Norman Mailer feels the party has been held back by its support of another group almost as numerous as homosexuals: women.

In fairness to Norman, it should be pointed out that while most heterosexual males are impressed only by white heterosexual males, Norman likes black ones as well; *Life* once called his article about Muhammad Ali "verbal fellatio."

I have gone on record as an admirer of young stuff often enough to avoid charges that I am prejudiced in favor of old-timers, and I thus make bold to express my adoration of another supporting player in *State of the Union*, Charles Lane, who was around 49 when he

made the picture. That I am not alone in liking him can be seen in the fact that it was Lane, of all the others in the party scene, that Capra chose for close-up reaction shots during Tracy's climactic speech. Lane always looked, lean, clean, and if not mean, at least pushy, and his neat, sharp features made him arguably the most photogenic actor in Hollywood history (this is not the same as saying he was the most beautiful).

While only lovers (of movies or of Lane) know his name, millions know his face; he made at least 308 pictures, and once saw himself on TV in an "oldie" he didn't even remember making. He worked also in TV shows, including *I Love Lucy*, *Petticoat Junction*, *The Pruitts of Southampton*, *"F" Troop*, and *Get Smart*, and primitive though some of these efforts be, especially *I Love Lucy*, they are worth watching in syndicated re-runs on local channels for Lane alone.

He still looked good in "The Character Actors," part of the series called *The Moviemakers*, at 7 p.m. October 21, 1985 on channel 13. It's fantastic that a man that old—he's around 87 at this writing (1986)—can be that healthy, that bright, that interesting.

Walter Goodman of the *Times* evaluates the *Moviemakers* series as shallow, but any program that is aware of Charles Lane is *ipso facto* authoritative and Walter himself was hardly profound when he complained in another *Times* "piece," as hacks call articles, that "with all the din about homosexuality… one may sigh for a return to a quieter time."

So keep it down, guys, and don't make Walter sigh. Real men don't sigh.

At least try to keep your activities as quiet as heterosexual ones, which do not seem too noisy to Walter (rape, war, mugging, wife beating, child abuse, violence in sports, and so on).

Naturally I hoped to find Lane encoded as "a confirmed bachelor" in his file at the Lincoln Center Library. It was a poignant experience to read that he is married and the father of two (one F., one M.).

That I have fallen for a player his age, fallen as I did for Bomba the Jungle Boy and at least two Dead End Kids, offers hope to senior sex objects that even they can find romance.

Lane, Turner, and Walburn are part of a blessed and enchanted group, numbering in the hundreds, who brought their own personalities to every picture they made and gave pretty much the same performance in every picture. They weren't, and couldn't be, scripted or directed. The genius of the directors—Capra in the case of *State of the Union*—lay in knowing these supporting players, knowing what they did, having a taste for it, putting them on camera, and letting them "go." The directors' genius in putting these specialty numbers in their pictures was executive rather than creative. It was the supporting players who created from scripts which may have had nothing more for them than such things as

Lulubelle Alexander: (Laughs.)

Just as men who have a fetish for athletic supporters find them more alluring than the hairy peekers and balls they support, so do movie lovers often find the supporting players more entertaining than the stars they support.

STEVE MCQUEEN

McQueen by Penina Spiegel
Doubleday, 376 pages, $17.95

My Husband, My Friend by Neile McQueen Toffel
Atheneum, 325 pages, $17.95

Steve McQueen (1930–1980) wore kotex; he "suffered from painfully inflamed hemorrhoids," Penina Spiegel writes in *McQueen*, "and had to wear two sanitary napkins to ease his discomfort while riding [motorcycles]."

Not only does this revelation lessen the allure of McQueen's butt; it symbolizes the fraudulence of the heterosexual front.

Ought Penny (for I prefer that over "Penina") to be telling us these things? Ought she, for instance, to quote a friend of Steve's saying, "I've been in a room with McQueen, three or four guys, one chick. One guy had it up her cunt, she was jacking two guys off, sucking another guy off. One guy was jacking on her." The purist would complain that this classic pornographic tableau lacked a "guy" giving it to the "chick" in the ass, but the ratio of "guys" to "chick" is already homosexual enough. In non-fiction, the truth is always in good taste, always in style; the whole truth; and this is that Steve McQueen was not only one of the most alluring movie stars but also one of the rottenest. As can be seen in Spiegel's book and in a book by one of his wives, *My Husband, My Friend* by Neile McQueen Toffel, he was beautiful but dumb, plus stingy, mean, petty, selfish, and hateful. McQueen's inflamed asshole underwent additional and regular invasions when he was dying in Mexico under the bizarre care of a dentist named William Donald Kelley, who had abandoned his original oral specialty and was concentrating, for some reason, on such anal procedures as coffee enemas and "rectal enzyme implants" in order to "cure" cancer. In submitting to this medical outlaw, McQueen demonstrated one last time that he is to be remembered more for his butt than his brains; earlier signs that he was neither bright nor educated were his fear that he was becoming "impudent" (impotent), his insistence that "obsequious" be removed from a script because he didn't know its meaning, his belief that the Dominican Republic (where he once worked as a "towel boy" in a whorehouse) was the Dominion Republic, and so on.

The question of whether his asshole had been invaded early in life, as it was so often at the end, is inevitable in light of the fact that, after being abandoned by his parents and becoming a hobo at age 14, he wound up in Boys Republic, a reform school in Chino, California, where newcomers had to serve as "slaves" for the older boys. The question is not answered in these books.

His work as a waiter in a Port Arthur, Texas, whorehouse balanced the nasty boys-only ambience of the reform school with nasty heterosexual role models. This was ideal background for the Marine Corps, which craves dirty low-down boys as much as many homosexuals do.

When he got out of the Marines, he had a somewhat sissy introduction to his profession; his letter of acceptance by the Neighborhood Playhouse, a New York acting school, instructed him to bring "shorts, a T-shirt, a dance belt, white cotton socks, and ballet slippers." He always felt that acting was a sissy profession, and I suppose he was right. As soon as he took up acting, he also took up motorcycles; they were his "balls." He would say, "Do these look like the hands of an actor?"

With unconvincing modesty, he said in public, "I sure don't get goose pimples when I look in the mirror." But he did, according to both books, like to look in the mirror. "His body," Mrs. McQueen writes, "was his religion. He worked out for two hours daily. He was vain.…"

A typical heterosexual, he "was desperately afraid of growing old."

"Turning forty," Mrs. McQueen writes, "was terribly bad for him."

He was short; a caption under a photograph showing Steve with four companions points out that "he's standing on tiptoes. Steve made everyone scrunch down so he wouldn't be the shortest."

> The blue jeans were bought three or four dozen at a time, washed many times over for shrinkage, and then especially bleached by the studio's wardrobe department to make them look well worn. They were tailored to his form afterward.

Like the boxer Muhammad Ali, Steve thought he was "beautiful," but where Ali may have been kidding at least a little bit, Steve meant it.

Dustin Hoffman he regarded as "one ugly cat. Good actor, yeah, but he sure is homely."

"Time after time," Mrs. McQueen writes, "Steve would stare at his image in the mirror and say to me, 'Look at that, baby, take a look at that face and that body and tell me the truth. Who would you pick, him [Hoffman] or me?"

In one of their numerous brawls, Mrs. McQueen broke the mirror in Steve's hotel room. It was the cruelest thing she could have done; comparable to pouring an alcoholic's bottle down the drain. An alcoholic can get another bottle, and Steve another mirror; but the wait is agony.

There are men so enamored of their own bodies and their own cocks that their own nudity, rather than any external sex object, gives them a hard-on, and almost any hole will do.

According to a friend, Steve "was the world's champ at getting laid in the bathroom of an airplane. He'd get on a plane and before it got to New York he'd be gettin' it on in the toilet."

Among other things, he liked what a friend called "poop shooting." (A variant spelling in some parts of the United States is "poop chuting.") Poop shooting is not entered in medical and psychiatric reference books here, but could conceivably be in Southern California. It means simply what in Pittsburgh is called "shit cocking" and elsewhere "butt fucking."

Steve boasted that he had sex with all of his "leading ladies." Mrs. McQueen says all but two. Suzanne Pleshette was one of the two and Candy Bergen perhaps the other. The only co-star Mrs. McQueen specifically identifies as having sex with Steve is Lee Remick, the dirty thing.

When Steve "lazily, sweetly" said to Pleshette, "Get me some popcorn," she was healthy and intelligent enough to say, "Get it yourself." Mrs. McQueen, possibly because she was Filipino, waited on Steve "hand and foot." So did another wife, Ali McGraw, at first, "fetching him his beer and giggling prettily with embarrassment when he burped hugely and openly." Does love mean wanting someone to wait on you? But it soon became apparent that Ali, an upper-income type, was slumming with Steve and betraying her early promise as the winner of the award given to that girl "who best reflects the highest ideals of Rosemary Hall" (her prep school). Steve McQueen was hardly one of the ideals of Rosemary Hall, and when he complained about her fried chicken she wisely picked up the platter and threw it at him.

"Private, personal lovemaking, a one-on-one experience with a woman," Spiegel writes, "was not nearly as titillating [to Steve] as sex with an audience. 'Steve liked groups,' says one of his intimates. 'He liked showing off his body and peepee. The first guy to take his shirt off was Steve; the first to drop his pants was Steve.'"

Spiegel attributes his fondness for orgies to a fondness for women, but it is a widely accepted view in psychology that these scenes—especially those in which several males have one woman—are a socially acceptable substitute for homosexuality, a way for men to enjoy being with other men when they are bareassed and in heat.

"We had some good times together," a friend of Steve's said. "We did some funny things with ladies.... He was screwing some broad from behind, she was sucking my cock, and we were looking and talking to each other. She was just a piece of ass, that's all." Forgetting "love" for the moment, who "likes" whom in this scene? Do the two males like the woman or does each male like the friend to whom he is talking? Note also the use of the flattering word "ladies"—common in rock music and show biz and thus in the general heterosexual population—to conceal contempt for women. Heterosexual males evidently feel it is so awful to be a woman they cannot even use the word woman, but must use "lady" (e.g., "M'lady she gives good head"), just as racist cops feel it's so awful to be Puerto Rican they don't use that word but rather "Spanish."

Steve, another friend said, enjoyed having sex with a woman "who was still warm as it were, from sex with his buddies." Coming this close to "sex with his buddies," he had what a therapist called a "deep-seated fear of homosexuality" and made an ostentatious public display of non-homosexuality. It was more than would seem necessary. When a friend embraced him on a set Steve pushed him away with "Not in front of the crew." When another friend, John Miller, asked if he'd ever had a gay experience, Steve was enraged; he offered to "prove" his heterosexuality by going over to Central Park West and beating up "two fags." But that might prove only that he had a homosexual problem. When he learned in an anonymous 'phone call that his name was on a list of homosexuals in an "underground book," Mrs. McQueen writes that the "blood drained from Steve's face. He was thunderstruck. There was a long pause and he looked at me unseeingly." Later when he referred to "that fuckin' list," Mrs. McQueen knew he was referring to the list of homosexuals:

> That fuckin' list had twisted my head so bad, baby, that I felt I had to prove to the whole goddam world I was Steve McQueen, super stud.

It was an odd reaction if there were in fact no gay experiences in his life, and it seems odd too that Mrs. McQueen regards the publication of the list as nothing less than a "point of no return" in their failing marriage.

In the absence of any reported gay experiences, the theory of one of Steve's friends seems the most reasonable: "Even if Steve were gay, he wouldn't have let himself be. He was such a macho bastard that if he had that tendency he wouldn't have done it." There are men called closet queens who have sex with other men but are too conventional and too insecure to talk about it; there are men more remote called vault queens who merely want sex with other men but are too conventional and insecure even to have it. McQueen's attitude and behavior are merely suspect, not conclusive. As I say, typically heterosexual.

He was a wife-beater, but, perhaps because she'd been imprisoned by the Japanese at age nine in World War II, "was forced to 'do certain things' that she still finds it hard to name and to watch fellow prisoners being tortured," and had no models to compare her own marriage to,

> Steve's behavior didn't strike Neile as being unusual. She just accepted the fact that all men are difficult creatures who require constant petting on the part of the female to make them even remotely civilized. "I thought my married life was normal," she says.

The horrible thing is that maybe it was.

JANE RUSSELL

Jane Russell's autobiography was published by Franklin Watts, Inc. in 1985 under the characteristically informative title, *Jane Russell*. The photograph reproduced there of Jane as a child shows an ease before the camera of a born star.

Though it was more than a half-century ago, the photograph is curiously contemporary. Her childish ensemble, with its lack of concern for lines which reveal the body, is "in" today.

The still of Jane in antique bloomers was made almost 40 years ago but it too is, ideologically, ultra-modern. It's from *The Paleface* (1948), 15 years before the "women's liberation movement," but it is still an image that is competitive with any that movement has generated. In light of the degradation of women inflicted by men who by definition, but only by definition, love them, there is nothing more inspiring than a woman wearing holsters on her underwear.

Between takes, Jane posed with her four brothers, who, sadly, were not posing in *their* underwear; the photograph shows that the three of them, like their sister, were lookers, and might well have looked good in Jockey shorts or even boxer shorts, to say nothing of jock straps.

The Jane Russell of *Paleface* is an alliterationist's dream: surly, sullen, scornful, snarling. How could she, armed with two heaters, seem enchanting while another pistol packin' mamma, Nancy Reagan, who slept with a gat under her pillow at the Reagan ranch in Pacific Palisades, seem, in some sense, an old cunt? I think it's that Jane was just being bratty for fun, while Nancy is mean for real. Nancy's warm smile (I have twice in my life wondered whether she and President Reagan wear that smile even whilst taking a shit) conceals a cold heart; Jane's sneer is a false front for affection.

While tangling assholes with such co-stars as Bob Hope, Vincent Price, Robert Mitchum, and Victor Mature (the last three of whom were ideal partners for her; the tragedy is that she never played opposite Sheldon Leonard), she is credibly contemptuous but it is clear that she really likes them. She also, she says in her book, liked them offscreen. But Nancy's nastiness—when, for example, she is giving a hotel manager hell for not having the Presidential Suite just so—is authentic.

I gather from the stills from such pictures as *The French Line* and *Gentlemen Prefer Blondes*, both released in 1953, that there was another Jane Russell, who could project a huge smile to the balcony after doing a strenuous dance number. But for some reason I find such efforts uninteresting, and Frank Rich of the *New York Times*, similarly, has taken to task Tommy Tune, the tuxedoed tap dancer from Texas, for this embarrassingly accommodating attitude toward the audience, this begging for its approval. There is something more impressive than a performer who tries so hard to please an audience and that is one who, like the Jane Russell of *The Paleface* and of three pictures released in 1952 (*Macao*, *The Las Vegas Story*, and *Son of Paleface*) seems disappointed that the audience has failed to please her. I realize that this attitude is annoying to managers of corporate profit centers, but I like it; I'm sorry.

Macao is triumphantly vulgar; it's overwhelming. *The Las Vegas Story* is almost as sleazy and almost as good; this absurd city is the perfect subject for Hollywood and Jane Russell and Victor Mature the perfect people to treat it seriously. The same people who designed the hotels could have designed Jane Russell. *Son of Paleface* must be a lesbian's dream, featuring both a feminine Jane Russell who sings at the Dirty Shame and a really tough Russell in black drag who leads a gang of robbers. Though not a lesbian, I enjoyed her too. Bob Hope's surreal humor lowers the tone of the picture, but he was popular among the peasants, including producers and network presidents. I am not trying here to insult producers and network presidents; I assume it is understood that to make a motion picture or a TV show that will meet the requirements of many millions of people, the executive must have the mind—don't you see?—of a peasant.

In *The Paleface*, seen at 2 a.m. October 29, 1985 on channel 5, Russell is discovered in an ideal setting for one so hard: jail. She is not merely standing behind bars as an ordinary movie star would, but standing with one foot up on a seat. Now there's a real jailbird.

She creates a rapidly and richly detailed portrait of a tough. Breaking out of jail, she takes time to throw water at the sherrif. Meeting the governor, she accepts a drink only after wiping the glass on her sleeve. Kissing Bob Hope, she gives him a knock-out blow on the back of his head.

Hope, a pot-bellied, wide-hipped sissy of 45, has come west from the effete east. The east may have been effete, but never this effete:

HOPE: We're Mr. and Mrs. Potter. I'm Mister.

His marriage to Jane, like many, perhaps most, marriages, is a marriage of convenience, the union of an especially overripe fruit and an especially tough fruit fly. Their relationship is established economically:

RUSSELL: Oh, shut up.

HOPE: Yes, ma'am.

When their wagon reaches its destination, Jane vaults out, Hope minces out. When a room clerk asks if they'd like a boy, meaning a bellboy, Hope giggles. After carrying her across the threshold, he says, "Tomorrow night you carry me."

One minute he's swishing, wetting a finger and running it over an eyebrow; the next minute he's horny for Jane, or what he thinks is Jane. "Smooth, smooth," he sighs as he feels some skin. It turns out to be that of a male Indian, but clearly, he will do; they kiss.

Unable to mask his natural nelliness, Hope solved the problem by exaggerating it, trying to show that all of it, even the part that existed before his burlesque, was an effort to be funny. He seldom attempted to portray a serious heterosexual relationship; in a Hope picture, it is heterosexuality that is campy. He has always seemed sexually inadequate, even sexually handicapped.

Hope's children are all adopted. That his wife, Delores, may not be disappointed in their marriage is suggested by the fact that the sort of man whose company she enjoys is a priest. When priests break their vows of chastity, they tend to do it with boys, not women.

I should add that it's perfectly understandable and fine that many women do not want "studs." Why should they? It's also fine if they do. Why not?

It is usually homosexuals who have to bear the burden of males who, like Bob Hope and William F. Buckley, Jr., seem to experience heterosexuality by attacking homosexuality. As recently as July 4, 1986, Hope said that the Statue of Liberty has AIDS but that he doesn't know whether she got it from the mouth of the Hudson or the Staten Island ferry. It is the joke of a man still, in his 83rd year, in sexual despair; a man whose material, designed when he was young to claim indirectly that he is heterosexual, now seems to claim that he once was. He is Hollywood's senior sissy and fag-baiter.

His sexual claim is a comic version of that made in all serious-ness on TV and in his *National Review* by Buckley and some curious creatures in his crowd—Joseph Sorban, Alan Sears, and

William Brookhiser. Were they to confine themselves to print, they would merely seem suspect; they are fools to appear on TV, where they can clearly be seen to fall into the range of male sexuality between eunuchoid and sissy.

There is no obvious motive for Jane Russell's charming churlishness on screen; it was often gratuitous, more than the script called for or than the director, I should think, would allow. It would seem, then, natural. But it wasn't; according to her book, to her TV "talk show" appearances, and to Arthur Bell, who had lunch with her, she was plain Jane in the best sense, a friendly, foul-mouthed, pious Christian. I can only theorize that she regarded the picture business as so shitty, as it were—and it arguably was and is—that she felt she should act accordingly.

Her first and longest marriage was to a Los Angeles Rams foot-ball player. He looked austere, asexual, uptight, inadequate. But isn't that why men play football? He was mean and nasty to Jane but not to football freaks. "I couldn't understand," she writes, "why Robert couldn't be with me instead of the boys at cocktail time."

At the opening of *The Las Vegas Story* in Las Vegas, "He wasn't content to just be with me. He kept looking for Kelly." Kelly was a friend of his, a sports announcer. After a fight in their hotel room, Robert left Jane. "I called Kelly's room," she writes, "and... Robert answered."

Jane had had an abortion earlier. She wanted a baby now but she and Robert couldn't make it.

A confident intellectual can afford to enjoy Jane's portrayals of gang leaders and club singers (sometimes whores in the original properties); her screen character was a little like Mae West's, the trustworthy tramp, the outlaw who's more moral than the pillars of society. The rising middle class, however, must use such people as Jane Russell as rungs in the ladder to respectability and must represent themselves as being cultured consumers of such officially established and approved artists as Meryl Streep. The *New York Times*, for example, regards Katharine Hepburn as a legitimate actress, though Jane Russell is more legitimate in the sense of being more real, just as the *Times* puts statements from the Pope on page one, even though they are the mad ravings of a sexual psychopath and numerous other men and women are healthier and more Christian representatives of Catholicism.

What sounds like the most enchanting Jane Russell performance ever is one we cannot see. But some lucky people saw it "in 1965 or 1966." I would welcome a letter from anyone who did or who can supply the newspaper reviews, which "slaughtered" it. Jane appeared in a hastily put together run of *Pal Joey* in Toronto. "None of us," she writes, "knew what the shit we were doing at all…. We must have looked like a bunch of clowns stumbling through our dances, fumbling lines, bumping into each other, forgetting crucial business, misplacing props." On the third night, she "turned to the orchestra pit and shouted, 'Hold it! I'm going to get this damn song ["Bewitched, Bothered, and Bewildered"] right if it's the last thing I do. Start over!'" That's my idea of a showstopping number and of a thrilling evening in the theater. The image of Jane "bumping into" other players is especially breathtaking.

She, of course, regarded it as a disaster. Nor does she seem to understand how incomparable her screen work is. But Robert Mitchum does; he calls her "an authentic original." "I got little artistic satisfaction from my work," she writes. "I was definitely a victim of Hollywood typecasting." William Wyler wanted her for *Friendly Persuasion* opposite Gary Cooper; had she done the part, "that could have broken the pattern." She also oughtn't to have turned down *Love Me or Leave Me* opposite Jimmy Cagney. She didn't get many offers that good; the number of producers and reviewers who are capable of comprehending the fact that a woman who looks like Jane Russell can also act is just too small.

But if she was a victim, we are the beneficiaries. Nothing is more threatening to a voyeur than an exhibitionist; Jane Russell seems unaware she's being watched.

LYNN BARI

I wrote just five words about Lynn Bari in a book review, but they were enough to produce a letter from a reader on 72nd Street. It's true that my evaluation of Bari was as ardent as it was brief; I called her "the greatest star of all." The reader agreed. He wanted to meet not only Bari but even me.

I can understand his response; I suppose most of us enjoy having our tastes validated by others. When, for example, I heard that the favorite movie stars of a certain man in Brooklyn are Sheldon Leonard, the Central Casting hood, and Bobby Jordan, the antsy Dead End Kid, I became more certain than ever before that they are two of my favorites also. The fact that the Brooklynite is in truck parts only enhanced his authority (and also his allure). It would have been sufficient if he'd just been in auto parts; to be in truck parts is even better. He would be exposed daily to blue collars who need these parts (or perhaps it is they who expose themselves to him), and his endorsement of the breathtakingly blue collar Sheldon Leonard and Bobby Jordan gives them, and my taste for them, an added authenticity.

I did meet the Bari fan from 72nd Street. He has a number of things going for him. A half-dozen that come to mind at once are that he is young, handsome, and has (in order of their importance to me, not to him) an interesting career, enough money, a good apartment, and a lover. Yet his two main interests in life appear to be Lynn Bari and Mary Beth Hughes. Though he was born after they made their pictures, he has fallen for them in recent years while watching their "oldies" on TV and *en cassette*.

Thus the revival at the Regency Theater in the fall of 1986 of a picture featuring both Bari and Hughes—*Sleepers West* (1941)—

was an important event in his life. (They were both *Orchestra Wives* [1942] also, a title which inspired Pauline Kael's brilliant observation that it "sounds like a statistical classification.") He alerted me to the Regency revival, and I went too.

In addition to the guaranteed glamour of Lynn Bari, *Sleepers West* offers the glamour of the old railroad sleeping and dining cars, which I believe are no longer available. After a glamorous transcontinental journey on one of those trains, Bari and her suitor, Lloyd Nolan, arrive in California, where Bari has the picture's last word: They are in a restaurant in San Francisco; Bari orders from the waitress, Mary Beth Hughes, a sandwich with onion; Nolan asks her not to have the onion; Bari (pert, perky, and peppy to the end) complies with his request by changing her order to the equally aromatic garlic.

Done by another actress, this finale could have seemed at least a little sordid; its theme, after all, is bad breath. But it is impossible that Bari—perfectly groomed, immaculate, heavily made up, and powerfully lit—could have bad breath. Not Lynn Bari.

In the same way, Bari's other roles would have been drastically different if played by other actresses. A Bari picture is memorable more for what she contributed to it than for what the writer and director did. Like such more successful players as Mae West, Bari played herself. Her popularity is thus a tribute to her not merely as an actress, but as a person; as a woman. She was popular also among the studio crews, who admired what Richard Lamparski calls her "unpretentious, direct manner."

In the magnificent *Mr. Moto's Gamble* (1938), seen on TV in 1986, Bari is a soft-bitten news hen surrounded by hard-bitten news hawks, one of whom makes a patronizing remark about women reporters. Bari de-balls him with one line—but she delivers it in such a good-natured way that the men enjoy laughing at her emasculation of them. What we have in this deceptively light little exchange is nothing less than the problem of the white heterosexual majority's maltreatment of minorities. Another actress might have turned it into a bitter, angry scene (and could certainly be forgiven for doing so, for white heterosexual males can be bitchy when they safely outnumber a victim). Bari's easy triumph over the men does not move the plot along but is entertaining to the humanist who is

less interested in plot than in people and in how they handle problems. Bari would make a good model for homosexuals to follow in dealing with males who represent themselves as being heterosexual.

In *Nocturne* (1946), seen at 3 a.m. December 5, 1983, on channel 9, Bari plays a small-time actress who earned only $68.00 for her last part in a picture, yet has (by 1986 Manhattan standards) a lavish apartment, and she casually tells George Raft, "If you'll pull that mink coat out of the closet I'll tag along with you." She could thus be, as played by certain other actresses, a slut. But the Lynn Bari who cannot have bad breath and cannot be cowed by hard-bitten news hawks also cannot be a slut. She is utterly credible when she says; "Can I help it if people give me things?" Her appearance and manner suggest that if she has been sleeping with some men, they were worth sleeping with; it was for affection, not gain, and they liked her too or they wouldn't have given her "things."

Another *Nocturne* scene invites a sluttish performance. George Raft is trying to befriend Bari by a swimming pool. She tells him he's "pretty dull" but amends her opinion after she sees him push another man into the pool: "Maybe not as dull as I thought." Raft pushed the man into the pool in anger, not in fun; but in Bari's reading, her character is not a slut who admires muscle, but rather, to use Dan Rather's inspired phrase for United States Senators, a merry prankster.

Even so, Raft suspects her of something much worse than bad breath (murder).

RAFT: Mom, how would you feel if I married a murderess?
MOM: I wouldn't mind so long as she's a nice girl.

Bari is a nice girl, but Raft remains skeptical. "That's great acting, sister," he tells her, "but you're going to have a tough audience: 12 citizens."

But perhaps it is her sister who killed the man.

BARI: She went there to say goodbye.
RAFT: You sure she didn't say it with a .38?

But it is Raft who, for reasons which need not concern us here, or for that matter need not concern us even while watching the picture, gets arrested. The cop apologizes: "I'm sorry. I like you, but …." Raft apologizes back—"I'm sorry, I like you too"—and then knocks the cop out cold.

Written by Jonathan Latimer, *Nocturne* is full of such enchanting action and dialogue, which is simultaneously tough and funny. The same cannot be said for another major Bari picture, *China Girl* (1943), written by the famous hack, Ben Hecht. Hecht was a snob of the worst kind, an economic and sexual snob. He boasted about how fast he wrote his scripts and how much money he made from them, but this is something to be ashamed of, not proud of. He seems to admire the Gene Tierney part he wrote for the picture because she's a missionary's daughter and went to Vassar, and seems to scorn Lynn Bari's part because she is not the sort of woman who can be forever fulfilled by one man (for example, Ben Hecht?) and is obviously not Ivy League, or even Big Ten. But "Vassar graduate" is an economic classification and not, as poor Hecht seems to think, an intellectual and moral one; after all, Nancy Reagan, the President's wife, went to a similar college, Smith, but all this means is that her stepfather, a surgeon, could afford it. It does not mean (especially in view of her coldness toward poor and unsuccessful people) that she is intellectual or moral.

But Bari, without even trying, sabotages Hecht's script and steals the show from that gorgeous zombie, Gene Tierney, as even the *New York Times* and Leonard Maltin in his *TV Movies* are aware. "Bari best item in film," Maltin writes in his Tarzan-like English. I'm glad to see that he noticed, but I cannot endorse his depiction of Bari as an "item." As can be seen in a still from the film, she is considerably more than an item. She captures the audience's attention, if not that of the men in the still, who seem more interested in George Montgomery (and he was, it is true, interesting). At first glance, the still looks like a scene in a gay bar that caters to men who like military drag. In unwitting, and unconvincing, compensation, Hecht has Montgomery say that there's "only one thing real about dames." Bari: "What?" Montgomery: "This" (he forces a kiss on her). The scene must have been excessively, and thus inadequately, heterosexual even in 1943 and seems especially so today, when more secrets of male sexuality are available than in Hecht's time and heterosexual pretense no longer goes, as it did then, unchallenged, but is vulnerable to growing suspicions that the more heterosexual a man acts the less heterosexual he is.

In her youth, Bari was a creature of admirable energy and sophistication. Her sophistication may have come not from an internal source, but from an external one—-from the mere fact that, as she told Lamparski, she "made as many as three pictures at a time. I'd go from one set to another shooting people and stealing husbands…. I never knew what the hell the plots were." This is bound to produce a certain cool detachment, visible on the screen.

I hope Fox paid her well for all her work. It must have; she spent a million on one divorce alone (from Sid Luft). It was not merely that their marriage didn't work, but that Sid didn't either; a 1958 Associated Press dispatch quotes Bari as saying that he worked only a total of nine months during her eight year marriage to him. She won custody of their son. In what must be everyone's dream, "he and his mother share a pretty apartment overlooking the Pacific Ocean in Marina Del Rey, California," according to Lamparski.

During World War II, Bari would sometimes get up at dawn, go to a friendly neighborhood military camp, and dance the night away with the troops. The Lincoln Center library has a clipping of a photograph from a fan magazine which shows Bari inspecting rifles at a troop formation; she was a real sport. I should think only the one-fourth or so of the troops who were gay would know who she was, but I must be wrong; there was a large audience of males who could pass for "straight" at the Regency's revival of *Sleepers West*. I hope any reader who contributes to the fan mail which, Bari told Lamparski, she still gets, will tell her that she is still big box office in Manhattan.

I've never seen the picrures in which, as she says, she went around "shooting people." I can't, and won't, believe she ever shot a man who didn't deserve it. I have, however, seen a picrure in which Bari gives a *tour de force* demonstration of a sudden shift in both acting styles, from a heroine to a "heavy." It is *Abbott and Costello Meet the Keystone Kops* (1955). After an effusive, ladylike exchange with Abbott and Costello, Bari abruptly turns hard with her accomplice, Fred Clark: "Let's make our getaway before these suckers turn us in to the bunko squad."

Her charm, and that of such playmates as Peter Lorre, Fred Clark, and Slapsie Maxie Rosenbloom, seems wasted on the *New York Times*, which tends, in its TV listings, to value plot over people. I can understand how, after a hard day at the *New York Times*, the last thing a *Times* employee would want to see is a person, on or off screen. But in light of the *Times* emphasis upon plot, it is most extraordinary that the paper identifies the murder victim in *Nocturne* as a woman. It was a man. There's a big difference, bigger even than the difference between North and South Dakota, which the *Times* also confused in its coverage of the November, 1986 elections. The paper reported that Thomas A. Daschle ran for the U.S. Senate against the incumbent from North Dakota, but Daschle ran against the incumbent from *South* Dakota. He won. This news, however garbled by the *Times*, is good news, for Daschle is, as Lamparski calls Lynn Bari, "liberal politically." Hail Thomas Daschle! Hail Lynn Bari!

HEARTBREAK RIDGE

Heartbreak Ridge (1986) starts out as a heterosexual training film, but in 128 long, loud minutes only gets as far as non-homosexuality. But it's popular; many men and boys are in the same sexual fix and can enjoy seeing their failure validated on screen.

The lead—the elderly California millionaire, Clint Eastwood— also produced and directed the thing. It is thus utterly his picture and its homosexual obsession is his obsession; it is part of his personality, not part of the plot.

The picture's allure for heterosexual trainees is the same as the allure of the Marine Corps, which is its *mise en scène*. The picture, like the Marines and like football on TV, offers the promise that feelings of, and a reputation for, heterosexuality can be achieved by violence, without the need to fuck pussy.

It is a Reagan Era kind of heterosexuality, expressed through relentless boasts of masculinity and through the discharge of bullets, not sperm. Although they sing about having "a handful of pussy and a mouthful of ass," the recruits in the picture do not once get, or even try to get, a piece of tail. The picture's meaning finally is that, hard though the Marine Corps training may be, it's not as hard as the older kind of heterosexuality (loving women).

The advertised desire of the Marine Corps is that it "wants a few good men." This is embarrassingly like the desire of homosexuals. Many well-functioning homosexuals have had more than a few good Marines. The Marine Corps is nowhere near as gay as the Navy, but the recruits in *Heartbreak Ridge* and their sergeant, Clint Eastwood, are anxious to make it clear that while they don't have sex with women, they wouldn't with men either.

Clint tells them, "I'm not doing this because I want to take long showers with you assholes." And later, "This doesn't mean we're going to be swapping spit in the shower." He's reminiscent of a doorman in Manhattan I've heard of who will shout "straight" in bars, "I'm not gay." His fellow barflies assume he *is*; no one accuses him of being gay and his denial is of an accusation that comes from within himself.

As women in the picture are selected for their beauty, to show that the producer and director appreciate it, the men in *Heartbreak Ridge* (and in the Tom Cruise locker room picture, *All the Right Moves*) seem to have been selected for their lack of it, to prove that the producer and director isn't interested in it. If made by a man who doesn't have homosexuality on his mind, a picture about the Marine Corps which includes barracks and toilet scenes, as this one does, would automatically show some alluring male flesh. The lack of it in *Heartbreak Ridge* seems to be the result of a conscientiously executed policy. Even the recruits in Jockey shorts wear the waistband pulled down to reveal soft bellies. There is not a bare butt nor a prick in sight; in this group the tongue, not the prick, is the primary sexual organ. I don't mean to suggest that they're dick lickers, merely that they only say, but don't show, that they're "straight."

It's curiously pre-sexual; childish; bratty. Among the things America's fighting men in *Heartbreak Ridge* are fighting is s-x.

Even jacking off is forbidden, jokingly. "Just one shake of those wangs," Clint says as he passes by the urinals. "Anything more constitutes pleasure."

A life so austre has its own built-in compensation: an unusually butch obscenity. It's not a positive, erotic obscenity, but a negative one: "I'll cut off your head and shit down your neck." And so on.

Clint calls his recruits "pussies" and "ladies." Clint is going to make "life takers and heart breakers" of them.

He has done no less than three tours of duty in Viet Nam. I thought it had been settled years ago that Viet Nam did more harm than good to both Asia and America. Now comes Eastwood being proud of it.

He is a little above Rambo; he doesn't wear Johnson's Baby Oil. But just not wearing baby oil is not enough. While in Viet Nam and Korea, he didn't write to his wife, Marsha Mason. "I swear, not knowing was the worst," she says, and slaps him—twice. I'd have thought knowing he didn't care enough to write was the worst.

Clint reads women's magazines in an effort to improve his relationship with Marsha. Never before has heterosexuality been shown so literally as unnatural, learned behavior.

At the end, Clint and Marsha walk off into the sunset with flags flying and a Marine band playing, not because they get along together but because he'll soon be retiring form the Corps and will have to have "something." She'll be able to handle him; she can shout "fuck" as well as any Marine. With such a skill, she could have become a bigger star in today's pictures than she is. But she may have been held back by her fleshy nose, which contrasts to Clint's exquisitely chiseled one.

He also has the crazed eyes of a fanatic sunbelt Republican, the same eyes as Lieutenant Colonel Oliver North, who, by coincidence, I saw on TV the same day I saw *Heartbreak Ridge*. In a televised congressional hearing, Ollie took the Fifth Amendment to avoid answering questions about smuggling arms and money to Iran and Nicaragua. The two Marines, Ollie in life and Clint on screen, share also the same paranoia about "Commie bastids" and the same regal grandeur of men who know what's best for us, sneaking around the Constitution and the will of Congress to achieve it. The same epitaph could be used for both: "At home and abroad, he helped increase the gunfire."

In contrast to Clint's high cheekbones and sunken cheeks (the look so prized by actresses), Ollie has the fat-headed look of a man who enjoys a good healthy shit and very little else.

But it was Ollie who talked President Reagan into the invasion which is the climax of *Hearbreak Ridge*, the invasion of the island of Grenada.

"The island of what?" a Marine asks when Eastwood announces that that's where they're going. This is where the charm of the blue collar male ends, in his willingness to ship out and shoot people in islands he's never heard of. Breathtakingly virile on the surface, he lacks the deeper strength of men who don't *have* to go to Grenada or Viet Nam. Professor Charles Shively of the University of Massachusens feels that the only result of the rescue of Grenada's American medical students, who'd been rejected by medical schools in the States, is the distribution throughout the health care business of incompetent medics; and he has expressed the fear that through their incompetence they may kill more Americans than would have been killed had the students been left in the hands of Commie bastids in Grenada. Better that an incompetent medic die at the hands of a Commie bastid than that a competent patient die at the hands of an incompetent doctor.

In addition to the general objections that even many heterosexuals have to people like Reagan and Clint Eastwood, I object on the specific ground that these professional anti-Communists are themselves sexual communists, who want the state to police sex in order to make all citizens share in the general sexual impoverishment of our culture. If communism is an assault by the poor against the rich, sexual communism is an assault by the sexually cold against the sexually gifted.

The sexual inadequacies of people like the Pope, Jerry Falwell, William F. Buckley, Jr., Patrick Buchanan, and Clint Eastwood would be none of my business if the afflicted would suffer in silence. But they try to punish the sexually healthy, often homosexuals.

There is something drastically wrong when a male comes out of the blue-collar class—or on second thought out of any class—

looking as exquisite as Clint Eastwood. Like his father, he worked in gas stations, but he obviously didn't belong there. In one of his first movies, *Francis Joins the Navy* (1955), he looked like a typical chorus boy and had an embarrassingly accommodating manner. With the mammoth commercial success of his cop and cowboy pictures, which he cranked out with the help of such kinky members of the Hollywood gun club as Michael Cimino and John Milius, he has long since ceased to be accommodating and has turned really nasty in a righteous, right-wing way. But he still looks as precious as he did as a chorus boy. There is not now, and was not then, any of the glamour of the gas station in his makeup. The glamour in his makeup is his makeup—Max Factor or whatever.

No less an authority than the *Village Voice* says that he looks homosexual; rumors that he *is* might not have reached print during his lifetime if his good friend, Burt Reynolds, had not acknowledged (and denied) them in interviews. Burt's denials—and thus inevitably the rumors—have been widely circulated.

Clint's bratty mind, like that of Hitler and Pope Paul, is not to be taken seriously. But the numbers, the following of these people, can be. The grosses of Clint's pictures are as gross as his message. *Heartbreak Ridge* won the approval of both the bourgeois reviewers and the man in the street. Interviewed for the *New York Post* Popcorn Panel, the man in the street felt the same way the indoor reviewers did (but did not use review lingo like "riveting"). The *Times* is normally opposed to the expression of heterosexuality through obscenity or gunfire, but an astonishingly decadent review in that paper by Vincent Canby evaluated *Heartbreak Ridge* as "hilariously obscene." This is like admiring Hitler for his oratorical style. Vince's street counterpart is Toby Axelrod, aged 20 and a member of the *Post* Popcorn Panel, who said, "I like Clint Eastwood, especially when he talks dirty. The nasty language was graphic and good." The plump, Teutonic Richard Schickel, who is well established in the *Times* as an admirer of butch males, found in *Heartbreak Ridge* that Clint's "toughness is all the tougher." *Cf.* Jeff Sherman, 22, of the *Post* Popcorn Panel: "Killing looked easy in this, and that'll appeal to a lot of people." Roger Ebert, the Rex

Reed of Chicago, is bullied enough and I won't add to it by quoting from his favorable review.

Perhaps things are not as bad as they seem; I had the impression that the hundreds of overweight but undeveloped young crackers in attendance at *Heartbreak Ridge* when I saw it at the RKO Warner December 9 would support any invasion of any island President Reagan cares to select but would rather watch than do it. They may be like the bar stool athletes drinking a bottle or a can of Coors, the heterosexual beer, who gain intimations of heterosexuality by watching football and hockey on TV, but don't actually want to play and have their teeth knocked out and their knees smashed.

In a dramatic illustration of the readiness of heterosexuals to call each other heroes, the Marine Corps awarded more medals for the Grenada invasion than there were troops in the invasion, according to the *New York Times*. If there are any medals left, President Reagan ought to give one to Clint Eastwood for making *Heartbreak Ridge*; like John Wayne and Reagan himself, Clint has confined his military heroism to the screen and has never had the opportunity to earn combat decorations except in second unit footage.

On screen and off, the problem is not that our military heroes are too heterosexual, but that they aren't—don't you see?—heterosexual enough.

ART FROM THE POST-HETEROSEXUAL AGE

It has just occurred to me, after years of using film stills from The Museum of Modern Art to illustrate my articles about "oldies" on TV, that I write not only about films but also about their stills. The stills themselves are art objects. They can be studied in silence and solitude at length, and can offer a more detailed experience of actors and acting than do fast moving pictures.

Sometimes stills reveal information that is hardly available in a motion picture, sometimes even information that is in conflict with the point of the movie. Years ago I made a second visit to an ordinary Eighth Avenue bar in Manhattan solely to see its enlarged photograph of the young Gary Cooper wearing lipstick, which I had earlier found fascinating. It was an image of advanced decadence, a shocking secret about one of America's most famous movie stars. While doing an article on Cooper recently, I remembered the barroom photograph and asked the Museum if it could supply a similar one. From its archive of literally a million stills, the Museum produced Figure 1. By enlarging Cooper from the still, we have perhaps America's best contribution to the artistic record of a rare type of man, a type that is more a Teutonic than an American specialty— the man who is at once beautiful and tough, the soldier in lipstick. It is an image as characteristic of Berlin 1930 as of Hollywood 1928, the year in which *Legion of the Condemned*, the film it illustrates, was released. It is competitive with the Nazis in lipstick and lingerie in *The Damned* (1969) and with the magnificent Colonel Alfred Redl, the World War I Austrian army ace, in whose apartment raiders found perfume, articles of feminine attire, and photographs of Redl having sex with other Austrian army men, sometimes nude, sometimes wearing women's clothing (and perhaps perfume). The police

Figure 1. Still from *Legion of the Condemned* with Gary Cooper, the soldier in lipstick.

in all cultures have the most moving photographs; in America, newspapers routinely report that police confiscate thousands of photographs taken by men of naked young boys.

Off camera Cooper fulfilled, at least a little bit, the erotic promise of the still—that a man who wears lipstick will do a lot of things with a lot of people who pay him the attention he is trying to get. According to the literature, Cooper had a big prick, the habit of hanging out nude off camera while making a picture, some sex with men, and a lot of it with women (Lupe Velez, Clara Bow, Patricia Neal, and so on).

I had suspected, but could not be sure, that some of the men in the old "talkies", including Cooper and even John Wayne, seemed to be wearing lipstick; the still from the Museum confirmed this. Sometimes, as in Figure 2, a still offers the chance to discover someone or something that is not noticeable at all in the movie it represents. To illustrate an article on *Stage Door Canteen* (1943), I asked the Museum for a still showing a group scene at this World War II center for the military. One face in the still it sent, which I hadn't noticed at all in the movie itself, arrested my attention. I examined the face, a sailor's, under a magnifying glass and found that it warranted enlarging. He looks like an actual person, rather than an actor; he looks more interesting, in fact, than many stars. He and his partner, dancing together but remote from each other, offer a harshly realistic image of heterosexuality as a duty more than

Figure 2. Still from *Stage Door Canteen*. Heterosexuality, more a duty than a desire.

a desire. I find this poignant, especially for the woman; women, unlike homosexuals, are brought up to expect something from men. The sailor and his dancing partner present a startling conflict with the joyous heterosexuality depicted in *Stage Door Canteen* and in films in general, and could be used to illustrate the dawning of the post-heterosexual age which began in World War II.

As I prefer people like the sailor in Figure 2, to actors, my bias also is for:

> anatomy against art,
> photographs against paintings,
> prose against poetry,
> the writing of non-writers against that of writers,
> the grace of people in the street against the excessive grace of dancers.

At a New York discotheque recently, when the male whores who had been commissioned to perform as strippers failed to show, members of the audience were pressed into service. I asked a young man I was talking to—handsome, stolid, blue collar, even oafish in appearance and manner—if he would strip. He said no. I said, "You know how to take your clothes off, don't you?" "Yeah, but I don't know how to dance." But that was his charm, that he looked to be the opposite of a dancer. He was simply a man I would enjoy watching undress. Had he done so, his act would have provided a more authentic exhibitionist-voyeur experience than did the men who stripped in time to the music, which set up an artistic barrier between the viewer and the object. Artistry, culture, and refinement frequently set up a barrier.

This is especially true in writing about sex. I prefer the work of people to that of "writers." The strongest writing about sex is on the men's room walls and I try to include this style of writing in my anthologies of men's sex histories. A man I know advertised in a New York sex paper for "dirty phone calls" from heterosexual (or, to use the hyperbolic slang, "straight") men. He received about 800 calls. He enjoyed them, as did the callers; a couple of hundred of them have become regular callers. They evidently have no other outlet for certain desires and behaviour. I asked the man if he would try to get his callers to write letters to me for anonymous publication in my books. Even though he is educated, and intelligent as well, he said no—they didn't sound like writers. But that is why I wanted them. I don't want artistic, cultured, and refined writers, who use "one" for "I" (one suspects, one hopes, one wishes, one wonders) and who continue all their lives to have that sense appropriate only in freshman French, the sense of *déjà vu*.

Figure 3 offers four masterpieces by that Divine Chiseler, Nature—the sculptor of billions of unspeakably erotic masterworks. The photographing of these four butts could be said to require even more artistry than painting them would; for while a painter can apply shading as he sees fit, light is the photographer's paint and he cannot be certain, be he a still photographer or a cinematographer, whether he has the shading he wants until he sees a positive print of the negative he has exposed. The shading in Figure 3—a still from *A Bigger Splash*—is maddening. Except for an imperfection on the left thigh of the figure on the right and one on the right nate of the figure that is second from the right, the youths have (and perhaps are) perfect asses, statuesque in the sense that they are hairless. The photograph can be even more satisfying than a statue that does not take the light or, as happens more often, has little light to take, or the wrong light. The thighs of the four youths are sufficiently closed to exempt them from charges of pornography (not that there is

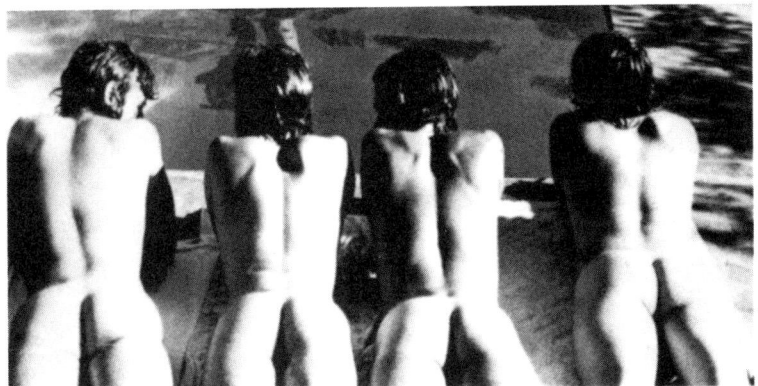

Figure 3. Four masterpieces by that Divine Chiseler, Nature.

anything wrong with pornography); the fact that their assholes are not displayed is not, I gather, the result of reluctance of the models or of the people who made *A Bigger Splash*, but rather is simply a restriction inherent in the medium of mainstream filmmaking. As in the case of the semi-literate men who do strong sexual writing and the handsome youth who could undoubtedly undress well, there are no bad artists, only bad media.

Many artists escape the restrictions of the media and do the work they want to do simply by calling it something other than what it is. It is best, for example, to call sexual writing sociology. People, bless them, are at least sometimes willing to let you define yourself and your work and willing to believe you are what you say you are and your work is what you say it is. The best policy is to establish abruptly, tersely, and immediately, at the very beginning, that your work is art, theater, dance, dance theater, whatever. The most beautiful display of naked male tissue recently in New York was that of Maxwell Caulfield at the prestigious Public Theater. There was no dramatic need for his nudity; but somebody, understandably, wanted to show Caulfield naked and Caulfield, who started as a stripper in a male club, didn't mind. Not only did the reviewers not complain that his nudity was not necessary; even the "straight" reviewers gave rave notices to his body. The play itself, *Salonika*, stirred less enthusiasm. I do not gloat over this sneaky triumph of the flesh, for the star, Jessica Tandy, was a great actress and she was no competition, poor thing, for Caulfield's flesh.

Figure 4. Anatomy against art.

But Caulfield must be a good actor too; he manages to look like a husky, milk-fed Midwestern American, but he's English, you know.

Stills from the dance world offer the same pleasures and opportunites that film stills do. Figure 4 is represented as (and the reviewers have been willing to regard it as) a performance, by the Sankai Juko dance troupe of Japan, of a number called "Kinkan Shonen", or "A Young Boy's Dream of the Origin of Life and Death." If this be a dream, it must be a wet dream; I naturally see it as a group of men offering their butts (and handsome butts they are, if I may say so). All of the reviewers concealed their bewilderment in bullshit of a very high order except Burt Supree, who alone dealt directly with the eroticism of the scene; he described in the *Village Voice* the four men as "writhing and howling as their skirts slipped down just below their buttocks and they waggle (sic) their asses with tauntingly sexual glee."

I doubt that any reviewer, even Burl Supree, would regard Figure 5 as a dance or theater scene. It is a photograph taken by Gene Bagnato at a Times Square male strip show. But it doesn't matter how anyone categorizes the entertainment; I say Bagnato's photograph of it is a work of art, a masterpiece, as moving a representation

Figure 5. Beauty in a forbidden setting.

of the male nude in action as any I've seen in painting, sculpture, or photography. Its central stroke of genius is the photographer's selection of a subject this unacceptable in the first place. It takes a high intelligence, and the confidence intelligence gives, to seek beauty in so forbidden a setting and to publish a photographic record of it.

That I am not alone in admiring also the valor of the—let us say—"dancer" is attested to by the man in the tuxedo.

But I don't want to encourage too much nudity. Nudity has great value only in a clothed society.

Bibliography

Vince Aletti, "Boyd McDonald's Natural Acts," *Village Voice*, March 25, 1981.

—— "Boyd McDonald, 1925–1993," *Village Voice*, October 12, 1993.

Kenneth Anger, *Hollywood Babylon*. (Phoenix, AZ: Associated Professional Services, 1965).

Arthur Bell, "Bell Tells," *Village Voice*, April 3, 1984.

Bruce Benderson, *Sex and Isolation: And Other Essays*. (Madison: University of Wisconsin Press, 2007).

Louise Brooks, *Lulu in Hollywood*. (New York: Alfred A. Knopf, 1982).

Roberto Calasso, *Literature and the Gods*. Translated by Tim Parks. (New York: Alfred A. Knopf, 2001).

David Callahan, "Museum of Modern Art Film Stills Archive Closes," *Film History*, Vol. 15, No. 1 (2003).

Mary Corliss, "Still and Moving," in Roger Ebert, *The Great Movies*. (New York: Broadway Books, 2002).

Richard Corliss, "The Case of the (Still) Missing Film Stills Archive," *Time*, January 11, 2012.

Juan Goytisolo, *Forbidden Territory*. Translated by Peter Bush. (San Francisco: North Point Press, 1989).

Stephen Greco, "Straight to Hell with Boyd McDonald," *The Advocate*, September 17, 1981.

Bruce Hainley, "Writing Survey (Part 2)," *Frieze*, issue 100 (June-August 2006).

—— "Second Life: Bruce Hainley Selects," *East of Borneo*, August 25, 2011.

J. Hoberman and Jonathan Rosenbaum, *Midnight Movies*. (New York: Harper & Row, 1983).

Andrew Holleran, "Obsessed," *Christopher Street*, issue 209 (January 1994).

Mark Jacobson, "In Praise of Film Freaks," *Village Voice*, June 16, 1975.

Anthony Kaufman, "Freeze Frame: MoMA Shuts Down Film Still Archive," *Village Voice*, January 22, 2002.

John Kobal, *People Will Talk*. (New York: Alfred A. Knopf, 1985).

Richard Lamparski, *Whatever Became Of...?* Volumes 1-11. (New York: Crown Publishers, 1966–1989).

Suzanne Jill Levine, *Manuel Puig and the Spider Woman*. (New York: Farrar, Straus and Giroux, 2000).

Stéphane Mallarmé, *Les dieux antiques*. (Paris: Gallimard, 1925).

Boyd McDonald, *Meat: True Homosexual Experiences from STH*. Introduction by Charles Shively. (San Francisco: Gay Sunshine Press, 1981).

———— *Cum: True Homosexual Experiences from STH Writers, Volume 4*. (San Francisco: Gay Sunshine Press, 1983).

———— *Scum: True Homosexual Experiences. An STH Chapbook, Volume 13*. Introduction by Edward T. Hougen. (Boston: Fidelity Publishing, 1993).

Motion Picture Producers and Distributors of America, "The Motion Picture Production Code of 1930," www.artsreformation.com/a001/hays-code.html.

Kliph Nesteroff, "Whatever Became Of... Richard Lamparski?" http://blog.wfmu.org, March 25, 2007.

Harry Alan Potamkin, "Film Cults," in *The Compound Cinema*. (New York: Teachers College Press, 1977).

Manuel Puig, *Kiss of the Spider Woman*. Translated by Thomas Colchie. (New York: Alfred A. Knopf, 1979).

Manuel Puig and Ronald Christ, "A Last Interview with Manuel Puig," *World Literature Today*, vol. 65, no. 4, (Autumn 1991).

Matthew Rettenmund, "Whatever Became Of... Richard Lamparski?: An Exclusive Interview with Mr. Yesterday," www.boyculture.com, October 23, 2012.

Andrew Sarris, *The American Cinema: Directors and Directions, 1929–1968*. (New York: Dutton, 1968).

Shirley Sealey, *Celebrity Sex Register*. (New York: Simon and Schuster, 1982).

Jason Simon, *Festschrift for an Archive*. (New York: Callicoon Fine Arts, 2012).

Stephanie Strom, "Donors Sweetened Director's Pay at MoMA," *New York Times*, February 16, 2007.

Kenneth Tynan, "The Girl in the Black Helmet," *The New Yorker*, June 11, 1979.

Alan Whyte, "Museum of Modern Art Workers on Strike in New York," http://www.wsws.org/en/articles/2000/05/moma-m08.html, May 8, 2000.

Photographic Credits

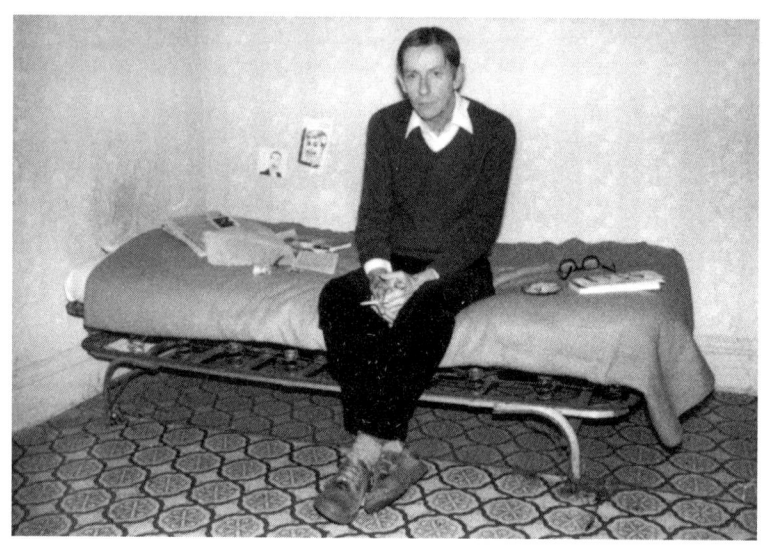

ABOUT THE AUTHOR

Boyd McDonald (1925–1993) was a writer for *Time Magazine* and IBM, a journalist, and founder and editor of *Straight to Hell*, a celebrated fanzine that bore a variety of subtitles, including "The Manhattan Review of Unnatural Acts" or "The New York Review of Cocksucking."